The Midnight Rider Rides Again
By
Derek Johnson

RattleTrap1776

Donald John Trump
has been your
President

the WHOLE time...

45 - 47

The End.

Just kidding.

About the End that is...

This book outlines the Chronological Blueprint of how *they* did **it**.

It = Military Occupation and Continuity of Operations Plan.

Forward

Our Constitution was made only for a moral and religious people. It is wholly inadequate to the government of any other.

John Adams
A Founding Father and
Second President of the United States

The America in which Adams wrote this, was very different to today.

It was just as divided, belligerent and just as populated by ne'er do wells and heroes. But it was, I believe, a more moral, more patriotic, more self-reliant, and if not better educated, it was certainly a 'smarter' America in many and important ways.

I believe that men and women of that America would not have allowed the current sad state of affairs to develop. Thankfully there are and remain enough moral, patriotic, self-reliant, educated, and smarter Americans ready to ride to the rescue of their beloved land.

Derek Johnson is one such American and America should be grateful for him.

Like his historical forebear in the Revolutionary War, Paul Revere and his Midnight Ride, Derek rode into the fray on an intelligence mission, the goal of which in his case was for the restoration of the American Republic.

He was well armed with the invincible combination of a courageous soldier's conviction, a tenacious lawyer's pedantry, and an investigator's dispassionate eye for the truth, truly worthy of Hercule Poirot or Sherlock Holmes.

Derek rode the social media airwaves with his message of hope and hard data in order to give the people a chance to make some sense of the confusing and calamitous situation in which the US and the world found itself.

He was doggedly determined. His forensic examination and painstaking deconstruction of the evidence resulted in the collapse, in the minds of many, of the false narrative being peddled by malevolent forces.

This book is the story of that ride. Derek is a one-man wrecking machine who moved and continues to move forward unflinchingly and inexorably through disinformation, misinformation and outright lies, smashing the deep state as he advances towards the truth, the whole truth and nothing but the truth.

This book is a must read for both contemporary and future historians, describing what happened and how it happened; from the timeline or 'Blueprint' to the various Acts that were passed and through to the intricate web of Executive Orders that set the traps.

It is a vital and invaluable lesson in history, in civics and in what it takes to reclaim and secure the intention of the founding fathers for the people of the United States.

It is also an engrossing account which provides a rich and comprehensive understanding of the theory and practice of US government and its rehabilitation of the relationship between the elected officials and the people, despite the fake news, through Military Occupancy and the Continuation of Government. An intriguing, fascinating and at times humorous journey through one of the most confusing and dangerous periods of the US history.

Derek Johnson radiates the revolutionary spirit of Paul Revere and unashamedly points a finger in the face of those who should, but do not act in the face of assaults on their beloved country. The United States would be more secure from threats both foreign and domestic if there were more Americans with the passion and knowledge of Derek Johnson.

But be warned. This book is only Part One and leaves the reader tantalisingly anticipating the next instalment.

By Lieutenant Colonel Riccardo Bosi (Ret)

The face of modern war is changing – again. Just as the attacks on the Twin Towers and Building 7 in New York on September 11, 2001, now twenty-two years ago, denoted a sea change in how wars would be fought going forward from large traditional military formations facing each other on the battlefield, such as during World War I and World War II, to asymmetric, Irregular Warfare operations targeting helpless civilians by surprise attack on undefended facilities. Though heated debate is still underway regarding who *perpetrated* the 9/11 attacks (inside job or foreign terrorists) and by what means (actual aircraft crashing into buildings or planned demolitions camouflaged by Computer Generated Imagery), the fact remains that, no matter who conducted the attacks, the targets were civilian innocents in non-military facilities. Without doubt, the 9/11 attacks were a classic example of Irregular Warfare that changed the paradigm of how wars would be fought from that point forward. And now the paradigm is changing, again.

While the threat of confrontation and/or conflict between large, standing national armies does still exist, actual events on the ground in recent years have shown an alarming new trend. International Criminal Organizations, many aligned with and supported by the Deep State Cabal, have taken root, and increased in power and influence in multiple Theaters of Operation worldwide. These Cartels are often transnational and not aligned with specifically recognized national borders. They increase their wealth, power, and influence through elaborately organized criminal enterprises, often involving participation by corrupt government officials and high-level, Deep State-aligned business and military leaders.

They are a threat to all humanity, as they have turned to human trafficking, especially of children, and the production, distribution, and sale of adrenochrome, a by-product of the extraction of adrenaline from tortured children, as their main source of income, resulting in a multi-trillion-dollar revenue stream.

These Cartel operations often use Cabal-aligned paramilitary elements or hired security forces to secure their activities. The worldwide threat posed by the Cabal and its various Cartels have forced White Hat militaries to adjust Strategy and Tactics to meet that threat. With the dispersal of the enemy in so many widespread, global locations, and with the current levels of corruption present within most civilian governments, the importance of effective Joint Operational Planning and Execution between the various White Hat militaries cannot be over-emphasized.

The ability to attack widespread targets in different Theaters, simultaneously, or nearly so, in multiple Operational Areas and tactical Zones of Action, will require the highest levels of collaboration and interactive C3I (Command, Control, Communications and Intelligence) among leaders at all levels from senior Commanders to junior unit leaders. Tools exist to assist in Joint Operation Planning. For example, within the US Military, the joint planning and execution community (JPEC) conducts joint planning to understand the strategic and operational environment (OE) and determine the best use of existing capabilities to achieve national (and international) objectives. Joint planning identifies military options that can integrate with other instruments of power (diplomatic, economic, informational) to achieve those objectives. In the process, likely benefits, costs, and risks associated with proposed military options are identified and analyzed. Again, success in the planning effort will require intense collaboration between vetted key leadership in all the militaries of the countries involved in the joint planning effort.

This book is an extraordinary analysis of the Birdseye view of the Operation that was put into place by the United States Military Commands with Donald John Trump at the helm of the Nation who is the pinnacle in World Leadership in Prosperity, Hope, Freedom and Peace, along with World Leaders, in a massive global cleanout Operation, a War on the Deep State, Global Elitists, would have enslaved the people of all Nations for too long.

This book will serve as a Military and Federal Laws and Orders in a devotional style to outline a chronological order of a War Room meets Legislation, which supports a code of honor and ethics as this is a War to free Humanity not a Corporate Banker War.

Derek Johnson changed the field when his video went globally viral on August 24, 2022, showing how "Joe Biden" received 3 Cannons, a 3-Volley Salute on January 20, 2021, while the whole world thought they witnessed an Inauguration, and all the current, bipartisan Legislation via Military and Federal Laws and Orders outlining the very strategic operation amongst other keen attention to detail and the ability to retain all of it and deliver to the people. His mark on the world is truly a pinpoint definition of a soldier keeping the Oath he took to the Constitution and his Nation. He's more than fulfilled the acronyms of the United States Army motto: LDRSHIP.

Loyalty. Duty. Respect. Selfless-Service. Honor. Integrity. Personal Courage.

By Colonel Charles "Chuck" Sellers (Ret).

Preface: What This Book's All About

I feel like the beginning should have some real cool yet head scratchin' saying that makes you wonder where it's going to lead like the opener in *Moby Dick*... *'They call me Ishmael.'* But it doesn't LOL. This is going to be the easiest book you've ever read in your life because Americans were programmed to have short attention spans and education removed to create the level of cognitive dissonance we reached and not for lack of better words just being straight up honest and real... It's for lack of better words, *pathetic*. And for that, I won't be apologizing. We need to '*Make America Read Again.*'

However, giving up on Americans simply because the enemy and evil people of the world duped us for so long would not be a trait of a true American either. We were all born into the corrupt matrix. We inherited this mess of the Swamp Rats Federal Corporation operating in their capacity in which they created problems they already had solutions to. And most of us know the vicious cycle was too chaotic for most people to figure out without any of that populus knowing much about their Government and Foundation to know any difference. These corrupt "leaders" and their cronies knew not many would seek a way out or know where to start to go against the '*authority*' that had been given to these ruthless and despicable people.

This is why it's very important and crucial to understand the words, "Life, Liberty, and the Pursuit of Happiness." This book is the SIMPLE version of the Blueprint of the Chronological Order of the main and key Military and Federal Laws and Orders of how Donald John Trump is also the dash in the middle, 45 – 47.

This book allows the average, everyday Americans, the chance, and opportunity to follow the simple principles of America, Military, and our government. I take the past and current Military and Federal Laws, Executive Orders, Statutes, Acts, Codes, Military Regulations, Military Customs, and the visual evidence they produce that form a Blueprint of this Continuity of Government and Military Occupancy and put it in the everyday American terms as simply as possible, because I too, am an average American.

They form a chronological order in what I coined '**The Blueprint**' to follow such as a cliff-note booklet designed to provide the tools to look up and read the full version of the Law, Order, Act, Code, Regulation, or Custom. It outlines how the Military Generals and Donald John Trump used our Foundation and our past Laws and Orders that SUPPORT the Constitution to reset on the Foundation as the Declaration of Independence gives us and the Military, the authority and power to do so. One does NOT have to be a Lawyer or Congress anything to understand the Laws and Orders that govern us. I mean, that's the whole point...? Why wouldn't anyone want to know the Laws and Orders that have been passed that have been turned and used against us not for us?

> Who writes the Law? Who gave them the authority to write it?
> What makes them the ONLY who can write them?
> What makes them the ONLY who can read and interpret?

See how simple this is. **People**. "*We the People.*" Guess who Congress works for? **Us**! 535 members of Congress work for us, millions! Let that sink in a bit. Think about ALL the complaints you've heard in your life and the way we can solve our problems is to take back control that the 535 people represent us... There's a saying that: "it's easier to con people than it is to convince them they've been conned."

Only 1.7% to 1.9% of the population of America fought in the Revolutionary War... kind of looks similar today does it not? Though it's a LOT worse with all the wagging tails and barking dog keyboard warriors who all want to use their voice, but not lift one hand in doing anything to help the cause and change.

It does not have EVERYTHING... if it did... nobody would read it. This is the cliff-notes version if you will. I also put the References directly under the source because nobody's gonna go to the back of a book these days. It's also a tribute to Paul Revere. I'm not sure I necessarily believe in time-traveling, but if you do, I'm not going to say it doesn't happen.

We're gonna kick off this book the right way! Visuals to get you excited that you've been watching a Military Operation and Continuity of Operations Plan – a plan that was put together long before 2016.

Ironically, the 'jab' did not cause this:

He went from Mr. Ed to Kenny Rogers in less than one year… and "Americans" believed Mainstream Media articles and FaceCrook CryBaby ("Factcheckers") that Joe received *Plastic Surgery*.

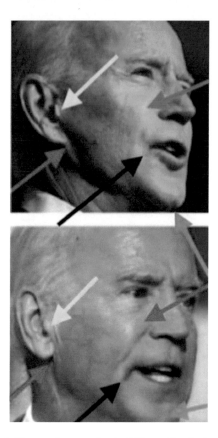

Plastic Surgery would peel your skin and face back like you just saw Rosie O'Donnell naked… It doesn't change your eye color, eye shape, smile structure and teeth, chin and bone structure, earlobes, and nose and bone structure.

How do you go from that smiles structure to no structure?

How do you go from that nose bone structure to another?

How do you go from a detached earlobe to an attached earlobe?

How do you go from a straight chin to a dent in your chin?

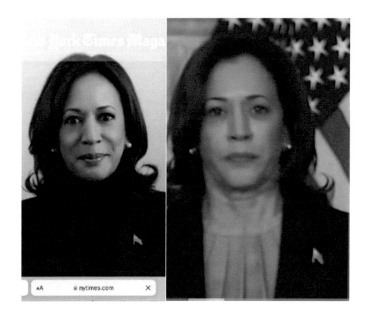

From debonair to linebacker for the Bears. How are people this naïve? Great job, Americans. Don't want to get called out? Start acting like a Proud American.

We're talking about BONE STRUCTURE <u>not</u> **skin**. Not only do you go from 3:00 AM Televangelist to Skinny Kenny... And ALLLLL of a sudden, after YEARS, "his" signature changed. Do we need to call in the signature expert that appears on the TV Show "Pawn Stars" or what?

ppropriations.

e) This order is not intended to, and does not, create any right or benefit, substantive or procedural, enforceable at law or in equity by any party against the United States, its departments, agencies, or entities, its officers, employees, or agents, or any other person.

THE WHITE HOUSE, October 30, 2023. Filed 10–31–23; 11:15 am]

[FR Doc. 2023–24283

Billing code 3395–F4–P

SE, October 30, 202

Political party	Democratic (since 1969)
Other political affiliations	Independent (before 1969)
Spouses	Neilia Hunter (m. 1966; died 1972) Jill Jacobs (m. 1977)
Children	Beau · Hunter · Naomi · Ashley
Relatives	Biden family
Residence	White House
Education	University of Delaware (BA) Syracuse University (JD)
Occupation	Politician · lawyer · author
Awards	Full list
Signature	
Website	Campaign website ☑ White House website ☑

Joe Biden's voice

▶ 6:23

Biden speaks on the U.S. withdrawal from Afghanistan and the fall of Kabul
Recorded August 16, 2021

HOW are Americans THIS naïve? COMPLETELY changes. Yet "his" website, JoeBiden.com, in 2023, has the same as his original. No… really… How NAÏVE are Americans? I was posting this LONG before I went viral August 24, 2022, and you wouldn't believe the comments I received even after people knew I was a Veteran.

Now… We may proceed to the heart of the book… now that I have your attention and your eyes.

Chapter 2: Paul Revere Tribute

'They' say "**history repeats itself**" and I'd have to more than 100% agree with this cool story.

I've always been a Paul Revere fan. There's just something about the original *Midnight Rider* and the impact he had on the Revolutionary War the night before Lexington and Concord.

Born on December 21, 1734, in the North End of Boston, Massachusetts, his name came from his Father, Apollos Rivoire, who changed it to Paul Revere, passing it down to him.

It is uncertain, but more than likely he finished school at thirteen and became his father's apprentice. After his father died on July 22,1754, at 19, Revere could not legally operate a shop for two more years, so in February 1756, he instead found a patriotic way to earn money. From February to November 1756, Second Lieutenant Paul Revere was an artillery officer in New York, joining thousands of Massachusetts men who served in New York and Canada during the Seven Years' War.

In February 1770, he made home in North Square in the North End. As a Son of Liberty and member of the North End Caucus, he engraved political cartoons and helped plan and implement resistance to British policies. (**Reference:** His most famous engraving was of the Boston Massacre in 1770. See Clarence S. Brigham, *Paul Revere's Engravings* (New York: Atheneum, 1969). Revere's Hichborn cousins and many of his artisan friends, neighbors, and fellow Freemasons were also Sons of Liberty and members of the North End Caucus. See Alan Day and Katherine Day "Another Look at the Boston Caucus," *Journal of American Studies* 5 (April 1971): 19-42.)).

His career as a "Messenger of the American Revolution" began on December 17, 1773, carrying news of the Boston Tea Party to New York. Thereafter, he regularly relayed information between the Boston Committee of Correspondence and the Continental Congress in Philadelphia. (**Reference:** Triber, *A True Republican*, 37-100; Appendix D, "Paul Revere's Role in the Revolutionary Movement," in David Hackett Fischer, *Paul Revere's Ride* (New York: Oxford University Press, 1994), 301-307)).

Revere's April 18-19, 1775, ride to Lexington was an intelligence mission directed by Boston's Revolutionary leader *Dr. Joseph Warren* and executed by Paul Revere, William Dawes, and a network of individuals. Based on spying by Revere and others, the likely object of a British expedition seemed to be either the arrest of John Hancock and Samuel Adams in Lexington or the seizure of munitions in nearby Concord. Although British soldiers captured Revere before he got to Concord, he had provided earlier warnings.

(**Reference:** Hancock and Adams were staying in Lexington at the parsonage of Reverend Jonas Clark while attending the Massachusetts Provincial Congress in Concord. Revere rode to Concord on April 8 and Lexington on April 16. On April 18, Warren ordered Revere and Dawes to ride to Lexington. They continued to Concord on their own, aided by Dr. Samuel Prescott of Concord. Revere wrote three accounts of his ride: a deposition for the Massachusetts Provincial Congress, written within a month of the event, a slightly revised deposition, and a more detailed 1798 letter to Jeremy Belknap of the Massachusetts Historical Society, in Paul Revere's *Three Accounts of his Famous Ride: A Massachusetts Historical Society Picture Book* (Boston: MHS, 1976). The most complete analysis of his ride is in Fischer, *Paul Revere's Ride*. See also, Triber, *A True Republican*, 101-105; Christian Di Spigna, *Founding Martyr: The Life and Death of Dr. Joseph Warren, the American Revolution's Lost Hero* (New York: Broadway Books, 2018), 163-167)).

Revere's Revolutionary service as Lieutenant Colonel of the Massachusetts Artillery ended in charges of insubordination, neglect of duty, and cowardice for his role in a massive amphibious assault to take Fort George in Penobscot Bay, Maine. After nearly taking the British fort on July 28, 1779, militia and naval officers spent over two weeks heatedly debating whether to continue the siege. In Councils of War on August 7 and 13, Revere voted with the minority to end the siege. British naval reinforcements arrived on August 13, resulting in a chaotic retreat, with high casualties and enormous cost.

(**Reference:** Orderly book (containing orders of General Solomon Lovell, commanding officer of the Penobscot Expedition, correspondence between Lovell and the Massachusetts Council and Council of War minutes), Solomon Lovell's Letterbook, July 7-12, 1779, and "State of facts respecting the Penobscot Expedition" by William Todd (one of Revere's chief accusers), all in Solomon Lovell Papers, MHS; *Revolution: Penobscot Expedition*, Vol. 145, *Massachusetts Archives Collection, passim*; Eldridge Henry Goss, *The Life of Colonel Paul Revere* (Boston: Joseph George Cupples, 1891), Vol. 2, Chapter 10 ("Penobscot Expedition), Chapter 11 "Revere's Diary of the Penobscot

Expedition; Russell Bourne, "The Penobscot Fiasco," *American Heritage* 25 (October 1974): 28-33, 100-101; William M. Fowler, Jr., "Disaster in Penobscot Bay," *Harvard Magazine* 81 (July-August 1979): 26-31; Triber, *True Republican*, 133-139)).

After the failed assault, a military court charged Revere with two charges of insubordination for ordering his men to retreat without orders from his commanding officer, General Solomon Lovell, and for not immediately turning over a boat to Brigadier General Peleg Wadsworth to evacuate the crew of a schooner drifting towards the enemy. Since he considered the siege over, Revere believed he was no longer under Lovell's command. He admitted not immediately obeying Wadsworth's order, saying "he had all his private baggage" on the boat "but afterwards ordered her to go." During his court-martial, Revere aggressively and successfully cross-examined witnesses who testified to his general military ineptitude. His best defense was the panicked retreat of the expedition. He was fully exonerated on February 19, 1782.

(*Reference:* After two civilian inquiries did not completely vindicate him, Revere spent nearly three years petitioning for a court-martial. He believed he was the victim of a "deep laid" plan by two accusers, disgruntled former members of his regiment. Revere's brash personality may have caused tension in the regiment and during the Penobscot Expedition. Disobeying the order from General Wadsworth was a perfect example of insubordination. Ironically, Wadsworth was the maternal grandfather of the poet Henry Wadsworth Longfellow, who made Revere famous. On Penobscot and the "deep laid plan," see Revere to General William Heath, October 24, 1779, William Heath Papers, *MHS Collections*, 7th ser., 4 (1904): 318-326; *Revolution: Penobscot Expedition*, Vol. 145; *Massachusetts Archives Collection*; Goss, *Life of Paul Revere*, Chapter 12 ("Investigation, Testimony, and Vindication"); Frederic Grant, Jr., "The Court-Martial of Paul Revere," *Boston Bar Journal* 21 (April 1977): 5-13; Michael M. Greenburg, *The Court-Martial of Paul Revere: A Son of Liberty and America's Forgotten Military Fiasco* (Lebanon, N.H: ForeEdge Press, 2014); Triber, *A True Republican*, 133-139)).

The post-Revolutionary Revere became a prosperous entrepreneur and respected citizen, owning a silver shop, hardware shop, foundry, and copper mill. He took pride in making useful manufactures for his country.

(*Reference:* After a brief foray as a hardware merchant in the early 1780s, he opened a foundry in 1788. He opened a copper mill in 1801, after several years of experimentation and a $10,000 loan from the United States government, which he repaid in copper sheeting. In his letters, he often bragged about the quality of his works, claiming they were equal to British manufactures. His trade card, c. 1796-1803, lists his work, including "Cast Bells and Brass Cannon…Manufacture Sheets (copper sheeting)… Bolts, Spikes, Nails, etc…." The most complete account of Revere's post-Revolutionary industrial career is Robert Martello, *Midnight Ride, Industrial Dawn: Paul Revere and the Growth of American Enterprise* (Baltimore: Johns Hopkins, 2010.) See also Triber, *A True Republican*, 141-146, 158, 165, Chapter 10, *passim*)).

Revere held several civic offices, including Grand Master of the Massachusetts Grand Lodge, Suffolk County Coroner, and President of the Boston Board of Health. (*Reference:* Triber, *A True Republican*, 168-176)).
Paul Revere died in Boston on May 10, 1818, at the age of eighty-three. The *Boston Intelligencer and Evening Gazette* called him "cool in thought, ardent in action" and noted both his benevolent character and service "in the early days of our Revolutionary drama…as well as at a later period of its progress.

It would take another forty-three years for Henry Wadsworth Longfellow to make Paul Revere a legend. (*Reference:* Longfellow visited the Old North Church steeple on April 5, 1860. Inspired by his visit, he began writing "Paul Revere's Ride" the next day. The poem appeared in *Atlantic Monthly* magazine (January 1861) and *Tales of a Wayside Inn* (1863). See Triber, *A True Republican*, 1)).

Born December 21, 1734…would have made him 4 days shy of 39, as he started his role as a "Messenger of the American Revolution" on December 17, 1773… which prepped him for his Midnight Ride which made him a Revolutionary Hero at age 40.

Born February 8, 1983, made me 39 years old on August 24, 2022, and my "Rant" Video grew my platform to thousands of followers, on past 40…

Are there Time Travelers? Stories like this make you wonder…

Rest in peace Hero and thank you for your inspiration. May this book glorify your life and all those with the same kindred hearts and spirits.

Paul Revere Story:
https://www.nps.gov/people/paul-revere.htm

Paul Revere Story 2 (Picture Reference):
https://www.paulreverehouse.org/the-real-story/

Chapter 3: So... Who the heck is Derek Johnson?

They call me Ishmael... *LOL* I'm not a plant. I'm not a bot. I'm not undercover. I'm not rich. I'm not a grifter. I'm not a fraud. I'm not a paid spokesperson.

I'm a direct, straightforward, no bullcrap kinda guy, who's a retired United States Army Veteran, simply keeping the Oath I proudly raised my right hand and swore to protect, who loves The United States of America and everything she stands for from the origins of her Foundation passed down by my ancestors who've been here since the beginning.

I grew up in small-town USA in Alabama, Mississippi, and Texas; 8 states total. I come from a long lineage of plowboys and cowboys. I grew up where 'Yes Sir' and 'No Ma'am' had nothing to do with your age... it has everything to do with respect. My Parents and Grandparents are and were blue-collared, small-town, country people who put a major emphasis on values, standards, integrity, respect, honor, loyalty, duty, hard-work, and education. My Father, Grandfather, Great-Grandfather, Uncle, several Great-Uncles, and many other family members served in the Armed Forces.

I earned my bachelor's degree in business management from THE University of Alabama, Roll Tide. And I earned my master's degree in business administration (MBA) from Colorado State University, in which I finished with National Academic and Military Honors for maintaining a 3.8 GPA and higher, Go Rams.

In 2020 and 2021, I scored two Billboard Country Airplay hits with my songs: "*Real Cool Kinda Hot*" and "*Right Beer Right Now*." In 2020, George Strait and I were the only two Military Veterans to chart Billboard Country Airplay hits. If Country Music Fans ONLY knew the politics of *that* cesspool, dirty system, they might support more artists and songwriters like me. But I look forward to being the one to enlighten many people and fans on what and how we did it without a major record label.

I did not get to serve as long as *I wanted*, but God had other plans. Had I still been in the Military, due to the Oath, National Security, the Uniform Code of Military Justice, Department of Defense Regulations, and Army Regulations, I would have NOT been able to say what I've said and do what I've been doing. We try to define our lives too much by titles, ranks, positions, accolades, and achievements with the results of those coming in material things versus how we treat one another and being good humans at the end of the day. Someday I'll expand on 'who' I am in depth... but for the integrity of this book and what it's intended for... is for you to see what happened '*right in front of ya*' and to lead a rally of Patriots in this Nation helping others appreciate their Freedoms, the pursuit of life, liberty, and happiness, and how those were established and how we maintain those versus getting on the brink of losing everything as we were.

Chapter 4: 'I Saw The Light'

I do believe the most asked question is definitely *"when or what was the light that came on that pointed all this out to you?"*

Well, for one, as far back as I can remember… I've always engaged in conversations about how our history was being misconstrued, butchered and rewritten. Too many people think and believe that our Foundation and Government cannot be *"just that simple."*

Well, it can… but always has a risk of happening? People always end up wanting more… and more… and more… that old saying: "you give 'em an inch, they take a mile." That's why our Founders established the saying *'checks and balances.'* Which also pairs with 'with great power comes great responsibility.' And along with the responsibility the other characteristics to accompany must have a foundation with:

1. Honesty
2. Integrity
3. Accountability
4. Consequences for abusing the power in all brackets

But as far as the 'turning point' or what I call the "light bulb moment?"

It was the 2016 Campaign Trail, during 2015, when there were around 16 candidates running for Presidency, which was a record, when Jeb Bush asked candidate Trump:

1. Who's going to vote for you?
2. Who's going to support you?
3. Who's going to back you?

And it was his response that lit the bulb… he said (and I paraphrase):

"That's a loaded question and if the moderator will allow me time, I'll answer that for you. One, the American people are tired of BS politicians like you, every single one of you on this stage has been in politics no less than 4 years and you tell the American people what they want to hear and never back it up. The American people will vote for me because I'm a businessman, not a politician. And who's going to support and back me? I have over 200 Generals backing me."

That last line: "I have over 200 Generals backing me."

That was a "Conspiracy Theory" for over 60 years after it had been passed down that 200 Generals had said, *"never again will we let happen to this Country what happened under JFK again."*

That comment plus December 6, 2017, when out of the blue CIC Trump declared Jerusalem the Capital of Israel.

Those two key moments in History gave me this sense in my heart and stomach to keep a dialogue of notes of legislation and events of what was happening because the latter took this to a whole new level, though it was already Biblical, as everything operates under God's creation, but that was the definite visual that it was a confirmed Biblical operation underway.

Chapter 5: Thinkin' Like RattleTrap1776

I'm going to paint a picture from the top down of how at the end of the day you can simplify life and create a balanced way of critical and logical thinking that will make one more successful at an equality of serious thinking but not being too serious about life either. You've always got to stick to the basics and what you can know.

The saying: *"common sense ain't so common anymore"* ... We're going to change that. This is just one scenario of how Derek Johnson / RattleTrap1776 thinks.

Space, Stars, Moon, Sun, Earth.

How old are they? How far are they? How close are they?

How come certain constellations never move? How does a <u>manmade</u> telescope tell us how far they are?

How do people believe when a scientist with a manmade telescope tells how far those are… but the same people will not believe in tangible things they can put their hands or brains on?

Mountains, Canyons, Rocks, Oceans, Seas, Lakes, Rivers, Ponds, Streams, Creeks, Geysers, Trees, Flowers.

How did they form? How old are they?

Some of these are out of man's control. Some of these have been created by man such as: lakes, ponds, and ways to crossbreed trees and flowers.

Wind, Rain, Sleet, Hail, Thunder, Lightning, Snow, Hurricanes, Tornadoes, Dust Bowls, Monsoons, Dew, Haze, Clouds, Humidity, Heat, Cold, Frozen Tundras, Ice.

Who controls these?

How are they on their cycle? How are they predictable every season? Why are some worse than others?

Can you stop a tornado? Can you stop a hurricane?

Why are so many people trying to play God, but a good percentage of those people don't believe in a God?

If the experts can tell you how old Earth is… how come, they cannot stop these natural disasters?

Infrastructure, Skyscrapers, Houses, Hospitals, Offices, Stores, Warehouses.

If the Earth is as old as "experts" claim… Why did it take so long to build and accumulate the number of these we have?

Trucks, Cars, Boats, Airplanes, ATVs, Bicycles, Motors, Engines.

If the Earth is as old as "experts" claim… Why did it take so long to create the technology to create these?

If the Wheel is as old as "experts" claim… Why did it take so long to create the technology to create these?

Technology, Phones, Computers, Power Supplies, Wires, Cords, Fiber Optics, Internet.

If the Earth is as old as "experts" claim… Why did it take so long to establish technology as we've seen in the past 30 years?

Why is it someone 35 years old can tell a 20-year-old… "back in my day?" Sure, there were changes all along the way… but from 1993 when AOL went public to present day… that change has been RAPID, VAST, and more change than anyone born from the 1960s and their childhoods prior had seen.

So, you're telling me from the first flight, December 17, 1903, to July 21, 1969, we put men on the moon? But from July 21, 1969, to the present day… with the technology boom… we cannot go back?

People. Humans.

Ever heard the Serenity Prayer?

"God grant me the serenity to accept the things I cannot change, courage to change the things I can, and the wisdom to know the difference, living one day at a time; enjoying one moment at a time; taking this world as it is and not as I would have it; trusting that You will make all things right if I surrender to Your will; so that I may be reasonably happy in this life and supremely happy with You forever in the next. Amen."

How come we have the best technology in the world… the most access to information, yet we have the cognitive dissonance aka the laziest and most argumentative people in the world?

Why do people seek change, but whine, gripe, fuss, argue, and try to debate those with solutions to the change?

My approach is unique and different. My approach gets outside of my comfort zone yet remains simple doing so. There's MANY things that just don't matter.

How old is Earth? Is it flat or round? Are there other life forms? How about who cares? Thousands of years on speculations, theories, and myths. Let's work with what we know and can manage and control.

We were all born into this world… the matrix… the problems… the issues… the everything. ***Good versus Evil.***

Whether you like it or not… the Bible is spot on accurate on these things. It's never been debunked. Many want to approach that you cannot prove there's a God… well, I say, you cannot prove there's not. I can prove I'm breathing, living, seeing all the things a man did not create. I can prove there's no half man, half monkeys. I can prove a man cannot build a bird or cow. I can prove via the timeline that's been passed down to us that Earth or Humans isn't as old as "experts" make people believe.

Once again, how come humans will believe a man just because their title is scientist when they all use man-made technology to tell you that this rock is 7 trillion years old, but the rock beside it, that looks just like it, is 1 trillion years less? That's all man made and man theories.

If the timeline we know is accurate… since it's the one most people know then here's a unique way of using your brain to let it wonder.

One example:

If you flew from New York to England today… It's roughly 7 hours and 5 minutes.

"History" tells us the Vikings discovered America around 1,000 A.D. and Christopher Columbus in 1492.

 That's a 492-year difference.

The Mayflower landed at Plymouth Rock in 1620.

 That's a 128-year difference.

The Revolutionary War started in 1775.

 That's a 155-year difference.

Delaware became the first state in the union, on December 7, 1787.

  That's a 12-year difference and 3 months after the Constitution.

California became a state in 1850.

 That's a 63-year difference.

The first Skyscraper was built in America, 1885.

 That's a 110-year difference from the start of the Revolutionary War.

Look at how far our cities have grown from 1885 to present day when the first scraper was built in 1885…

Arizona did not become a state until 1912.

The "United" States of America is NOT that old ladies and gentlemen. If the Native Americans were the first occupants of the United States… then that means the population and technology of the world did not have a capacity for man to sail to discover a land that's only a 7-hour flight from where the founders came from. The point is NOT they thought the world was flat and the map fell off where they assumed the ocean ended. It's the discovery process we're addressing here… why did it take so long to discover and develop America or a new land period if the Earth is as OLD as "experts" claim it is. And the end of the day… that still does not matter either. This is just a critical yet simple way of addressing what we have and what we know exists.

The United States of America… is NOT that old, ladies and gentlemen. And it's NOT that old to look the way it looks right now. We look like a bunch of childish, snot nose children to the rest of the world with the Freedoms and Liberties we have yet cannot get it together due to the laziness and cognitive dissonance people CHOOSE to stay in versus any alternative of doing something about this broken, manmade, system that was cast upon us with their agendas.

The only way to eliminate evil is to be able to identify, address, and control the levels. NOT doing anything about it because you're afraid is the reason why we're where we are. The adage, "give'em an inch, they'll take a mile," is why we are where we are.

Anyone who knows anything about destruction knows it's a lot more effective to destroy from within. A former President once said, "*if we ever lose America, we will lose it from within.*"

Never be afraid to challenge your mind to think.

"Any man who reads too much and uses his own brain too little falls into lazy habits of thinking."

– Albert Einstein

Don't read just to read. Read to empower yourself and your mind.

Chapter 6: So, who were our Founders?

Our Founders weren't a bunch of young guys like hotheads you see in bars talking smack and not doing anything about it. They weren't a bunch of young punks who just wanted to fight and be jotted down for history's sake. The founders were not a bunch of poor men. They were wealthy and successful men with nothing to gain, but everything to lose.

"*Give me liberty or give me death.*"

How many rich people today do you hear willing to lose everything for the cost of Freedom? Nine out of 10 answers would be: Crickets or "I would if I had to." America is an idea on a piece of paper in the Smithsonian… That paper does not defend or fight for us… We do. Daily. Our Founders were very brilliant men. And they weren't a bunch of youngsters who just wanted to flex their muscles, beat their chests, and fight…

These men were weathered and filled with wisdom but were also resilient and knew what it would take to produce something as great as America… which is why they established the Military first. Ironically, they did things backwards with kicking the Revolutionary War off with the Battle of Lexington and Concord. Everything those Founders did was unconventionally backwards.

> Started war in April 1775; Battle of Lexington and Concord.
> Established first branch, Army
> Wrote War Articles (Military Laws)
> Established second and third branch (Navy and Marine Corps)
> Created Flag
> Wrote the Declaration of Independence
> Fought 7 more years
> Wrote the Articles of Confederation in 1777
> Drafted the Constitution 10 years after AOC in 1787
> Elected first President, 1789
> The Constitution enacted 1789
> The Bill of Rights, 1791
> The Battle of 1812, British revolt and defeated in 1814

The founders literally started the war with the 'Shot heard around the world' at the Battle of Lexington and Concord, April 19, 1775; Less than 2 months before they established the first branch of Military, the United States Army, June 14, 1775;

16 days later, the first 69 articles of War were published, June 30, 1775; The Navy was established, October 13, 1775, and the Marine Corps, November 10, 1775; The Grand Union Flag was established, December 3, 1775.

Notice those are long before the Declaration of Independence and the Constitution? The Declaration of Independence came one year and 2 months *after* the Revolutionary War kicked off and the establishment of the Armed Forces were formed. The Declaration was written in future tense; always alive; always moving forward. It gives every American Patriot the command to reset any government that goes against the Foundation. It specifically says, 'it's their right and duty' to do so.

Using words such as '*their*' is very powerful as it's a command plus forever future tense to always know your Foundation and how we came to know this great Nation. It also shows the hearts of warriors in the Military throughout the years to always fight for that premise and Foundation. When one really marinates on the above then applies that the Founders started fighting, established Military and Military Law, wrote the Declaration of Independence, then fought SEVEN more years before the Revolutionary War ended… that should tell you how extraordinary their vision and mission was. Understanding the History and Foundation of our Nation is VITAL. Without knowing that simple gist above… It's hard to understand the full Operation because every intricate detail is vitally important. Military came first in our Nation.

Do you really think a man as successful as Donald John Trump would have just walked away *that* easily without anything to say, but *"You know I won Joe?"*

Yeahhhh… no. Not a snowball's chance even in the outskirts of hades. However, one would not even remotely have to think in such a manner if they had just been paying attention to what was being written and laid out in front of them.

CIC DJT had to look a certain way throughout this. Too many Patriots and those who 'claim' to be awake have been focused on him playing the game to win those who are asleep. He could never resemble a dictator throughout this operation which would go against the integrity of the grain and fabric of our Nation's foundation and history. But these quotes weren't just 'slogans' of a four years.

"We have it all. We've caught them all."

*"The **best** is yet to come."*

"There's a storm coming. Wait for it."
        "Be careful what you wish for."

And if claim to be "awake" and you think he simply 'walked' away knowing he would just rerun in 2024… without a plan in place… you're almost not worthy of calling yourself a true 'Trump Supporter' much less a Patriot. I cannot apologize for that. I won't.

And all the 'holier than thou people' out there who point a finger at CIC Trump's past clearly have not read or applied the passage…

    "He that is without sin among you, let him first cast a stone at her." - **John 8:7**

Status, wealth, and fame have nothing to do with judgment. Judgment is still judgment. Donald is still a man worthy of forgiveness and the Cross no different than anyone else.

He was chosen and put into the position for a reason. He was an outsider to the system. That same system people whine, fuss, and argue about, yet do not want to help clean up or fix. He's there to do a job. It's no easy job no matter how many supports him because there's always that percentage of people who just cannot help but be ignorant.

Look at all of those who ridiculed, mocked, shunned, spit on, and threw rocks at Christ on the way to the Cross.
    "Amen, I say to you, no prophet is accepted in his own native place." - **Luke 4:24**

If they treated Jesus Christ this way…, how do you think they're going to do with those who stand for Christ? Has anyone not taken a gander at all the filth in the world? Has anyone not noticed all the people who mock Christ and Christians? So, how do you think half the Nation of filth and corruption will adhere to a President taking us back to our Foundation, morals, and principles?

Have you not seen the attempt to rewrite History of how our Founders were evil and bad men? Have you not seen the attempts to rewrite all our history? Have you not seen how 'woke' people are? Yet those sameee people all want change, yet want to keep their Freedoms and Liberties...

Do you see how many people celebrate the 4th of July... yet many of them are those who hate CIC Donald Trump... the keenest President on the Declaration of Independence than any other President combined? Remember, July 4th isn't celebrating the Constitution.

What a confused Nation we are... when it's simple. Go back to the basics. And that's what CIC Donald John Trump and the Military are doing. It's not HOW MANY are on board... too many people are focused on the wrong things. Who holds the keys to the Military Bases? That's ALL that matters.

CIC Trump and the Generals have that control. And there's MORE than enough proof to prove so. That's why at the end of the day... It's simple. All that matters is what's in place. And that's what I'm going to lay out for everyone.

This book is not everything once again, but it's in place to get you to digging...and that's by design and for a reason.

Also, for those who spew off: "That's not Donald Trump, but nice look alike." You're the ones who are in DIRE need of this book but more specifically focus on the Military Special Operations.

WHY would Security put the actual Donald Trump at rallies where a sniper at 1,000 yards could attempt a shot VERSUS Donald Trump at his privately secured, MEMBERS ONLY, Country Club with a wall that looks like the Great Wall of China around it, with LOADED Secret Service swarming the premises?

A MASS majority saying this... don't know much about simple Legislation... much less National Security and Special Operations. This Plan was drafted LONG BEFORE November 8, 2016, and that would include body doubles.

Also, the mass majority saying such have never been around a Trump Trash Can much less his private COUNTRY CLUB.

This book is designed to help you use your brain and cognitively think... that's a good one to start with.

Too many people want to ask a gazillion questions like:

'Why would it look like this?'

'Why would President Trump let America look like this if what you say is true?'

'Why would anyone let this happen… when there's people suffering and dying?'

If you have that kind of time to question… you are killing time when you could be contributing. The better question is… HOW did we let America look like this and reach this point? That's the question we should always keep as a precedent and priority to address to make sure she never gets that way again.

Anyone who has a business mind reading this knows… Any great business executive who takes over a company that's faltering or on the decline does not walk right in the door demanding any kind of change in supply, production, manufacturing, management, mission, goals, etc. A great business mind will watch and observe the process of all those functions, assess and identify goals and how to meet those goals, via the process of which the company functions, THEN adjust where needed to meet those requirements, the mission, and goals for productivity.

Now bring back those questions above and any like those you've heard in the ballpark…

'Why would it look like this?'

'Why would President Trump let America look like this if what you say is true?'

'Why would anyone let this happen… when there's people suffering and dying?'

Let's take a gander at the 'HOW' did we let America look like this and reach this point with a little bit of our History and Foundation. That's *our* right *and* our duty. That's why the Declaration of Independence is so important.

Think about this… our Founders declared Independence with the Declaration of Independence 7 years before the Revolutionary War ended.

The "shot heard around the world" that was the first shots fired in battle as noted by Ralph Waldo Emerson in his "Concord Hymn" described the shots fired by the Patriots at North Bridge at Concord & Lexington, the first battle of the Revolutionary War, April 19, 1775.

Let's look at the *Declaration*:

Declaration of Independence

In Congress, July 4, 1776:
The unanimous Declaration of the thirteen united States of America, When in the Course of human events, it becomes necessary for one people to dissolve the political bands which have connected them with another, and to assume among the powers of the earth, the separate and equal station to which the Laws of Nature and of Nature's God entitle them, a decent respect to the opinions of mankind requires that they should declare the causes which impel them to the separation.

We hold these truths to be self-evident, that all men are created equal, that they are endowed by their Creator with certain unalienable Rights, that among these are Life, Liberty and the pursuit of Happiness.--That to secure these rights, Governments are instituted among Men, deriving their just powers from the consent of the governed, --That whenever any Form of Government becomes destructive of these ends, it is the Right of the People to alter or to abolish it, and to institute new Government, laying its foundation on such principles and organizing its powers in such form, as to them shall seem most likely to effect their Safety and Happiness. Prudence, indeed, will dictate that Governments long established should not be changed for light and transient causes; and accordingly all experience hath shewn, that mankind are more disposed to suffer, while evils are sufferable, than to right themselves by abolishing the forms to which they are accustomed. But when a long train of abuses and usurpations, pursuing invariably the same Object evinces a design to reduce them under absolute Despotism, it is their right, it is their duty, to throw off such Government, and to provide new Guards for their future security.--Such has been the patient sufferance of these Colonies; and such is now the necessity which constrains them to alter their former Systems of Government. The history of the present King of Great Britain is a history of repeated injuries and usurpations, all having in direct object the establishment of an absolute Tyranny over these States. To prove this, let Facts be submitted to a candid world.

He has refused his Assent to Laws, the most wholesome and necessary for the public good.
He has forbidden his Governors to pass Laws of immediate and pressing importance, unless suspended in their operation till his Assent should be obtained; and when so suspended, he has utterly neglected to attend to them.

He has refused to pass other Laws for the accommodation of large districts of people, unless those people would relinquish the right of Representation in the Legislature, a right inestimable to them and formidable to tyrants only.

He has called together legislative bodies at places unusual, uncomfortable, and distant from the depository of their public Records, for the sole purpose of fatiguing them into compliance with his measures.

He has dissolved Representative Houses repeatedly, for opposing with manly firmness his invasions on the rights of the people.

He has refused for a long time, after such dissolutions, to cause others to be elected; whereby the Legislative powers, incapable of Annihilation, have returned to the People at large for their exercise; the State remaining in the meantime exposed to all the dangers of invasion from without, and convulsions within.

He has endeavored to prevent the population of these States; for that purpose obstructing the Laws for Naturalization of Foreigners; refusing to pass others to encourage their migrations hither, and raising the conditions of new Appropriations of Lands.

He has obstructed the Administration of Justice, by refusing his Assent to Laws for establishing Judiciary powers.

He has made Judges dependent on his Will alone, for the tenure of their offices, and the amount and payment of their salaries.

He has erected a multitude of New Offices, and sent hither swarms of Officers to harass our people, and eat out their substance.

He has kept among us, in times of peace, Standing Armies without the Consent of our legislatures.

He has affected to render the Military independent of and superior to the Civil power.

He has combined with others to subject us to a jurisdiction foreign to our constitution, and unacknowledged by our laws; giving his Assent to their Acts of pretended Legislation:

For Quartering large bodies of armed troops among us:
For protecting them, by a mock Trial, from punishment for any Murders which they should commit on the Inhabitants of these States:
For cutting off our Trade with all parts of the world:
For imposing Taxes on us without our Consent:
For depriving us in many cases, of the benefits of Trial by Jury:
For transporting us beyond Seas to be tried for pretended offences
For abolishing the free System of English Laws in a neighbouring Province, establishing therein an Arbitrary government, and enlarging its Boundaries so as to render it at once an example and fit instrument for introducing the same absolute rule into these Colonies:

For taking away our Charters, abolishing our most valuable Laws, and altering fundamentally the Forms of our Governments:

For suspending our own Legislatures, and declaring themselves invested with power to legislate for us in all cases whatsoever.

He has abdicated Government here, by declaring us out of his Protection and waging War against us.

He has plundered our seas, ravaged our Coasts, burnt our towns, and destroyed the lives of our people.

He is at this time transporting large Armies of foreign Mercenaries to compleat the works of death, desolation and tyranny, already begun with circumstances of Cruelty & perfidy scarcely paralleled in the most barbarous ages, and totally unworthy the Head of a civilized nation.

He has constrained our fellow Citizens taken Captive on the high Seas to bear Arms against their Country, to become the executioners of their friends and Brethren, or to fall themselves by their Hands.

He has excited domestic insurrections amongst us, and has endeavoured to bring on the inhabitants of our frontiers, the merciless Indian Savages, whose known rule of warfare, is an undistinguished destruction of all ages, sexes and conditions.

In every stage of these Oppressions We have Petitioned for Redress in the most humble terms: Our repeated Petitions have been answered only by repeated injury. A Prince whose character is thus marked by every act which may define a Tyrant, is unfit to be the ruler of a free people.

Nor have We been wanting in attentions to our Brittish brethren. We have warned them from time to time of attempts by their legislature to extend an unwarrantable jurisdiction over us. We have reminded them of the circumstances of our emigration and settlement here. We have appealed to their native justice and magnanimity, and we have conjured them by the ties of our common kindred to disavow these usurpations, which, would inevitably interrupt our connections and correspondence. They too have been deaf to the voice of justice and of consanguinity. We must, therefore, acquiesce in the necessity, which denounces our Separation, and hold them, as we hold the rest of mankind, Enemies in War, in Peace Friends.

We, therefore, the Representatives of the united States of America, in General Congress, Assembled, appealing to the Supreme Judge of the world for the rectitude of our intentions, do, in the Name, and by Authority of the good People of these Colonies, solemnly publish and declare, That these United Colonies are, and of Right ought to be Free and Independent States; that they are Absolved from all Allegiance to the British Crown, and that all political connection between them and the State of Great Britain, is and ought to be totally dissolved; and that as Free and Independent States, they have full Power to levy War, conclude Peace, contract Alliances, establish Commerce, and to do all other Acts and Things which Independent States may of right do. And for the support of this Declaration, with a firm reliance on the protection of divine Providence, we mutually pledge to each other our Lives, our Fortunes and our sacred Honor.

*Note: Misspellings reflect the original Declaration of Independence draft. And all Mississippians say: Heck yeahhh!

Now, let's look at a few key and powerful lines:

"That whenever any Form of Government becomes destructive of these ends, it is the Right of the People to alter or to abolish it, and to institute new Government, laying its foundation on such principles and organizing its powers in such form, as to them shall seem most likely to effect their Safety and Happiness."

Notice the capitalization of these words:

> *It is the Right of the People…* **Right**, big R capitalized.

Notice these words and think of their definitions:

> *To alter or to abolish it, and to institute a new Government.*

Alter: change or cause to change in character or composition, typically in a comparatively small but significant way. - Oxford Languages.

Abolish: formally put an end to (a system, practice, or institution). - Oxford Languages.

The power of words… Which is why it's important to read and understand your Foundation of this Nation that everyone 'claims' to love, yet the majority know nothing about.

"But when a long train of abuses and usurpations, pursuing invariably the same Object evinces a design to reduce them under absolute Despotism, it is their right, it is their duty, to throw off such Government, and to provide new Guards for their future security."

It is our right and it is our duty to throw off such Government, and to provide new Guards for their future…

Throw Off: rid oneself of something.

This line right here gives us the authority to alter or abolish, meaning destroy, any Government that goes against the Foundation of our Principles… Amazing when people read and understand our Foundation. The Revolutionary War was the turning point in America, yet it was the beginning of the United States of America. Those Founders came together, banned together, declared Independence 7 years before the War ended, and wouldn't take no for an answer that became known as our Foundation and History, the start to this "Free" Nation.

The problem we've had are people who became lazy, complacent, and full of excuses, as I had heard, as I know you had to, people say "that's Congress' job" or "that's above my paygrade" and other comments through the years as to suggest that Government, Infrastructure, and Systems created themselves, and weren't controllable by man.

That's how America got the way it did. People afraid of discipline and structure, people afraid of responsibility and accountability, because they were scared, they'd offend someone or hurt their feelings… the 'Woke Culture.'

"They love our milk and honey, but they preach about another way of living…" - lyrics from "Fightin' Side of Me' by Merle Haggard.

How do you think our Founders had enough of what they were living through? Keep in mind, it was their ancestors, and not as long ago before that period, that their people had fled persecution, risked unknown voyages on ships to come to this new land…

Do you not see what happened? The Patriots were from all descents basically fighting the old ideologies of people who fled and came over and went back to their old ideology of living… defeating the point of many who fled to escape those.

That's why it's important to understand that at any point does a group of people who believe in our Foundation, ban together, and stand together, then fight together if we must, we can always re-establish our Foundation as the Declaration says.

Our Foundation and History is not that complicated. My Dad and Grandpa always said, "life is what we make of it." But why do we make it so complicated? We don't have to.

We are the ones who made the power of the dollar so powerful. Everything we have is manmade. We cannot blame systems. Systems do not make people choose or decide.

WE have that right. WE have that duty. WE establish government, systems, and infrastructure.

WE must not allow America to go down the drain as it did… We must take this responsibility and always maintain integrity, honesty, and accountability always.

America is an idea on a piece of paper in the Smithsonian… it does NOT simply govern without People who keep that dream alive and fight for it daily, weekly, monthly, yearly.

Chapter 9: Articles of Confederation

The Articles of Confederation served as the FIRST United States Constitution. They were adopted by Congress on November 15, 1777.

Keep in mind the timeline of Military Branches and War Articles then the Articles here… And everyone thought Donald John Trump was announcing a "2024 Presidential Campaign" … on November 15, 2022, lol. That speech was LOADED with all Comms from Laws and Orders that form the Blueprint in which you'll read in Chapters below. Every number and timeline matters. If numbers don't matter… stop checking your bank accounts.

The Articles established a "league of friendship" for the 13 sovereign and independent states. It also outlined a Congress with representation not based on population – each state would have one vote in Congress.
Ratification by all 13 states was necessary to set the Confederation into motion. Because of disputes over representation, voting, and the western lands claimed by some states, ratification was delayed. When Maryland ratified it on March 1, 1781, the Congress of the Confederation came into being.

Just a few years after the Revolutionary War, however, James Madison and George Washington were among those who feared their young country was on the brink of collapse. With the states retaining considerable power, the central government had insufficient power to regulate commerce. It could not tax and was generally impotent in setting commercial policy. Nor could it effectively support a war effort. Congress was attempting to function with a depleted treasury; and paper money was flooding the country, creating extraordinary inflation.
The states were on the brink of economic disaster; and the central government had little power to settle quarrels between states. Disputes over territory, war pensions, taxation, and trade threatened to tear the country apart.

So, let's take a gander at the first Constitution of the United States, *the Articles of Confederation*.

Articles of Confederation, November 15, 1777:

"To all to whom these Presents shall come, we, the undersigned Delegates of the States affixed to our Names send greeting. Whereas the Delegates of the United States of America in Congress assembled did on the fifteenth day of November in the year of our Lord One Thousand Seven Hundred and Seventy seven, and in the Second Year of the Independence of America agree to certain articles of Confederation and perpetual Union between the States of Newhampshire, Massachusetts-bay, Rhodeisland and Providence Plantations, Connecticut, New York, New Jersey, Pennsylvania, Delaware, Maryland, Virginia, North Carolina, South Carolina, and Georgia in the Words following, viz. "Articles of Confederation and perpetual Union between the States of Newhampshire, Massachusetts-bay, Rhodeisland and Providence Plantations, Connecticut, New York, New Jersey, Pennsylvania, Delaware, Maryland, Virginia, North Carolina, South Carolina, and Georgia.

Article I. The Stile of this confederacy shall be, "The United States of America."

Article II. Each state retains its sovereignty, freedom and independence, and every Power, Jurisdiction and right, which is not by this confederation expressly delegated to the United States, in Congress assembled.

Article III. The said states hereby severally enter into a firm league of friendship with each other, for their common defence, the security of their Liberties, and their mutual and general welfare, binding themselves to assist each other, against all force offered to, or attacks made upon them, or any of them, on account of religion, sovereignty, trade, or any other pretence whatever.

Article IV. The better to secure and perpetuate mutual friendship and intercourse among the people of the different states in this union, the free inhabitants of each of these states, paupers, vagabonds and fugitives from Justice excepted, shall be entitled to all privileges and immunities of free citizens in the several states; and the people of each state shall have free ingress and regress to and from any other state, and shall enjoy therein all the privileges of trade and commerce, subject to the same duties, impositions and restrictions as the inhabitants thereof respectively, provided that such restrictions shall not extend so far as to prevent the removal of property imported into any state, to any other State of which the Owner is an inhabitant; provided also that no imposition, duties or restriction shall be laid by any state, on the property of the united states, or either of them.

If any Person guilty of, or charged with, treason, felony, or other high misdemeanor in any state, shall flee from Justice, and be found in any of the united states, he shall upon demand of the Governor or executive power of the state from which he fled, be delivered up, and removed to the state having jurisdiction of his offence.

Full faith and credit shall be given in each of these states to the records, acts and judicial proceedings of the courts and magistrates of every other state.

Article V. For the more convenient management of the general interests of the united states, delegates shall be annually appointed in such manner as the legislature of each state shall direct, to meet in Congress on the first Monday in November, in every year, with a power reserved to each state to recall its delegates, or any of them, at any time within the year, and to send others in their stead, for the remainder of the Year.

No State shall be represented in Congress by less than two, nor by more than seven Members; and no person shall be capable of being delegate for more than three years, in any term of six years; nor shall any person, being a delegate, be capable of holding any office under the united states, for which he, or another for his benefit receives any salary, fees or emolument of any kind.

Each State shall maintain its own delegates in a meeting of the states, and while they act as members of the committee of the states.

In determining questions in the united states, in Congress assembled, each state shall have one vote.

Freedom of speech and debate in Congress shall not be impeached or questioned in any Court, or place out of Congress, and the members of congress shall be protected in their persons from arrests and imprisonments, during the time of their going to and from, and attendance on congress, except for treason, felony, or breach of the peace.

Article VI. No State, without the Consent of the united States, in congress assembled, shall send any embassy to, or receive any embassy from, or enter into any conference, agreement, alliance, or treaty, with any King prince or state; nor shall any person holding any office of profit or trust under the united states, or any of them, accept of any present, emolument, office, or title of any kind whatever, from any king, prince, or foreign state; nor shall the united states, in congress assembled, or any of them, grant any title of nobility.

No two or more states shall enter into any treaty, confederation, or alliance whatever between them, without the consent of the united states, in congress assembled, specifying accurately the purposes for which the same is to be entered into, and how long it shall continue.

No State shall lay any imposts or duties, which may interfere with any stipulations in treaties, entered into by the united States in congress assembled, with any king, prince, or State, in pursuance of any treaties already proposed by congress, to the courts of France and Spain.

No vessels of war shall be kept up in time of peace, by any state, except such number only, as shall be deemed necessary by the united states, in congress assembled, for the defence of such state, or its trade; nor shall any body of forces be kept up, by any state, in time of peace, except such number only as, in the judgment of the united states, in congress assembled, shall be deemed requisite to garrison the forts necessary for the defence of such state; but every state shall always keep up a well regulated and disciplined militia, sufficiently armed and accoutred, and shall provide and constantly have ready for use, in public stores, a due number of field pieces and tents, and a proper quantity of arms, ammunition, and camp equipage.

No State shall engage in any war without the consent of the united States in congress assembled, unless such State be actually invaded by enemies, or shall have received certain advice of a resolution being formed by some nation of Indians to invade such State, and the danger is so imminent as not to admit of a delay till the united states in congress assembled, can be consulted: nor shall any state grant commissions to any ships or vessels of war, nor letters of marque or reprisal, except it be after a declaration of war by the united states in congress assembled, and then only against the kingdom or State, and the subjects thereof, against which war has been so declared, and under such regulations as shall be established by the united states in congress assembled, unless such state be infested by pirates, in which case vessels of war may be fitted out for that occasion, and kept so long as the danger shall continue, or until the united states in congress assembled shall determine otherwise.

Article VII. When land forces are raised by any state, for the common defence, all officers of or under the rank of colonel, shall be appointed by the legislature of each state respectively by whom such forces shall be raised, or in such manner as such state shall direct, and all vacancies shall be filled up by the state which first made appointment.

Article VIII. All charges of war, and all other expenses that shall be incurred for the common defence or general welfare, and allowed by the united states in congress assembled, shall be defrayed out of a common treasury, which shall be supplied by the several states, in proportion to the value of all land within each state, granted to or surveyed for any Person, as such land and the buildings and improvements thereon shall be estimated, according to such mode as the united states, in congress assembled, shall, from time to time, direct and appoint. The taxes for paying that proportion shall be laid and levied by the authority and direction of the legislatures of the several states within the time agreed upon by the united states in congress assembled.

Article IX. The united states, in congress assembled, shall have the sole and exclusive right and power of determining on peace and war, except in the cases mentioned in the sixth article - of sending and receiving ambassadors - entering into treaties and alliances, provided that no treaty of commerce shall be made, whereby the legislative power of the respective states shall be restrained from imposing such imposts and duties on foreigners, as their own people are subjected to, or from prohibiting the exportation or importation of any species of goods or commodities whatsoever - of establishing rules for deciding, in all cases, what captures on land or water shall be legal, and in what manner prizes taken by land or naval forces in the service of the united Sates, shall be divided or appropriated - of granting letters of marque and reprisal in times of peace - appointing courts for the trial of piracies and felonies committed on the high seas; and establishing courts; for receiving and determining finally appeals in all cases of captures; provided that no member of congress shall be appointed a judge of any of the said courts.

The united states, in congress assembled, shall also be the last resort on appeal, in all disputes and differences now subsisting, or that hereafter may arise between two or more states concerning boundary, jurisdiction, or any other cause whatever; which authority shall always be exercised in the manner following. Whenever the legislative or executive authority, or lawful agent of any state in controversy with another, shall present a petition to congress, stating the matter in question, and praying for a hearing, notice thereof shall be given, by order of congress, to the legislative or executive authority of the other state in controversy, and a day assigned for the appearance of the parties by their lawful agents, who shall then be directed to appoint, by joint consent, commissioners or judges to constitute a court for hearing and determining the matter in question: but if they cannot agree, congress shall name three persons out of each of the united states, and from the list of such persons each party shall alternately strike out one, the petitioners beginning, until the number shall be reduced to thirteen; and from that number not less than seven, nor more than nine names, as congress shall direct, shall, in the presence of congress, be drawn out by lot, and the persons whose names shall be so drawn, or any five of them, shall be commissioners or judges, to hear and finally determine the controversy, so always as a major part of the judges, who shall hear the cause, shall agree in the determination: and if either party shall neglect to attend at the day appointed, without showing reasons which congress shall judge sufficient, or being present, shall refuse to strike, the congress shall proceed to nominate three persons out of each State, and the secretary of congress shall strike in behalf of such party absent or refusing; and the judgment and sentence of the court, to be appointed in the manner before prescribed, shall be final and conclusive; and if any of the parties shall refuse to submit to the authority of such court, or to appear or defend their claim or cause, the court shall nevertheless proceed to pronounce sentence, or judgment, which shall in like manner be final and decisive; the judgment or sentence and other proceedings being in either case transmitted to congress, and lodged among the acts of congress, for the security of the parties concerned: provided that every commissioner, before he sits in judgment, shall take an oath to be administered by one of the judges of the supreme or superior court of the State where the cause shall be tried, "well and truly to hear and determine the matter in question, according to the best of his judgment, without favour, affection, or hope of reward: "provided, also, that no State shall be deprived of territory for the benefit of the united states.

All controversies concerning the private right of soil claimed under different grants of two or more states, whose jurisdictions as they may respect such lands, and the states which passed such grants are adjusted, the said grants or either of them being at the same time claimed to have originated antecedent to such settlement of jurisdiction, shall, on the petition of either party to the congress of the united states, be finally determined, as near as may be, in the same manner as is before prescribed for deciding disputes respecting territorial jurisdiction between different states.

The united states, in congress assembled, shall also have the sole and exclusive right and power of regulating the alloy and value of coin struck by their own authority, or by that of the respective states - fixing the standard of weights and measures throughout the united states - regulating the trade and managing all affairs with the Indians, not members of any of the states; provided that the legislative right of any state, within its own limits, be not infringed or violated - establishing and regulating post-offices from one state to another, throughout all the united states, and exacting such postage on the papers passing through the same, as may be requisite to defray the expenses of the said office - appointing all officers of the land forces in the service of the united States, excepting regimental officers - appointing all the officers of the naval forces, and commissioning all officers whatever in the service of the united states; making rules for the government and regulation of the said land and naval forces, and directing their operations.

The united States, in congress assembled, shall have authority to appoint a committee, to sit in the recess of congress, to be denominated, "A Committee of the States," and to consist of one delegate from each State; and to appoint such other committees and civil officers as may be necessary for managing the general affairs of the united states under their direction - to appoint one of their number to preside; provided that no person be allowed to serve in the office of president more than one year in any term of three years; to ascertain the necessary sums of money to be raised for the service of the united states, and to appropriate and apply the same for defraying the public expenses; to borrow money or emit bills on the credit of the united states, transmitting every half year to the respective states an account of the sums of money so borrowed or emitted, - to build and equip a navy - to agree upon the number of land forces, and to make requisitions from each state for its quota, in proportion to the number of white inhabitants in such state, which requisition shall be binding; and thereupon the legislature of each state shall appoint the regimental officers, raise the men, and clothe, arm, and equip them, in a soldier-like manner, at the expense of the united states; and the officers and men so clothed, armed, and equipped, shall march to the place appointed, and within the time agreed on by the united states, in congress assembled; but if the united states, in congress assembled, shall, on consideration of circumstances, judge proper that any state should not raise men, or should raise a smaller number than its quota, and that any other state should raise a greater number of men than the quota thereof, such extra number shall be raised, officered, clothed, armed, and equipped in the same manner as the quota of such state, unless the legislature of such state shall judge that such extra number cannot be safely spared out of the same, in which case they shall raise, officer, clothe, arm, and equip, as many of such extra number as they judge can be safely spared. And the officers and men so clothed, armed, and equipped, shall march to the place appointed, and within the time agreed on by the united states in congress assembled.

The united states, in congress assembled, shall never engage in a war, nor grant letters of marque and reprisal in time of peace, nor enter into any treaties or alliances, nor coin money, nor regulate the value thereof nor ascertain the sums and expenses necessary for the defence and welfare of the united states, or any of them, nor emit bills, nor borrow money on the credit of the united states, nor appropriate money, nor agree upon the number of vessels of war to be built or purchased, or the number of land or sea forces to be raised, nor appoint a commander in chief of the army or navy, unless nine states assent to the same, nor shall a question on any other point, except for adjourning from day to day, be determined, unless by the votes of a majority of the united states in congress assembled.

The congress of the united states shall have power to adjourn to any time within the year, and to any place within the united states, so that no period of adjournment be for a longer duration than the space of six Months, and shall publish the Journal of their proceedings monthly, except such parts thereof relating to treaties, alliances, or military operations, as in their judgment require secrecy; and the yeas and nays of the delegates of each State, on any question, shall be entered on the Journal, when it is desired by any delegate; and the delegates of a State, or any of them, at his or their request, shall be furnished with a transcript of the said Journal, except such parts as are above excepted, to lay before the legislatures of the several states.

Article X. The committee of the states, or any nine of them, shall be authorized to execute, in the recess of congress, such of the powers of congress as the united states, in congress assembled, by the consent of nine states, shall, from time to time, think expedient to vest them with; provided that no power be delegated to the said committee, for the exercise of which, by the articles of confederation, the voice of nine states, in the congress of the united states assembled, is requisite.

Article XI. Canada acceding to this confederation, and joining in the measures of the united states, shall be admitted into, and entitled to all the advantages of this union: but no other colony shall be admitted into the same, unless such admission be agreed to by nine states.

Article XII. All bills of credit emitted, monies borrowed, and debts contracted by or under the authority of congress, before the assembling of the united states, in pursuance of the present confederation, shall be deemed and considered as a charge against the united States, for payment and satisfaction whereof the said united states and the public faith are hereby solemnly pledged.

Article XIII. Every State shall abide by the determinations of the united states, in congress assembled, on all questions which by this confederation are submitted to them. And the Articles of this confederation shall be inviolably observed by every state, and the union shall be perpetual; nor shall any alteration at any time hereafter be made in any of them, unless such alteration be agreed to in a congress of the united states, and be afterwards con-firmed by the legislatures of every state.

And Whereas it hath pleased the Great Governor of the World to incline the hearts of the legislatures we respectively represent in congress, to approve of, and to authorize us to ratify the said articles of confederation and perpetual union, Know Ye, that we, the undersigned delegates, by virtue of the power and authority to us given for that purpose, do, by these presents, in the name and in behalf of our respective constituents, fully and entirely ratify and confirm each and every of the said articles of confederation and perpetual union, and all and singular the matters and things therein contained. And we do further solemnly plight and engage the faith of our respective constituents, that they shall abide by the determinations of the united states in congress assembled, on all questions, which by the said confederation are submitted to them. And that the articles thereof shall be inviolably observed by the states we respectively represent, and that the union shall be perpetual. In Witness whereof, we have hereunto set our hands, in Congress. Done at Philadelphia, in the State of Pennsylvania, the ninth Day of July, in the Year of our Lord one Thousand seven Hundred and Seventy eight, and in the third year of the Independence of America."

*Note: Spacing, Punctuation, and Grammar reflect the original Articles. And all Mississippians say?

Chapter 10: The Constitution

Did you know the highest Law in the land is the United States Constitution? The timeline is very important. Which is why ALL Laws are supposed to support *that* Constitution. Which is why Marbury vs. Madison, 1803, is *vitally* important to understand.

The case of Marbury vs. Madison established the principle of **judicial review** in the United States, meaning that American courts have the power to strike down laws and statutes that they find to violate the Constitution of the United States.

Here's the ruling on Marbury vs. Madison, 1803:

The powers of the legislature are defined and limited; and that those limits may not be mistaken or forgotten, the constitution is written. ... Certainly all those who have framed written constitutions contemplate them as forming the fundamental and paramount law of the nation, and consequently the theory of every such government must be, that an act of the legislature, repugnant to the constitution, is void. — Marbury, 5 U.S. at 176–77

Repugnant definition: unacceptable, in conflict with, and incompatible with.

Imagine that… Here's a Founding Father having to defend in Federal Court what a Law looks like in support of the United States Constitution a mere 20 years after the Revolutionary War ended and 13 years from when it went into effect which was 2 years after it was drafted.

Now do you understand why America looks the way it has 240 years since 1776 (using 2016 when the line was drawn in the sand with this Operation)? This is why the Declaration of Independence terminology is always in future tense… "it is *their* right and *their* duty to throw off such government…" and "it is the Right of the people to alter or abolish it"…

Their = future tense and generations to come.

Right = capitalized.

Right definition = restore to normal, upright position.

Duty definition = a moral or legal obligation; a responsibility.

Alter definition = change or cause to change in character or composition, typically in a comparatively small but significant way.

Abolish definition = formally put an end to (a system, practice, or institution).

You want to bring it even more home…? Do you want to take a Guilt Trip with me? This is the SAME Declaration of Independence and foundation all Americans drink their beer, raise a toast to Veterans who protected and fought, and current Military fighting to do the same, eat their BBQ and tater salads, chips, and blow-up hard-earned money in celebratory fashion on July 4, 1776… people should feel guilty.

How many know what Freedom costs? Take a look at America the past 35 years alone… Now, pay attention to the Laws and Orders that support the Constitution that form the Blueprint of what Donald John Trump and the Generals are doing.

*Note: The spelling and punctuation reflect the original Constitution below.

The United States Constitution, September 17, 1787:

We the People of the United States, in Order to form a more perfect Union, establish Justice, insure domestic Tranquility, provide for the common defence, promote the general Welfare, and secure the Blessings of Liberty to ourselves and our Posterity, do ordain and establish this Constitution for the United States of America.
Article. I.
Section. 1.
All legislative Powers herein granted shall be vested in a Congress of the United States, which shall consist of a Senate and House of Representatives.

Section. 2.

The House of Representatives shall be composed of Members chosen every second Year by the People of the several States, and the Electors in each State shall have the Qualifications requisite for Electors of the most numerous Branch of the State Legislature.

No Person shall be a Representative who shall not have attained to the Age of twenty five Years, and been seven Years a Citizen of the United States, and who shall not, when elected, be an Inhabitant of that State in which he shall be chosen.

Representatives and direct Taxes shall be apportioned among the several States which may be included within this Union, according to their respective Numbers, which shall be determined by adding to the whole Number of free Persons, including those bound to Service for a Term of Years, and excluding Indians not taxed, three fifths of all other Persons. The actual Enumeration shall be made within three Years after the first Meeting of the Congress of the United States, and within every subsequent Term of ten Years, in such Manner as they shall by Law direct. The Number of Representatives shall not exceed one for every thirty Thousand, but each State shall have at Least one Representative; and until such enumeration shall be made, the State of New Hampshire shall be entitled to chuse three, Massachusetts eight, Rhode-Island and

Providence Plantations one, Connecticut five, New-York six, New Jersey four, Pennsylvania eight, Delaware one, Maryland six, Virginia ten, North Carolina five, South Carolina five, and Georgia three.

When vacancies happen in the Representation from any State, the Executive Authority thereof shall issue Writs of Election to fill such Vacancies.

The House of Representatives shall chuse their Speaker and other Officers; and shall have the sole Power of Impeachment.

Section. 3.

The Senate of the United States shall be composed of two Senators from each State, chosen by the Legislature thereof, for six Years; and each Senator shall have one Vote.

Immediately after they shall be assembled in Consequence of the first Election, they shall be divided as equally as may be into three Classes. The Seats of the Senators of the first Class shall be vacated at the Expiration of the second Year, of the second Class at the Expiration of the fourth Year, and of the third Class at the Expiration of the sixth Year, so that one third may be chosen every second Year; and if Vacancies happen by Resignation, or otherwise, during the Recess of the Legislature of any State, the Executive thereof may make temporary Appointments until the next Meeting of the Legislature, which shall then fill such Vacancies.

No Person shall be a Senator who shall not have attained to the Age of thirty Years, and been nine Years a Citizen of the United States, and who shall not, when elected, be an Inhabitant of that State for which he shall be chosen.
The Vice President of the United States shall be President of the Senate, but shall have no Vote, unless they be equally divided.

The Senate shall chuse their other Officers, and also a President pro tempore, in the Absence of the Vice President, or when he shall exercise the Office of President of the United States.

The Senate shall have the sole Power to try all Impeachments. When sitting for that Purpose, they shall be on Oath or Affirmation. When the President of the United States is tried, the Chief Justice shall preside: And no Person shall be convicted without the Concurrence of two thirds of the Members present.
Judgment in Cases of Impeachment shall not extend further than to removal from Office, and disqualification to hold and enjoy any Office of honor, Trust or Profit under the United States: but the Party convicted shall nevertheless be liable and subject to Indictment, Trial, Judgment and Punishment, according to Law.

Section. 4.

The Times, Places and Manner of holding Elections for Senators and Representatives, shall be prescribed in each State by the Legislature thereof; but the Congress may at any time by Law make or alter such Regulations, except as to the Places of chusing Senators.

The Congress shall assemble at least once in every Year, and such Meeting shall be on the first Monday in December, unless they shall by Law appoint a different Day.

Section. 5.

Each House shall be the Judge of the Elections, Returns and Qualifications of its own Members, and a Majority of each shall constitute a Quorum to do Business; but a smaller Number may adjourn from day to day, and may be authorized to compel the Attendance of absent Members, in such Manner, and under such Penalties as each House may provide.
Each House may determine the Rules of its Proceedings, punish its Members for disorderly Behaviour, and, with the Concurrence of two thirds, expel a Member.
Each House shall keep a Journal of its Proceedings, and from time to time publish the same, excepting such Parts as may in their Judgment require Secrecy; and the Yeas and Nays of the Members of either House on any question shall, at the Desire of one fifth of those Present, be entered on the Journal.

Neither House, during the Session of Congress, shall, without the Consent of the other, adjourn for more than three days, nor to any other Place than that in which the two Houses shall be sitting.

Section. 6.

The Senators and Representatives shall receive a Compensation for their Services, to be ascertained by Law, and paid out of the Treasury of the United States. They shall in all Cases, except Treason, Felony and Breach of the Peace, be privileged from Arrest during their Attendance at the Session of their respective Houses, and in going to and returning from the same; and for any Speech or Debate in either House, they shall not be questioned in any other Place.

No Senator or Representative shall, during the Time for which he was elected, be appointed to any civil Office under the Authority of the United States, which shall have been created, or the Emoluments whereof shall have been encreased during such time; and no Person holding any Office under the United States, shall be a Member of either House during his Continuance in Office.

Section. 7.

All Bills for raising Revenue shall originate in the House of Representatives; but the Senate may propose or concur with Amendments as on other Bills.

Every Bill which shall have passed the House of Representatives and the Senate, shall, before it become a Law, be presented to the President of the United States; If he approve he shall sign it, but if not he shall return it, with his Objections to that House in which it shall have originated, who shall enter the Objections at large on their Journal, and proceed to reconsider it. If after such Reconsideration two thirds of that House shall agree to pass the Bill, it shall be sent, together with the Objections, to the other House, by which it shall likewise be reconsidered, and if approved by two thirds of that House, it shall become a Law. But in all such Cases the Votes of both Houses shall be determined by yeas and Nays, and the Names of the Persons voting for and against the Bill shall be entered on the Journal of each House respectively. If any Bill shall not be returned by the President within ten Days (Sundays excepted) after it shall have been presented to him, the Same shall be a Law, in like Manner as if he had signed it, unless the Congress by their Adjournment prevent its Return, in which Case it shall not be a Law.

Every Order, Resolution, or Vote to which the Concurrence of the Senate and House of Representatives may be necessary (except on a question of Adjournment) shall be presented to the President of the United States; and before the Same shall take Effect, shall be approved by him, or being disapproved by him, shall be repassed by two thirds of the Senate and House of Representatives, according to the Rules and Limitations prescribed in the Case of a Bill.

Section. 8.

The Congress shall have Power To lay and collect Taxes, Duties, Imposts and Excises, to pay the Debts and provide for the common Defence and general Welfare of the United States; but all Duties, Imposts and Excises shall be uniform throughout the United States;

To borrow Money on the credit of the United States;

To regulate Commerce with foreign Nations, and among the several States, and with the Indian Tribes;

To establish an uniform Rule of Naturalization, and uniform Laws on the subject of Bankruptcies throughout the United States;

To coin Money, regulate the Value thereof, and of foreign Coin, and fix the Standard of Weights and Measures;

To provide for the Punishment of counterfeiting the Securities and current Coin of the United States;

To establish Post Offices and post Roads;

To promote the Progress of Science and useful Arts, by securing for limited Times to Authors and Inventors the exclusive Right to their respective Writings and Discoveries;

To constitute Tribunals inferior to the supreme Court;

To define and punish Piracies and Felonies committed on the high Seas, and Offences against the Law of Nations;

To declare War, grant Letters of Marque and Reprisal, and make Rules concerning Captures on Land and Water;

To raise and support Armies, but no Appropriation of Money to that Use shall be for a longer Term than two Years;

To provide and maintain a Navy;

To make Rules for the Government and Regulation of the land and naval Forces;
To provide for calling forth the Militia to execute the Laws of the Union, suppress Insurrections and repel Invasions;

To provide for organizing, arming, and disciplining, the Militia, and for governing such Part of them as may be employed in the Service of the United States, reserving to the States respectively, the Appointment of the Officers, and the Authority of training the Militia according to the discipline prescribed by Congress;

To exercise exclusive Legislation in all Cases whatsoever, over such District (not exceeding ten Miles square) as may, by Cession of particular States, and the Acceptance of Congress, become the Seat of the Government of the United States, and to exercise like Authority over all Places purchased by the Consent of the Legislature of the State in which the Same shall be, for the Erection of Forts, Magazines, Arsenals, dock-Yards, and other needful Buildings;—And
To make all Laws which shall be necessary and proper for carrying into Execution the foregoing Powers, and all other Powers vested by this Constitution in the Government of the United States, or in any Department or Officer thereof.

Section. 9.

The Migration or Importation of such Persons as any of the States now existing shall think proper to admit, shall not be prohibited by the Congress prior to the Year one thousand eight hundred and eight, but a Tax or duty may be imposed on such Importation, not exceeding ten dollars for each Person.

The Privilege of the Writ of Habeas Corpus shall not be suspended, unless when in Cases of Rebellion or Invasion the public Safety may require it.

No Bill of Attainder or ex post facto Law shall be passed.

No Capitation, or other direct, Tax shall be laid, unless in Proportion to the Census or enumeration herein before directed to be taken.

No Tax or Duty shall be laid on Articles exported from any State.

No Preference shall be given by any Regulation of Commerce or Revenue to the Ports of one State over those of another: nor shall Vessels bound to, or from, one State, be obliged to enter, clear, or pay Duties in another.

No Money shall be drawn from the Treasury, but in Consequence of Appropriations made by Law; and a regular Statement and Account of the Receipts and Expenditures of all public Money shall be published from time to time.

No Title of Nobility shall be granted by the United States: And no Person holding any Office of Profit or Trust under them, shall, without the Consent of the Congress, accept of any present, Emolument, Office, or Title, of any kind whatever, from any King, Prince, or foreign State.

Section. 10.

No State shall enter into any Treaty, Alliance, or Confederation; grant Letters of Marque and Reprisal; coin Money; emit Bills of Credit; make any Thing but gold and silver Coin a Tender in Payment of Debts; pass any Bill of Attainder, ex post facto Law, or Law impairing the Obligation of Contracts, or grant any Title of Nobility.

No State shall, without the Consent of the Congress, lay any Imposts or Duties on Imports or Exports, except what may be absolutely necessary for executing it's inspection Laws: and the net Produce of all Duties and Imposts, laid by any State on Imports or Exports, shall be for the Use of the Treasury of the United States; and all such Laws shall be subject to the Revision and Controul of the Congress.

No State shall, without the Consent of Congress, lay any Duty of Tonnage, keep Troops, or Ships of War in time of Peace, enter into any Agreement or Compact with another State, or with a foreign Power, or engage in War, unless actually invaded, or in such imminent Danger as will not admit of delay.

Article. II.

Section. 1.

The executive Power shall be vested in a President of the United States of America. He shall hold his Office during the Term of four Years, and, together with the Vice President, chosen for the same Term, be elected, as follows

Each State shall appoint, in such Manner as the Legislature thereof may direct, a Number of Electors, equal to the whole Number of Senators and Representatives to which the State may be entitled in the Congress: but no Senator or Representative, or Person holding an Office of Trust or Profit under the United States, shall be appointed an Elector.

The Electors shall meet in their respective States, and vote by Ballot for two Persons, of whom one at least shall not be an Inhabitant of the same State with themselves. And they shall make a List of all the Persons voted for, and of the Number of Votes for each; which List they shall sign and certify, and transmit sealed to the Seat of the Government of the United States, directed to the President of the Senate. The President of the Senate shall, in the Presence of the Senate and House of Representatives, open all the Certificates, and the Votes shall then be counted. The Person having the greatest Number of Votes shall be the President, if such Number be a Majority of the whole Number of Electors appointed; and if there be more than one who have such Majority, and have an equal Number of Votes, then the House of Representatives shall immediately chuse by Ballot one of them for President; and if no Person have a Majority, then from the five highest on the List the said House shall in like Manner chuse the President. But in chusing the President, the Votes shall be taken by States, the Representation from each State having one Vote; A quorum for this Purpose shall consist of a Member or Members from two thirds of the States, and a Majority of all the States shall be necessary to a Choice. In every Case, after the Choice of the President, the Person having the greatest Number of Votes of the Electors shall be the Vice President. But if there should remain two or more who have equal Votes, the Senate shall chuse from them by Ballot the Vice President.

The Congress may determine the Time of chusing the Electors, and the Day on which they shall give their Votes; which Day shall be the same throughout the United States.

No Person except a natural born Citizen, or a Citizen of the United States, at the time of the Adoption of this Constitution, shall be eligible to the Office of President; neither shall any Person be eligible to that Office who shall not have attained to the Age of thirty five Years, and been fourteen Years a Resident within the United States.

In Case of the Removal of the President from Office, or of his Death, Resignation, or Inability to discharge the Powers and Duties of the said Office, the Same shall devolve on the Vice President, and the Congress may by Law provide for the Case of Removal, Death, Resignation or Inability, both of the President and Vice President, declaring what Officer shall then act as President, and such Officer shall act accordingly, until the Disability be removed, or a President shall be elected.

The President shall, at stated Times, receive for his Services, a Compensation, which shall neither be encreased nor diminished during the Period for which he shall have been elected, and he shall not receive within that Period any other Emolument from the United States, or any of them.

Before he enter on the Execution of his Office, he shall take the following Oath or Affirmation:—"I do solemnly swear (or affirm) that I will faithfully execute the Office of President of the United States, and will to the best of my Ability, preserve, protect and defend the Constitution of the United States."

Section. 2.

The President shall be Commander in Chief of the Army and Navy of the United States, and of the Militia of the several States, when called into the actual Service of the United States; he may require the Opinion, in writing, of the principal Officer in each of the executive

Departments, upon any Subject relating to the Duties of their respective Offices, and he shall have Power to grant Reprieves and Pardons for Offences against the United States, except in Cases of Impeachment.

He shall have Power, by and with the Advice and Consent of the Senate, to make Treaties, provided two thirds of the Senators present concur; and he shall nominate, and by and with the Advice and Consent of the Senate, shall appoint Ambassadors, other public Ministers and Consuls, Judges of the supreme Court, and all other Officers of the United States, whose Appointments are not herein otherwise provided for, and which shall be established by Law: but the Congress may by Law vest the Appointment of such inferior Officers, as they think proper, in the President alone, in the Courts of Law, or in the Heads of Departments.

The President shall have Power to fill up all Vacancies that may happen during the Recess of the Senate, by granting Commissions which shall expire at the End of their next Session.

Section. 3.

He shall from time to time give to the Congress Information of the State of the Union, and recommend to their Consideration such Measures as he shall judge necessary and expedient; he may, on extraordinary Occasions, convene both Houses, or either of them, and in Case of Disagreement between them, with Respect to the Time of Adjournment, he may adjourn them to such Time as he shall think proper; he shall receive Ambassadors and other public Ministers; he shall take Care that the Laws be faithfully executed, and shall Commission all the Officers of the United States.

Section. 4.

The President, Vice President and all civil Officers of the United States, shall be removed from Office on Impeachment for, and Conviction of, Treason, Bribery, or other high Crimes and Misdemeanors.
Article. III. Section. 1.

The judicial Power of the United States, shall be vested in one supreme Court, and in such inferior Courts as the Congress may from time to time ordain and establish. The Judges, both of the supreme and inferior Courts, shall hold their Offices during good Behaviour, and shall, at stated Times, receive for their Services, a Compensation, which shall not be diminished during their Continuance in Office.

Section. 2.

The judicial Power shall extend to all Cases, in Law and Equity, arising under this Constitution, the Laws of the United States, and Treaties made, or which shall be made, under their Authority;—to all Cases affecting Ambassadors, other public Ministers and Consuls;—to all Cases of admiralty and maritime Jurisdiction;—to Controversies to which the United States shall be a Party;—to Controversies between two or more States;— between a State and Citizens of another State,—between Citizens of different States,—between Citizens of the same State claiming Lands under Grants of different States, and between a State, or the Citizens thereof, and foreign States, Citizens or Subjects.

In all Cases affecting Ambassadors, other public Ministers and Consuls, and those in which a State shall be Party, the supreme Court shall have original Jurisdiction. In all the other Cases before mentioned, the supreme Court shall have appellate Jurisdiction, both as to Law and Fact, with such Exceptions, and under such Regulations as the Congress shall make.

The Trial of all Crimes, except in Cases of Impeachment, shall be by Jury; and such Trial shall be held in the State where the said Crimes shall have been committed; but when not committed within any State, the Trial shall be at such Place or Places as the Congress may by Law have directed.

Section. 3.

Treason against the United States, shall consist only in levying War against them, or in adhering to their Enemies, giving them Aid and Comfort. No Person shall be convicted of Treason unless on the Testimony of two Witnesses to the same overt Act, or on Confession in open Court.

The Congress shall have Power to declare the Punishment of Treason, but no Attainder of Treason shall work Corruption of Blood, or Forfeiture except during the Life of the Person attainted.
Article. IV.
Section. 1.

Full Faith and Credit shall be given in each State to the public Acts, Records, and judicial Proceedings of every other State. And the Congress may by general Laws prescribe the Manner in which such Acts, Records and Proceedings shall be proved, and the Effect thereof.

Section. 2.

The Citizens of each State shall be entitled to all Privileges and Immunities of Citizens in the several States.
A Person charged in any State with Treason, Felony, or other Crime, who shall flee from Justice, and be found in another State, shall on Demand of the executive Authority of the State from which he fled, be delivered up, to be removed to the State having Jurisdiction of the Crime.

No Person held to Service or Labour in one State, under the Laws thereof, escaping into another, shall, in Consequence of any Law or Regulation therein, be discharged from such Service or Labour, but shall be delivered up on Claim of the Party to whom such Service or Labour may be due.

Section. 3.

New States may be admitted by the Congress into this Union; but no new State shall be formed or erected within the Jurisdiction of any other State; nor any State be formed by the Junction of two or more States, or Parts of States, without the Consent of the Legislatures of the States concerned as well as of the Congress.

The Congress shall have Power to dispose of and make all needful Rules and Regulations respecting the Territory or other Property belonging to the United States; and nothing in this Constitution shall be so construed as to Prejudice any Claims of the United States, or of any particular State.

Section. 4.

The United States shall guarantee to every State in this Union a Republican Form of Government, and shall protect each of them against Invasion; and on Application of the Legislature, or of the Executive (when the Legislature cannot be convened) against domestic Violence.
Article. V.
The Congress, whenever two thirds of both Houses shall deem it necessary, shall propose Amendments to this Constitution, or, on the Application of the Legislatures of two thirds of the several States, shall call a Convention for proposing Amendments, which, in either Case, shall be valid to all Intents and Purposes, as Part of this Constitution, when ratified by the Legislatures of three fourths of the several States, or by Conventions in three fourths thereof, as the one or the other Mode of Ratification may be proposed by the Congress; Provided that no Amendment which may be made prior to the Year One thousand eight hundred and eight shall in any Manner affect the first and fourth Clauses in the Ninth Section of the first Article; and that no State, without its Consent, shall be deprived of its equal Suffrage in the Senate.
Article. VI.
All Debts contracted and Engagements entered into, before the Adoption of this Constitution, shall be as valid against the United States under this Constitution, as under the Confederation.

This Constitution, and the Laws of the United States which shall be made in Pursuance thereof; and all Treaties made, or which shall be made, under the Authority of the United States, shall be the supreme Law of the Land; and the Judges in every State shall be bound thereby, any Thing in the Constitution or Laws of any State to the Contrary notwithstanding.

The Senators and Representatives before mentioned, and the Members of the several State Legislatures, and all executive and judicial Officers, both of the United States and of the several States, shall be bound by Oath or Affirmation, to support this Constitution; but no religious Test shall ever be required as a Qualification to any Office or public Trust under the United States.
Article. VII.
The Ratification of the Conventions of nine States, shall be sufficient for the Establishment of this Constitution between the States so ratifying the Same.
The Word, "the," being interlined between the seventh and eighth Lines of the first Page, The Word "Thirty" being partly written on an Erazure in the fifteenth Line of the first Page, The Words "is tried" being interlined between the thirty second and thirty third Lines of the first Page and the Word "the" being interlined between the forty third and forty fourth Lines of the second Page.
Attest William Jackson Secretary
done in Convention by the Unanimous Consent of the States present the Seventeenth Day of September in the Year of our Lord one thousand seven hundred and Eighty seven and of the Independance of the United States of America the Twelfth In witness whereof We have hereunto subscribed our Names,
G°. Washington
Presidt and deputy from Virginia

Note: *Misspellings and Spacings are the original context.*

Chapter 11: The Bill of Rights

Bet you didn't know the Bill of Rights were written as a 3rd Constitution… Supporters of the Constitution, known as Federalists, opposed a bill of rights for much of the ratification period, in part because of the procedural uncertainties it would create (https://archive.org/details/originalmeanings00rako_0).

Many were concerned that a strong national government was a threat to individual rights and that the President would become a king. Jefferson wrote to Madison advocating a Bill of Rights:

"Half a loaf is better than no bread. If we cannot secure all our rights, let us secure what we can."

The pseudonymous Anti-Federalist "Brutus" (probably Robert Yates) wrote:

"We find they have, in the ninth section of the first article declared, that the writ of habeas corpus shall not be suspended, unless in cases of rebellion—that no bill of attainder, or ex post facto law, shall be passed—that no title of nobility shall be granted by the United States, etc. If every thing which is not given is reserved, what propriety is there in these exceptions? Does this Constitution any where grant the power of suspending the habeas corpus, to make ex post facto laws, pass bills of attainder, or grant titles of nobility? It certainly does not in express terms. The only answer that can be given is, that these are implied in the general powers granted. With equal truth it may be said, that all the powers which the bills of rights guard against the abuse of, are contained or implied in the general ones granted by this Constitution.

Ought not a government, vested with such extensive and indefinite authority, to have been restricted by a declaration of rights? It certainly ought. So clear a point is this, that I cannot help suspecting that persons who attempt to persuade people that such reservations were less necessary under this Constitution than under those of the States, are wilfully endeavoring to deceive, and to lead you into an absolute state of vassalage."

Alexander Hamilton's opposition to the Bill of Rights, from ***Federalist No. 84***:

"I go further, and affirm that bills of rights, in the sense and to the extent in which they are contended for, are not only unnecessary in the proposed Constitution, but would even be dangerous. They would contain various exceptions to powers not granted; and, on this very account, would afford a colorable pretext to claim more than were granted. For why declare that things shall not be done which there is no power to do? Why, for instance, should it be said that the liberty of the press shall not be restrained, when no power is given by which restrictions may be imposed? I will not contend that such a provision would confer a regulating power; but it is evident that it would furnish, to men disposed to usurp, a plausible pretense for claiming that power. They might urge with a semblance of reason, that the Constitution ought not to be charged with the absurdity of providing against the abuse of an authority which was not given, and that the provision against restraining the liberty of the press afforded a clear implication, that a power to prescribe proper regulations concerning it was intended to be vested in the national government. This may serve as a specimen of the numerous handles which would be given to the doctrine of constructive powers, by the indulgence of an injudicious zeal for bills of rights."

Madison argued against such an inclusion, suggesting that state governments were sufficient guarantors of personal liberty, in No. 46 of *The Federalist Papers*, a series of essays promoting the Federalist position.
Hamilton opposed a bill of rights in *The Federalist No. 84*, stating that:

> *"The constitution is itself in every rational sense, and to every useful purpose, a bill of rights."*

He stated that ratification did not mean the American people were surrendering their rights, making protections unnecessary:

> *"Here, in strictness, the people surrender nothing, and as they retain everything, they have no need of particular reservations."*

Patrick Henry criticized the Federalist point of view, writing that the legislature must be firmly informed:

> *"Of the extent of the rights retained by the people ... being in a state of uncertainty, they will assume rather than give up powers by implication."*

Other anti-Federalists pointed out that earlier political documents, in particular the Magna Carta, had protected specific rights. In response, Hamilton argued that the Constitution was inherently different:
Bills of rights are in their origin, stipulations between kings and their subjects, abridgments of prerogative in favor of privilege, reservations of rights not surrendered to the prince. Such was the Magna Charta, obtained by the Barons, swords in hand, from King John.

The Bill of Rights were primarily written by James Madison along with members of the 1st Congress. Proposed following the often bitter 1787 – 88 debate over the ratification of the Constitution and written to address the objections raised by Anti-Federalists, the Bill of Rights amendments add to the Constitution specific guarantees of personal freedoms and rights, clear limitations on the government's power in judicial and other proceedings, and explicit declarations that all powers not specifically granted to the federal government by the Constitution are reserved to the states or the people.

The concepts codified in these amendments are built upon those in earlier documents, especially the Virginia Declaration of Rights (1776), as well as the Northwest Ordinance (1787) (***Reference:*** Bryan, Dan (April 8, 2012). "The Northwest Ordinance of 1787 and its Effects". American History USA. Retrieved February 23, 2023.)), the English Bill of Rights (1689), and Magna Carta (1215) (***Reference:*** "Bill of Rights". history.com. A&E Television Networks. Archived from the original on February 25, 2019. Retrieved February 24, 2019).

Largely because of the efforts of Representative James Madison, who studied the deficiencies of the Constitution pointed out by anti-federalists and then crafted a series of corrective proposals, Congress approved twelve articles of amendment on September 25, 1789, and submitted them to the states for ratification.

Contrary to Madison's proposal that the proposed amendments be incorporated into the main body of the Constitution (at the relevant articles and sections of the document), they were proposed as supplemental additions (codicils) to it. (***Reference:*** England, Trent; Spalding, Matthew. "Essays on Article V: Amendments". The Heritage Foundation. Archived from the original on July 1, 2018. Retrieved February 24, 2019).

Articles Three through Twelve were ratified as additions to the Constitution on December 15, 1791, and became Amendments One through Ten of the Constitution. Article Two became part of the Constitution on May 5, 1992, as the Twenty-seventh Amendment. Article One is still pending before the states.

Bill of Rights December 15, 1791:

1. **First Amendment:** Congress shall make no law respecting an establishment of religion, or prohibiting the free exercise thereof; or abridging the freedom of speech, or of the press; or the right of the people peaceably to assemble, and to petition the Government for a redress of grievances.
2. **Second Amendment:** A well regulated Militia, being necessary to the security of a free State, the right of the people to keep and bear Arms, shall not be infringed.
3. **Third Amendment:** No Soldier shall, in time of peace be quartered in any house, without the consent of the Owner, nor in time of war, but in a manner to be prescribed by law.
4. **Fourth Amendment:** The right of the people to be secure in their persons, houses, papers, and effects, against unreasonable searches and seizures, shall not be violated, and no Warrants shall issue, but upon probable cause, supported by Oath or affirmation, and particularly describing the place to be searched, and the persons or things to be seized.
5. **Fifth Amendment:** No person shall be held to answer for a capital, or otherwise infamous crime, unless on a presentment or indictment of a Grand Jury, except in cases arising in the land or naval forces, or in the Militia, when in actual service in time of War or public danger; nor shall any person be subject for the same offence to be twice put in jeopardy of life or limb; nor shall be compelled in any criminal case to be a witness against himself, nor be deprived of life, liberty, or property, without due process of law; nor shall private property be taken for public use, without just compensation.
6. **Sixth Amendment:** In all criminal prosecutions, the accused shall enjoy the right to a speedy and public trial, by an impartial jury of the State and district wherein the crime shall have been committed, which district shall have been previously ascertained by law, and to be informed of the nature and cause of the accusation; to be confronted with the witnesses against him; to have compulsory process for obtaining witnesses in his favor, and to have the Assistance of Counsel for his defence.
7. **Seventh Amendment:** In Suits at common law, where the value in controversy shall exceed twenty dollars, the right of trial by jury shall be preserved, and no fact tried by a jury, shall be otherwise re-examined in any Court of the United States, than according to the rules of the common law.
8. **Eighth Amendment:** Excessive bail shall not be required, nor excessive fines imposed, nor cruel and unusual punishments inflicted.
9. **Ninth Amendment:** The enumeration in the Constitution, of certain rights, shall not be construed to deny or disparage others retained by the people.
10. **Tenth Amendment:** The powers not delegated to the United States by the Constitution, nor prohibited by it to the States, are reserved to the States respectively, or to the people.

Note: spelling and punctuation are original context.

Every conservative and republican hang their hat on the 2nd Amendment, and rightfully so, but funny how that 3rd Amendment slides in there for soldiers and those who housed them…

Amazing how that was *so* INTRICATE, IMPORTANT and PRECEDENT enough to place in Amendments to the Constitution.

Chapter 12: 3 Branches of Government

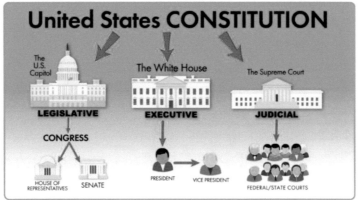

LEGISLATIVE

★Makes laws

★Approves presidential appointments

★Two senators from each state

★The number of congressmen is based on population

EXECUTIVE

★Signs laws

★Vetoes laws

★Pardons people

★Appoints federal judges

★Elected every four years

JUDICIAL

★Decides if laws are constitutional

★Are appointed by the president

★There are 9 justices

★Can overturn rulings by other judges

How the United States is Governed
The three branches of U.S. government

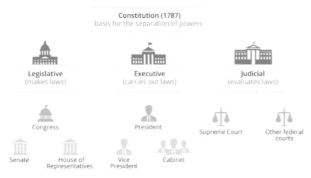

Constitution (1787)
basis for the separation of powers

Legislative (makes laws)   Executive (carries out laws)   Judicial (evaluates laws)

Congress   President   Supreme Court   Other federal courts

Senate   House of Representatives   Vice President   Cabinet

statista

Legislative Branch

An assembly with the authority to make laws for a political entity such as a country or city. They are often contrasted with the executive and judicial powers of government.

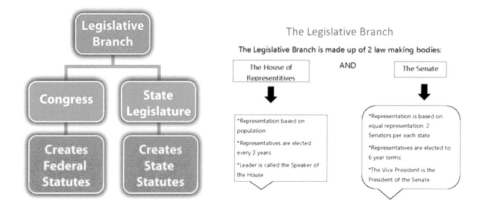

Established by Article I of the Constitution, the Legislative Branch consists of the House of Representatives and the Senate, which together form the United States Congress. The Constitution grants Congress the sole authority to enact legislation and declare war, the right to confirm or reject many Presidential appointments, and substantial investigative powers.

The House of Representatives is made up of 435 elected members, divided among the 50 states in proportion to their total population. In addition, there are 6 non-voting members, representing the District of Columbia, the Commonwealth of Puerto Rico, and four other territories of the United States: American Samoa, Guam, the U.S. Virgin Islands, and the Commonwealth of Northern Mariana Islands. The presiding officer of the chamber is the Speaker of the House, elected by the Representatives. He or she is third in the line of succession to the Presidency.

Members of the House are elected every two years and must be 25 years of age, a U.S. citizen for at least seven years, and a resident of the state (but not necessarily the district) they represent.

The House has several powers assigned exclusively to it, including the power to initiate revenue bills, impeach federal officials, and elect the President in the case of an Electoral College tie.

The Senate is composed of 100 Senators, 2 for each state. Until the ratification of the 17th Amendment in 1913, Senators were chosen by state legislatures, not by popular vote. Since then, they have been elected to six-year terms by the people of each state. Senators' terms are staggered so that about one-third of the Senate is up for reelection every two years. Senators must be 30 years of age, U.S. citizens for at least nine years, and residents of the state they represent.

The Vice President of the United States serves as President of the Senate and may cast the decisive vote in the event of a tie in the Senate.

The Senate has the sole power to confirm those of the President's appointments that require consent, and to provide advice and consent to ratify treaties. There are, however, two exceptions to this rule: the House must also approve appointments to the Vice Presidency and any treaty that involves foreign trade. The Senate also tries impeachment cases for federal officials referred to it by the House.

In order to pass legislation and send it to the President for his or her signature, both the House and the Senate must pass the same bill by majority vote. If the President vetoes a bill, they may override his veto by passing the bill again in each chamber with at least two-thirds of each body voting in favor.

The Legislative Process

The first step in the legislative process is the introduction of a bill to Congress. Anyone can write it, but only members of Congress can introduce legislation. Some important bills are traditionally introduced at the request of the President, such as the annual federal budget. During the legislative process, however, the initial bill can undergo drastic changes.

After being introduced, a bill is referred to the appropriate committee for review. There are 17 Senate committees, with 70 subcommittees, and 23 House committees, with 104 subcommittees. The committees are not set in stone, but change in number and form with each new Congress as required for the efficient consideration of legislation. Each committee oversees a specific policy area, and the subcommittees take on more specialized policy areas. For example, the House Committee on Ways and Means includes subcommittees on Social Security and Trade.

A bill is first considered in a subcommittee, where it may be accepted, amended, or rejected entirely. If the members of the subcommittee agree to move a bill forward, it is reported to the full committee, where the process is repeated again. Throughout this stage of the process, the committees and subcommittees call hearings to investigate the merits and flaws of the bill. They invite experts, advocates, and opponents to appear before the committee and provide testimony, and can compel people to appear using subpoena power if necessary.

If the full committee votes to approve the bill, it is reported to the floor of the House or Senate, and the majority party leadership decides when to place the bill on the calendar for consideration. If a bill is particularly pressing, it may be considered right away. Others may wait for months or never be scheduled at all.

When the bill comes up for consideration, the House has a very structured debate process. Each member who wishes to speak only has a few minutes, and the number and kind of amendments are usually limited. In the Senate, debate on most bills is unlimited — Senators may speak to issues other than the bill under consideration during their speeches, and any amendment can be introduced. Senators can use this to filibuster bills under consideration, a procedure by which a Senator delays a vote on a bill — and by extension its passage — by refusing to stand down. A supermajority of 60 Senators can break a filibuster by invoking cloture, or the cession of debate on the bill, and forcing a vote. Once debate is over, the votes of a simple majority pass the bill.

A bill must pass both houses of Congress before it goes to the President for consideration. Though the Constitution requires that the two bills have the exact same wording, this rarely happens in practice. To bring the bills into alignment, a Conference Committee is convened, consisting of members from both chambers. The members of the committee produce a conference report, intended as the final version of the bill. Each chamber then votes again to approve the conference report. Depending on where the bill originated, the final text is then enrolled by either the Clerk of the House or the Secretary of the Senate, and presented to the Speaker of the House and the President of the Senate for their signatures. The bill is then sent to the President.

When receiving a bill from Congress, the President has several options. If the President agrees substantially with the bill, he or she may sign it into law, and the bill is then printed in the Statutes at Large. If the President believes the law to be bad policy, he or she may veto it and send it back to Congress. Congress may override the veto with a two-thirds vote of each chamber, at which point the bill becomes law and is printed. There are two other options that the President may exercise. If Congress is in session and the President takes no action within 10 days, the bill becomes law. If Congress adjourns before 10 days are up and the President takes no action, then the bill dies and Congress may not vote to override. This is called a pocket veto, and if Congress still wants to pass the legislation, they must begin the entire process anew.

Powers of Congress

Congress, as one of the three coequal branches of government, is ascribed significant powers by the Constitution. All legislative power in the government is vested in Congress, meaning that it is the only part of the government that can make new laws or change existing laws. Executive Branch agencies issue regulations with the full force of law, but these are only under the authority of laws enacted by Congress. The President may veto bills Congress passes, but Congress may also override a veto by a two-thirds vote in both the Senate and the House of Representatives.

Article I of the Constitution enumerates the powers of Congress and the specific areas in which it may legislate. Congress is also empowered to enact laws deemed "necessary and proper" for the execution of the powers given to any part of the government under the Constitution.

Part of Congress's exercise of legislative authority is the establishment of an annual budget for the government. To this end, Congress levies taxes and tariffs to provide funding for essential government services. If enough money cannot be raised to fund the government, then Congress may also authorize borrowing to make up the difference. Congress can also mandate spending on specific items: legislatively directed spending, commonly known as "earmarks," specifies funds for a particular project, rather than for a government agency.

Both chambers of Congress have extensive investigative powers, and may compel the production of evidence or testimony toward whatever end they deem necessary. Members of Congress spend much of their time holding hearings and investigations in committee. Refusal to cooperate with a congressional subpoena can result in charges of contempt of Congress, which could result in a prison term.

The Senate maintains several powers to itself: It consents to the ratification of treaties by a two-thirds supermajority vote and confirms the appointments of the President by a majority vote. The consent of the House of Representatives is also necessary for the ratification of trade agreements and the confirmation of the Vice President.

Government Oversight

Oversight of the executive branch is an important Congressional check on the President's power and a balance against his or her discretion in implementing laws and making regulations.

One primary way that Congress conducts oversight is through hearings. The House Committee on Oversight and Government Reform and the Senate Committee on Homeland Security and Government Affairs are both devoted to overseeing and reforming government operations, and each committee conducts oversight in its policy area.

Congress also maintains an investigative organization, the Government Accountability Office (GAO). Founded in 1921 as the General Accounting Office, its original mission was to audit the budgets and financial statements sent to Congress by the Secretary of the Treasury and the Director of the Office of Management and Budget. Today, the GAO audits and generates reports on every aspect of the government, ensuring that taxpayer dollars are spent with the effectiveness and efficiency that the American people deserve.

The Executive Branch also polices itself: Sixty-four Inspectors General, each responsible for a different agency, regularly audit and report on the agencies to which they are attached.

Executive Branch

The part of government which enforces the law and has overall responsibility for the governance of a state.

The power of the Executive Branch is vested in the President of the United States, who also acts as head of state and Commander-in-Chief of the armed forces. The President is responsible for implementing and enforcing the laws written by Congress and, to that end, appoints the heads of the federal agencies, including the Cabinet. The Vice President is also part of the Executive Branch, ready to assume the Presidency should the need arise.

The Cabinet and independent federal agencies are responsible for the day-to-day enforcement and administration of federal laws. These departments and agencies have missions and responsibilities as widely divergent as those of the Department of Defense and the Environmental Protection Agency, the Social Security Administration and the Securities and Exchange Commission.

Including members of the armed forces, the Executive Branch employs more than 4 million Americans.

The President

The President is both the head of state and head of government of the United States of America, and Commander-in-Chief of the armed forces.

Under Article II of the Constitution, the President is responsible for the execution and enforcement of the laws created by Congress. Fifteen executive departments — each led by an appointed member of the President's Cabinet — carry out the day-to-day administration of the federal government. They are joined in this by other executive agencies such as the CIA and Environmental Protection Agency, the heads of which are not part of the Cabinet, but who are under the full authority of the President. The President also appoints the heads of more than 50 independent federal commissions, such as the Federal Reserve Board or the Securities and Exchange Commission, as well as federal judges, ambassadors, and other federal offices. The Executive Office of the President (EOP) consists of the immediate staff to the President, along with entities such as the Office of Management and Budget and the Office of the United States Trade Representative.

The President has the power either to sign legislation into law or to veto bills enacted by Congress, although Congress may override a veto with a two-thirds vote of both houses. The Executive Branch conducts diplomacy with other nations and the President has the power to negotiate and sign treaties, which the Senate ratifies. The President can issue executive orders, which direct executive officers or clarify and further existing laws. The President also has the power to extend pardons and clemencies for federal crimes.

With these powers come several responsibilities, among them a constitutional requirement to "from time to time give to the Congress Information of the State of the Union, and recommend to their Consideration such Measures as he shall judge necessary and expedient." Although the President may fulfill this requirement in any way he or she chooses, Presidents have traditionally given a State of the Union address to a joint session of Congress each January (except in inaugural years) outlining their agenda for the coming year.

The Constitution lists only three qualifications for the Presidency — the President must be at least 35 years of age, be a natural born citizen, and must have lived in the United States for at least 14 years. And though millions of Americans vote in a presidential election every four years, the President is not, in fact, directly elected by the people. Instead, on the first Tuesday after the first Monday in November of every fourth year, the people elect the members of the Electoral College. Apportioned by population to the 50 states — one for each member of their congressional delegation (with the District of Columbia receiving 3 votes) — these Electors then cast the votes for President. There are currently 538 electors in the Electoral College.

Today, the President is limited to two four-year terms, but until the 22nd Amendment to the Constitution, ratified in 1951, a President could serve an unlimited number of terms. Franklin Delano Roosevelt was elected President four times, serving from 1932 until his death in 1945; he is the only President ever to have served more than two terms.

By tradition, the President and the First Family live in the White House in Washington, D.C., also the location of the President's Oval Office and the offices of his or her senior staff. When the President travels by plane, his or her aircraft is designated Air Force One; the President may also use a Marine Corps helicopter, known as Marine One while the President is on board. For ground travel, the President uses an armored presidential limousine.

The Vice President

The primary responsibility of the Vice President of the United States is to be ready at a moment's notice to assume the Presidency if the President is unable to perform his or her duties. This can be because of the President's death, resignation, or temporary incapacitation, or if the Vice President and a majority of the Cabinet judge that the President is no longer able to discharge the duties of the presidency.

The Vice President is elected along with the President by the Electoral College. Each elector casts one vote for President and another for Vice President. Before the ratification of the 12th Amendment in 1804, electors only voted for President, and the person who received the second greatest number of votes became Vice President.

The Vice President also serves as the President of the United States Senate, where he or she casts the deciding vote in the case of a tie. Except in the case of tie-breaking votes, the Vice President rarely actually presides over the Senate. Instead, the Senate selects one of their own members, usually junior members of the majority party, to preside over the Senate each day.

The duties of the Vice President, outside of those enumerated in the Constitution, are at the discretion of the current President. Each Vice President approaches the role differently — some take on a specific policy portfolio, others serve simply as a top adviser to the President. Of the 48 previous Vice Presidents, nine have succeeded to the Presidency, and five have been elected to the Presidency in their own right.

The Vice President has an office in the West Wing of the White House, as well as in the nearby Eisenhower Executive Office Building. Like the President, he or she also maintains an official residence, at the United States Naval Observatory in Northwest Washington, D.C. This peaceful mansion has been the official home of the Vice President since 1974 — previously, Vice Presidents had lived in their own private residences. The Vice President also has his or her own limousine, operated by the United States Secret Service, and flies on the same aircraft the President uses — but when the Vice President is aboard, the craft are referred to as Air Force Two and Marine Two.

Executive Office of the President

Every day, the President of the United States is faced with scores of decisions, each with important consequences for America's future. To provide the President with the support that he or she needs to govern effectively, the Executive Office of the President (EOP) was created in 1939 by President Franklin D. Roosevelt. The EOP has responsibility for tasks ranging from communicating the President's message to the American people to promoting our trade interests abroad.

The EOP, overseen by the White House Chief of Staff, has traditionally been home to many of the President's closest advisers. While Senate confirmation is required for some advisers, such as the Director of the Office of Management and Budget, most are appointed with full Presidential discretion. The individual offices that these advisors oversee have grown in size and number since the EOP was created. Some were formed by Congress, others as the President has needed them — they are constantly shifting as each President identifies his or her needs and priorities. Perhaps the most visible parts of the EOP are the White House Communications Office and Press Secretary's Office. The Press Secretary provides daily briefings for the media on the President's activities and agenda. Less visible to most Americans is the National Security Council, which advises the President on foreign policy, intelligence, and national security.

There are also a number of offices responsible for the practicalities of maintaining the White House and providing logistical support for the President. These include the White House Military Office, which is responsible for services ranging from Air Force One to the dining facilities, and the Office of Presidential Advance, which prepares sites remote from the White House for the President's arrival.

Many senior advisors in the EOP work near the President in the West Wing of the White House. However, the majority of the staff is housed in the Eisenhower Executive Office Building, just a few steps away and part of the White House compound.

The Cabinet

The Cabinet is an advisory body made up of the heads of the 15 executive departments. Appointed by the President and confirmed by the Senate, the members of the Cabinet are often the President's closest confidants. In addition to running major federal agencies, they play an important role in the Presidential line of succession — after the Vice President, Speaker of the House, and Senate President pro tempore, the line of succession continues with the Cabinet offices in the order in which the departments were created. All the members of the Cabinet take the title Secretary, excepting the head of the Justice Department, who is styled Attorney General.

DEPARTMENT OF AGRICULTURE

The U.S. Department of Agriculture (USDA) develops and executes policy on farming, agriculture, and food. Its aims include meeting the needs of farmers and ranchers, promoting agricultural trade and production, assuring food safety, protecting forests and other natural resources, fostering rural prosperity, and ending hunger in America and abroad.

The USDA employs nearly 100,000 people and has an annual budget of approximately $150 billion. It consists of 16 agencies, including the Animal and Plant Health Inspection Service, the Food and Nutrition Service, and the Forest Service. The bulk of the department's budget goes towards mandatory programs that provide services required by law, such as programs designed to provide nutrition assistance, promote agricultural exports, and conserve our environment.

The USDA also plays an important role in overseas aid programs by providing surplus foods to developing countries.

The United States Secretary of Agriculture administers the USDA.

DEPARTMENT OF COMMERCE

The Department of Commerce is the government agency tasked with creating the conditions for economic growth and opportunity. The department supports U.S. business and industry through a number of services, including gathering economic and demographic data, issuing patents and trademarks, improving understanding of the environment and oceanic life, and ensuring the effective use of scientific and technical resources. The agency also formulates telecommunications and technology policy and promotes U.S. exports by assisting and enforcing international trade agreements.

The United States Secretary of Commerce oversees a $8.9 billion budget and more than 41,000 employees.

DEPARTMENT OF DEFENSE

The mission of the Department of Defense (DOD) is to provide the military forces needed to deter war and to protect the security of our country. The department's headquarters is at the Pentagon.

The DOD consists of the Departments of the Army, Navy, and Air Force, as well as many agencies, offices, and commands, including the Joint Chiefs of Staff, the Pentagon Force Protection Agency, the National Security Agency, and the Defense Intelligence Agency. The DOD occupies the vast majority of the Pentagon building in Arlington, Virginia.

The DOD is the largest government agency, with more than 1.4 million men and women on active duty, more than 700,000 civilian personnel, and 1.1 million citizens who serve in the National Guard and Reserve forces. Together, the military and civilian arms of DOD protect national interests through war-fighting, providing humanitarian aid, and performing peacekeeping and disaster relief services.

DEPARTMENT OF EDUCATION

The mission of the Department of Education is to promote student learning and preparation for college, careers, and citizenship in a global economy by fostering educational excellence and ensuring equal access to educational opportunity.

The Department administers federal financial aid for higher education, oversees educational programs and civil rights laws that promote equity in student learning opportunities, collects data and sponsors research on America's schools to guide improvements in education quality, and works to complement the efforts of state and local governments, parents, and students.

The U.S. Secretary of Education oversees the Department's 4,200 employees and $68.6 billion budget.

DEPARTMENT OF ENERGY

The mission of the Department of Energy (DOE) is to advance the national, economic, and energy security of the United States.

The DOE promotes America's energy security by encouraging the development of reliable, clean, and affordable energy. It administers federal funding for scientific research to further the goal of discovery and innovation — ensuring American economic competitiveness and improving the quality of life for Americans. The DOE is also tasked with ensuring America's nuclear security, and with protecting the environment by providing a responsible resolution to the legacy of nuclear weapons production.

The United States Secretary of Energy oversees a budget of approximately $23 billion and more than 100,000 federal and contract employees.

DEPARTMENT OF HEALTH AND HUMAN SERVICES

The Department of Health and Human Services (HHS) is the United States government's principal agency for protecting the health of all Americans and providing essential human services, especially for those who are least able to help themselves. Agencies of HHS conduct health and social science research, work to prevent disease outbreaks, assure food and drug safety, and provide health insurance.

In addition to administering Medicare and Medicaid, which together provide health coverage to one in four Americans, HHS also oversees the National Institutes of Health, the Food and Drug Administration, and the Centers for Disease Control.

The Secretary of Health and Human Services oversees a budget of approximately $700 billion and approximately 65,000 employees. The Department's programs are administered by 11 operating divisions, including eight agencies in the U.S. Public Health Service, two human services agencies, and the Centers for Medicare and Medicaid Services.

DEPARTMENT OF HOMELAND SECURITY

The Department of Homeland Security (DHS) protects the American people from a wide range of foreign and domestic threats. DHS has a broad and diverse mission set, including to prevent and disrupt terrorist attacks, protect critical infrastructure and civilian computer networks, facilitate lawful trade and travel, respond to and recover from natural disasters, protect our borders, and regulate the migration of individuals to and from our country.

The third largest Cabinet department, DHS employs more than 250,000 people and deploys an $58 billion annual budget across more than 20 components, including the U.S. Secret Service, Transportation Security Administration, Federal Emergency Management Agency, U.S. Coast Guard, U. S. Customs and Border Protection, U.S. Immigration and Customs Enforcement, U.S. Citizenship and Immigration Services, and the Cybersecurity and Infrastructure Security Agency. The Homeland Security Act of 2002 established the Department in response to the terrorist attacks of September 11, 2001 and brought together 22 executive branch agencies.

The Assistant to the President for Homeland Security and the Secretary of Homeland Security coordinate policy, including through the Homeland Security Council at the White House and in cooperation with other defense and intelligence agencies.

DEPARTMENT OF HOUSING AND URBAN DEVELOPMENT

The Department of Housing and Urban Development (HUD) is the federal agency responsible for national policies and programs that address America's housing needs, improve and develop the nation's communities, and enforce fair housing laws. The Department plays a major role in supporting homeownership for low- and moderate-income families through its mortgage insurance and rent subsidy programs.

Offices within HUD include the Federal Housing Administration, which provides mortgage and loan insurance; the Office of Fair Housing and Equal Opportunity, which ensures all Americans equal access to the housing of their choice; and the Community Development Block Grant Program, which helps communities with economic development, job opportunities, and housing rehabilitation. HUD also administers public housing and homeless assistance.

The Secretary of Housing and Urban Development oversees more than 9,000 employees with a budget of approximately $40 billion.

DEPARTMENT OF THE INTERIOR

The Department of the Interior (DOI) is the nation's principal conservation agency. Its mission is to protect America's natural resources, offer recreation opportunities, conduct scientific research, conserve and protect fish and wildlife, and honor the U.S. government's responsibilities to American Indians, Alaskan Natives, and to island communities.

DOI manages approximately 500 million acres of surface land, or about one-fifth of the land in the United States and manages hundreds of dams and reservoirs. Agencies within the DOI include the Bureau of Indian Affairs, the Fish and Wildlife Service, and the U.S. Geological Survey. The DOI manages the national parks and is tasked with protecting endangered species.

The Secretary of the Interior oversees about 70,000 employees and 200,000 volunteers on a budget of approximately $16 billion. Every year it raises billions in revenue from energy, mineral, grazing, and timber leases, as well as recreational permits and land sales.

DEPARTMENT OF JUSTICE

The mission of the Department of Justice (DOJ) is to enforce the law and defend the interests of the United States according to the law; to ensure public safety against threats foreign and domestic; to provide federal leadership in preventing and controlling crime; to seek just punishment for those guilty of unlawful behavior; and to ensure fair and impartial administration of justice for all Americans.

The DOJ is made up of 40 component organizations, including the Drug Enforcement Administration, the Federal Bureau of Investigation, the U.S. Marshals, and the Federal Bureau of Prisons. The Attorney General is the head of the DOJ and chief law enforcement officer of the federal government. The Attorney General represents the United States in legal matters, advises the President and the heads of the executive departments of the government, and occasionally appears in person before the Supreme Court.

With a budget of approximately $25 billion, the DOJ is the world's largest law office and the central agency for the enforcement of federal laws.

DEPARTMENT OF LABOR

The Department of Labor oversees federal programs for ensuring a strong American workforce. These programs address job training, safe working conditions, minimum hourly wage and overtime pay, employment discrimination, and unemployment insurance.

The Department of Labor's mission is to foster and promote the welfare of the job seekers, wage earners, and retirees of the United States by improving their working conditions, advancing their opportunities for profitable employment, protecting their retirement and health care benefits, helping employers find workers, strengthening free collective bargaining, and tracking changes in employment, prices, and other national economic measurements.

Offices within the Department of Labor the Occupational Safety & Health Administration, which promotes the safety and health of America's working men and women, and the Bureau of Labor Statistics, the federal government's principal statistics agency for labor economics, and.

The Secretary of Labor oversees 15,000 employees on a budget of approximately $12 billion.

DEPARTMENT OF STATE

The Department of State plays the lead role in developing and implementing the President's foreign policy. Major responsibilities include United States representation abroad, foreign assistance, foreign military training programs, countering international crime, and a wide assortment of services to U.S. citizens and foreign nationals seeking entrance to the United States.

The U.S. maintains diplomatic relations with approximately 180 countries — each posted by civilian U.S. Foreign Service employees — as well as with international organizations. At home, more than 5,000 civil employees carry out the mission of the Department.

The Secretary of State serves as the President's top foreign policy adviser and oversees 30,000 employees and a budget of approximately $35 billion.

DEPARTMENT OF TRANSPORTATION

The mission of the Department of Transportation (DOT) is to ensure a fast, safe, efficient, accessible and convenient transportation system that meets our vital national interests and enhances the quality of life of the American people.

Organizations within the DOT include the Federal Highway Administration, the Federal Aviation Administration, the National Highway Traffic Safety Administration, the Federal Transit Administration, the Federal Railroad Administration and the Maritime Administration.

The U.S. Secretary of Transportation oversees nearly 55,000 employees and a budget of approximately $70 billion.

DEPARTMENT OF THE TREASURY

The Department of the Treasury is responsible for promoting inclusive economic prosperity for all Americans.

The Department advances U.S. and global economic growth to raise American standards of living, support communities, promote racial justice, combat climate change, and foster financial stability. The Department operates systems that are critical to the nation's financial infrastructure, such as the production of coin and currency, the disbursement of payments owed to the American public, the collection of necessary taxes, and the borrowing of funds required by congressional enactments to run the federal government. The Treasury Department also performs a critical role in enhancing national security by safeguarding our financial systems, implementing economic sanctions against foreign threats to the U.S., and identifying and targeting financial support networks that threaten our national security.

The Secretary of the Treasury oversees a budget of approximately $13 billion and a staff of more than 100,000 employees.

DEPARTMENT OF VETERANS AFFAIRS

The Department of Veterans Affairs is responsible for administering benefit programs for veterans, their families, and their survivors. These benefits include pension, education, disability compensation, home loans, life insurance, vocational rehabilitation, survivor support, medical care, and burial benefits. Veterans Affairs became a cabinet-level department in 1989.

Of the 25 million veterans currently alive, nearly three of every four served during a war or an official period of hostility. About a quarter of the nation's population — approximately 70 million people — are potentially eligible for V.A. benefits and services because they are veterans, family members, or survivors of veterans.

The Secretary of Veterans Affairs oversees a budget of approximately $90 billion and a staff of approximately 235,000 employees.

Judicial Branch

The third branch of government is the Judicial branch. The Judiciary is made up of courts -- Supreme, Circuit, the magistrate (local) and municipal (city) courts. The Judicial branch interprets the laws.

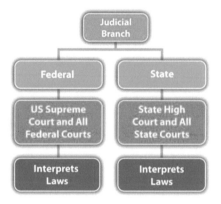

Where the executive and legislative branches are elected by the people, members of the Judicial Branch are appointed by the President and confirmed by the Senate.

The duties of the judicial branch include:

Interpreting state laws;

Settling legal disputes;

Punishing violators of the law;

Hearing civil cases;

Protecting individual rights granted by the state constitution;

Determining the guilt or innocence of those accused of violating the criminal laws of the state;

Acting as a check upon the legislative and executive branches of state government.

Article III of the Constitution, which establishes the Judicial Branch, leaves Congress significant discretion to determine the shape and structure of the federal judiciary. Even the number of Supreme Court Justices is left to Congress — at times there have been as few as six, while the current number (nine, with one Chief Justice and eight Associate Justices) has only been in place since 1869. The Constitution also grants Congress the power to establish courts inferior to the Supreme Court, and to that end Congress has established the United States district courts, which try most federal cases, and 13 United States courts of appeals, which review appealed district court cases.

Federal judges can only be removed through impeachment by the House of Representatives and conviction in the Senate. Judges and Justices serve no fixed term — they serve until their death, retirement, or conviction by the Senate. By design, this insulates them from the temporary passions of the public, and allows them to apply the law with only justice in mind, and not electoral or political concerns.

Generally, Congress determines the jurisdiction of the federal courts. In some cases, however — such as in the example of a dispute between two or more U.S. states — the Constitution grants the Supreme Court original jurisdiction, an authority that cannot be stripped by Congress.

The courts only try actual cases and controversies — a party must show that it has been harmed in order to bring suit in court. This means that the courts do not issue advisory opinions on the constitutionality of laws or the legality of actions if the ruling would have no practical effect. Cases brought before the judiciary typically proceed from district court to appellate court and may even end at the Supreme Court, although the Supreme Court hears comparatively few cases each year.

Federal courts enjoy the sole power to interpret the law, determine the constitutionality of the law, and apply it to individual cases. The courts, like Congress, can compel the production of evidence and testimony through the use of a subpoena. The inferior courts are constrained by the decisions of the Supreme Court — once the Supreme Court interprets a law, inferior courts must apply the Supreme Court's interpretation to the facts of a particular case.

The Supreme Court of the United States

The Supreme Court of the United States is the highest court in the land and the only part of the federal judiciary specifically required by the Constitution.

The Constitution does not stipulate the number of Supreme Court Justices; the number is set instead by Congress. There have been as few as six, but since 1869 there have been nine Justices, including one Chief Justice. All Justices are nominated by the President, confirmed by the Senate, and hold their offices under life tenure. Since Justices do not have to run or campaign for re-election, they are thought to be insulated from political pressure when deciding cases. Justices may remain in office until they resign, pass away, or are impeached and convicted by Congress.

The Court's caseload is almost entirely appellate in nature, and the Court's decisions cannot be appealed to any authority, as it is the final judicial arbiter in the United States on matters of federal law. However, the Court may consider appeals from the highest state courts or from federal appellate courts. The Court also has original jurisdiction over limited types of cases, including those involving ambassadors and other diplomats, and in cases between states.

Although the Supreme Court may hear an appeal on any question of law provided it has jurisdiction, it usually does not hold trials. Instead, the Court's task is to interpret the meaning of a law, to decide whether a law is relevant to a particular set of facts, or to rule on how a law should be applied. Lower courts are obligated to follow the precedent set by the Supreme Court when rendering decisions.

In almost all instances, the Supreme Court does not hear appeals as a matter of right; instead, parties must petition the Court for a writ of certiorari. It is the Court's custom and practice to "grant cert" if four of the nine Justices decide that they should hear the case. Of the approximately 7,500 requests for certiorari filed each year, the Court usually grants cert to fewer than 150. These are typically cases that the Court considers sufficiently important to require their review; a common example is the occasion when two or more of the federal courts of appeals have ruled differently on the same question of federal law.

If the Court grants certiorari, Justices accept legal briefs from the parties to the case, as well as from amicus curiae, or "friends of the court." These can include industry trade groups, academics, or even the U.S. government itself. Before issuing a ruling, the Supreme Court usually hears oral arguments, where the various parties to the suit present their arguments and the Justices ask them questions. If the case involves the federal government, the Solicitor General of the United States presents arguments on behalf of the United States. The Justices then hold private conferences, make their decision, and (often after a period of several months) issue the Court's opinion, along with any dissenting arguments that may have been written.

The Judicial Process

Article III of the Constitution of the United States guarantees that every person accused of wrongdoing has the right to a fair trial before a competent judge and a jury of one's peers.

The Fourth, Fifth, Sixth, and Eighth Amendments to the Constitution provide additional protections for those accused of a crime. These include:

A guarantee that no person shall be deprived of life, liberty, or property without the due process of law

Protection against being tried for the same crime twice ("double jeopardy")

The right to a speedy trial by an impartial jury

The right to cross-examine witnesses, and to call witnesses to support their case

The right to legal representation

The right to avoid self-incrimination

Protection from excessive bail, excessive fines, and cruel and unusual punishments

Criminal proceedings can be conducted under either state or federal law, depending on the nature and extent of the crime. A criminal legal procedure typically begins with an arrest by a law enforcement officer. If a grand jury chooses to deliver an indictment, the accused will appear before a judge and be formally charged with a crime, at which time he or she may enter a plea.

The defendant is given time to review all the evidence in the case and to build a legal argument. Then, the case is brought to trial and decided by a jury. If the defendant is determined to be not guilty of the crime, the charges are dismissed. Otherwise, the judge determines the sentence, which can include prison time, a fine, or even execution.

Civil cases are similar to criminal ones, but instead of arbitrating between the state and a person or organization, they deal with disputes between individuals or organizations. In civil cases, if a party believes that it has been wronged, it can file suit in civil court to attempt to have that wrong remedied through an order to cease and desist, alter behavior, or award monetary damages. After the suit is filed and evidence is gathered and presented by both sides, a trial proceeds as in a criminal case. If the parties involved waive their right to a jury trial, the case can be decided by a judge; otherwise, the case is decided and damages awarded by a jury.

After a criminal or civil case is tried, it may be appealed to a higher court — a federal court of appeals or state appellate court. A litigant who files an appeal, known as an "appellant," must show that the trial court or administrative agency made a legal error that affected the outcome of the case. An appellate court makes its decision based on the record of the case established by the trial court or agency — it does not receive additional evidence or hear witnesses. It may also review the factual findings of the trial court or agency, but typically may only overturn a trial outcome on factual grounds if the findings were "clearly erroneous." If a defendant is found not guilty in a criminal proceeding, he or she cannot be retried on the same set of facts.

Federal appeals are decided by panels of three judges. The appellant presents legal arguments to the panel, in a written document called a "brief." In the brief, the appellant tries to persuade the judges that the trial court made an error, and that the lower decision should be reversed. On the other hand, the party defending against the appeal, known as the "appellee" or "respondent," tries in its brief to show why the trial court decision was correct, or why any errors made by the trial court are not significant enough to affect the outcome of the case.

The court of appeals usually has the final word in the case, unless it sends the case back to the trial court for additional proceedings. In some cases the decision may be reviewed en banc — that is, by a larger group of judges of the court of appeals for the circuit.

A litigant who loses in a federal court of appeals, or in the highest court of a state, may file a petition for a "writ of certiorari," which is a document asking the U.S. Supreme Court to review the case. The Supreme Court, however, is not obligated to grant review. The Court typically will agree to hear a case only when it involves a new and important legal principle, or when two or more federal appellate courts have interpreted a law differently. (There are also special circumstances in which the Supreme Court is required by law to hear an appeal.) When the Supreme Court hears a case, the parties are required to file written briefs and the Court may hear oral argument.

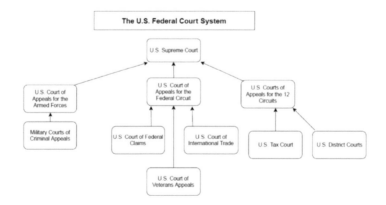

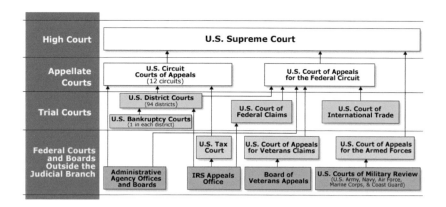

Conclusion:

It's best to know how your government was set up, how things have been adjusted and amended throughout the years, and how these things function and coincide with one another before you attempt to utilize your First Amendment freedom of expression.

Not knowing how the government operates and functions is why there's many null and void speeches. If your "freedom of speech" does not support the Constitution, but mine does, yours is null and void.

The same applies with Marbury vs. Madison, 1803: "All laws which are repugnant to the Constitution are null and void." In layman's terms, 'any statute that looks like a law, but does not support the Constitution, is null and void.' If one does not like our Foundation… then that's where one must find others who feel the same way and do something about it as our Founders did many years ago when they organized and fought the Revolutionary War which brought about all the Government and process everyone currently operates under.

Which is why it's always so baffling to hear some farfetched liberal who doesn't like guns and wants gun control, spewing their "First Amendment Rights" when that First Amendment was written by the same who wrote the Second Amendment as an absolute means to **protect** and **defend** the first.

Chapter 13: State and Local Government

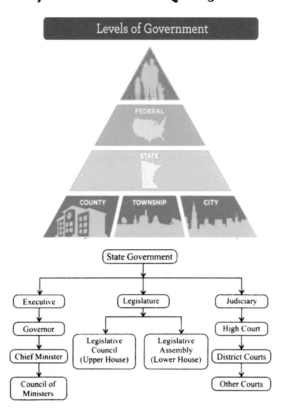

Powers not granted to the Federal government are reserved for States and the people, which are divided between State and local governments.

Most Americans have more frequent contact with their State and local governments than with the Federal Government. Police departments, libraries, and schools—not to mention driver's licenses and parking tickets—usually fall under the oversight of State and local governments. Each state has its own written constitution, and these documents are often far more elaborate than their Federal counterpart. The Alabama Constitution, for example, contains 310,296 words—more than 40 times as many as the U.S. Constitution.

All State governments are modeled after the Federal Government and consist of three branches: executive, legislative, and judicial. The U.S. Constitution mandates that all States uphold a "republican form" of government, although the three-branch structure is not required.

Executive Branch

In every state, the Executive Branch is headed by a governor who is directly elected by the people. In most states, other leaders in the executive branch are also directly elected, including the lieutenant governor, the attorney general, the secretary of state, and auditors and commissioners. States reserve the right to organize in any way, so they often vary greatly with regard to executive structure.

Legislative Branch

All 50 States have legislatures made up of elected representatives, who consider matters brought forth by the governor or introduced by its members to create legislation that becomes law. The legislature also approves a state's budget and initiates tax legislation and articles of impeachment. The latter is part of a system of checks and balances among the three branches of government that mirrors the Federal system and prevents any branch from abusing its power.

Except for one State, Nebraska, all States have a bicameral legislature made up of two chambers: a smaller upper house and a larger lower house. Together the two chambers make State laws and fulfill other governing responsibilities. (Nebraska is the lone state that has just one chamber in its legislature.) The smaller upper chamber is always called the Senate, and its members generally serve longer terms, usually four years. The larger lower chamber is most often called the House of Representatives, but some states call it the Assembly or the House of Delegates. Its members usually serve shorter terms, often two years.

Judicial Branch

State judicial branches are usually led by the State supreme court, which hears appeals from lower-level State courts. Court structures and judicial appointments/elections are determined either by legislation or the State constitution. The supreme court focuses on correcting errors made in lower courts and therefore holds no trials. Rulings made in State supreme courts are normally binding; however, when questions are raised regarding consistency with the U.S. Constitution, matters may be appealed directly to the United States Supreme Court.

Local Government

Local governments generally include two tiers: counties, also known as boroughs in Alaska and parishes in Louisiana, and municipalities, or cities/towns. In some States, counties are divided into townships. Municipalities can be structured in many ways, as defined by State constitutions, and are called, variously, townships, villages, boroughs, cities, or towns. Various kinds of districts also provide functions in local government outside county or municipal boundaries, such as school districts or fire protection districts.

Municipal governments—those defined as cities, towns, boroughs (except in Alaska), villages, and townships—are generally organized around a population center and in most cases correspond to the geographical designations used by the United States Census Bureau for reporting of housing and population statistics. Municipalities vary greatly in size, from the millions of residents of New York City and Los Angeles to the few hundred people who live in Jenkins, Minnesota.

Municipalities generally take responsibility for parks and recreation services, police and fire departments, housing services, emergency medical services, municipal courts, transportation services (including public transportation), and public works (streets, sewers, snow removal, signage, and so forth).

Whereas the Federal Government and State governments share power in countless ways, a local government must be granted power by the State. In general, mayors, city councils, and other governing bodies are directly elected by the people.

Chapter 14: Executive Orders

Executive orders are official documents, numbered consecutively, through which the President of the United States manages the operations of the Federal Government. Many executive orders are proposed by federal agencies before being issued by the president.

Like both legislative statutes and the regulations promulgated by government agencies, executive orders are subject to judicial review and may be overturned if the orders lack support by statute or the Constitution. Some policy initiatives require approval by the legislative branch, but executive orders have significant influence over the internal affairs of government, deciding how and to what degree legislation will be enforced, dealing with emergencies, waging wars, and in general fine-tuning policy choices in the implementation of broad statutes. As the head of state and head of government of the United States, as well as commander-in-chief of the United States Armed Forces, only the president of the United States can issue an executive order.

Presidential executive orders, once issued, remain in force until they are canceled, revoked, adjudicated unlawful, or expire on their terms. At any time, the president may revoke, modify, or make exceptions from any executive order, whether the order was made by the current president or a predecessor.

The Military with Executive Orders: **Department of Defense of Military and Associated Terms, March 2017**

n. Must be consistent with US law, treaties, international agreements, and **executive orders**.

DOD Dictionary of Military and Associated Terms: https://www.tradoc.army.mil/wp-content/uploads/2020/10/AD1029823-DOD-Dictionary-of-Military-and-Associated-Terms-2017.pdf

Chapter 15: Presidential Emergency Action Documents

PEADs are draft classified executive orders, proclamations, and messages to Congress that are prepared for the President of the United States to exercise or expand powers in anticipation of a range of emergency hypothetical worst-case scenarios, so that they are ready to sign and put into effect the moment one of those scenarios comes to pass.

They originated in the Eisenhower Administration in response to fears of the Cold War and nuclear war, and are part of what is often referred to as Continuity of Government (COG) planning.
No PEADs have been declassified, however they are referenced in FBI memoranda that were obtained through the Freedom of Information Act, agency manuals, and court records.
The orders are classified, and none have ever been publicly released or leaked. They are therefore obscure and generally unknown to average Americans, scholars, and even Executive branch officials, and are sometimes referred to as "secret powers" of the President.

PEADS write up on Wikipedia:
https://en.wikipedia.org/wiki/Presidential_Emergency_Action_Documents#cite_note-FEMA_Manual_111-1

Here's some excerpts from an Interview with CBS with Democratic Senator Gary Hart.

"Even though I've had security clearances for the better part of 50 years and been in and out of national security matters during that half-century, I had never heard of these 'secret powers,'" said former Senator Gary Hart.

"Sunday Morning" special contributor Ted Koppel asked, "Do you know what they are, now that you've heard of them?"

"Only vaguely, due to research done at the Brennan Center for Justice at New York University Law School," Hart said. "What these secret powers are, apparently, based on the research, is suspension of the Constitution, basically. And that's what's worrying, particularly on the eve of a national election."

Koppel asked, "Several times during his administration, President Trump has made allusions to secret powers that he has that we don't know about. Is he making that up?"

"Well, not exactly," Goitein replied. "And what's alarming about that is that no one really knows what the limits of those claimed authorities might be, because they are often developed and kept in secret."

"You're saying they are not consulting with Congress?" Koppel asked. "Exactly," said Goitein. "Congress is not aware of these documents, and from public sources we know that at least in the past these documents have purported to do things that are not permitted by the Constitution – things like martial law and the suspension of habeas corpus and the roundup and detention of people not suspected of any crime."

"I want them public, because they affect the freedom and liberty and rights of every American citizen," he said. "I can't say it any better. This is a blueprint for dictatorship. Now, I think the more attention it gets, the less likely those in power are going to use them."

Presidential Powers:
https://www.cbsnews.com/news/rewriting-the-limits-of-presidential-powers/

There's a Democratic Senator, who ran for President in 1984, who also achieve the rank of Lieutenant in the Navy, claiming security clearances for 50 years and never heard of a Presidential Emergency Action Document.

In articles like this… you must remove your emotions, find the keywords that link to the Laws and Orders being signed that his book outlines shortly.

Such as: The National Emergencies Act (NEA), which allows the president to declare a national emergency, which then unlocks more than 130 statutory authorities scattered throughout the U.S. Code.
Now, let's look at this other article:

"Washington (May 5, 2020) – Today, Senator Edward J. Markey (D-Mass.) announced he will be introducing the *Restraint of Executive In Governing Nation (REIGN) Act*, legislation that requires President Donald Trump, and future presidents, to turn over all presidential emergency action documents (PEADS) that may give the President extraordinary powers.

PEADS are draft executive orders, proclamations, and messages to the U.S. Congress prepared by a presidential administration in advance of anticipated emergencies. Although Congress has made available to the President a number of emergency powers upon the declaration of a national emergency, the content of most PEADS have never been made public or shared with Congress, raising concerns that President Trump could use such documents to claim authority during the coronavirus pandemic that exceeds those given by Congress.

Specifically, the *REIGN Act* requires the President turn over PEADS to Congress not later than 30 days after the approval, adoption, or revision of any PEAD, and requires the President to submit to Congress all PEADS currently in existence."

"Unlawful Presidential Emergency Powers:"
https://www.markey.senate.gov/news/press-releases/senator-markey-introduces-bill-to-rein-in-unlawful-presidential-emergency-powers

Your initial thought is to say how bias the 'media' is to President Trump. However, that's where I'm here to show you, these are all Optics because what's in Military and Federal Laws and Orders on bipartisan Legislation paper, but might as well be stone, is where the rubber meets the road.

Did you notice what the one DemoRat said, "What these secret powers are, apparently, based on the research, is *suspension* of the Constitution, basically." Remember the press grilling CIC Trump about saying "suspending the Constitution" and his reply was "I've never said anything about suspending the Constitution, you said that?" Listen to the man. Everything he says has meaning, *everything*.

It's a simple mindset. No need to be mad. When you know the Legislation via both sectors of Laws and Orders that were already in place long before these interviews… you'd see the Optic and Comm Candy all day long.

These powers have been around for MANY years in their corrupt system, but ALL OF A SUDDEN, they need to be changed because of *abuse of power?* LOL

They're telling you all day long without telling you. Why else would this have even been a topic in 2020? You'll see in pages ahead. Think about it though… If a Senator of 50 years, former Presidential candidate, and Navy Veteran, claims he didn't know about these exclusive and secretive Presidential Powers… why would we need an Act to limit the power that 99.9999999999999999% of Americans have never heard of?

All planned. All an operation.

Chapter 16: National Emergencies

A National Emergency is a <u>United States federal law</u> passed to end all previous <u>national emergencies</u> and to formalize the emergency powers of the President.

The Act empowers the President to activate special powers during a crisis but imposes certain procedural formalities when invoking such powers. The perceived need for the law arose from the scope and number of laws granting special powers to the <u>executive</u> in times of national emergency. <u>Congress</u> can terminate an emergency declaration with a joint resolution enacted into law. It's under 50 United States Code Chapter 34 Section 1601, 1621 and 1622 where National Emergencies are defined.

§1622. National emergencies

(a) Termination methods

Any national emergency declared by the President in accordance with this subchapter shall terminate if—
(1) there is enacted into law a joint resolution terminating the emergency; or
(2) the President issues a proclamation terminating the emergency.

Any national emergency declared by the President shall be terminated on the date specified in any joint resolution referred to in clause (1) or on the date specified in a proclamation by the President terminating the emergency as provided in clause (2) of this subsection, whichever date is earlier, and any powers or authorities exercised by reason of said emergency shall cease to be exercised after such specified date, except that such termination shall not affect—

(A) any action taken or proceeding pending not finally concluded or determine on such date;
(B) any action or proceeding based on any act committed prior to such date; or
(C) any rights or duties that matured or penalties that were incurred prior to such date.

(b) Termination review of national emergencies by Congress

Not later than six months after a national emergency is declared, and not later than the end of each six-month period thereafter that such emergency continues, each House of Congress shall meet to consider a vote on a joint resolution to determine whether that emergency shall be terminated.

(c) Joint resolution; referral to Congressional committees; conference committee in event of disagreement; filing of report; termination procedure deemed part of rules of House and Senate

(1) A joint resolution to terminate a national emergency declared by the President shall be referred to the appropriate committee of the House of Representatives or the Senate, as the case may be. One such joint resolution shall be reported out by such committee together with its recommendations within fifteen calendar days after the day on which such resolution is referred to such committee, unless such House shall otherwise determine by the yeas and nays.
 (2) Any joint resolution so reported shall become the pending business of the House in question (in the case of the Senate the time for debate shall be equally divided between the proponents and the opponents) and shall be voted on within three calendar days after the day on which such resolution is reported, unless such House shall otherwise determine by yeas and nays.
 (3) Such a joint resolution passed by one House shall be referred to the appropriate committee of the other House and shall be reported out by such committee together with its recommendations within fifteen calendar days after the day on which such resolution is referred to such committee and shall thereupon become the pending business of such House and shall be voted upon within three calendar days after the day on which such resolution is reported, unless such House shall otherwise determine by yeas and nays.
(4) In the case of any disagreement between the two Houses of Congress with respect to a joint resolution passed by both Houses, conferees shall be promptly appointed and the committee of conference shall make and file a report with respect to such joint resolution within six calendar days after the day on which managers on the part of the Senate and the House have been appointed. Notwithstanding any rule in either House concerning the printing of conference reports or concerning any delay in the consideration of such reports, such report shall be acted on by both Houses not later than six calendar days after the conference report is filed in the House in which such report is filed first. In the event the conferees are unable to agree within forty-eight hours, they shall report back to their respective Houses in disagreement.
(5) Paragraphs (1)–(4) of this subsection, subsection (b) of this section, and section 1651(b) of this title are enacted by Congress—

(A) as an exercise of the rulemaking power of the Senate and the House of Representatives, respectively, and as such they are deemed a part of the rules of each House, respectively, but applicable only with respect to the procedure to be followed in the House in the case of resolutions described by this subsection; and they supersede other rules only to the extent that they are inconsistent therewith; and
(B) with full recognition of the constitutional right of either House to change the rules (so far as relating to the procedure of that House) at any time, in the same manner, and to the same extent as in the case of any other rule of that House.

(A) Automatic termination of national emergency; continuation notice from President to Congress; publication in Federal Register

Any national emergency declared by the President in accordance with this subchapter, and not otherwise previously terminated, shall terminate on the anniversary of the declaration of that emergency if, within the ninety day period prior to each anniversary date, the

President does not publish in the Federal Register and transmit to the Congress a notice stating that such emergency is to continue in effect after such anniversary. (Pub. L. 94–412, title II, §202, Sept. 14, 1976, 90 Stat. 1255; Pub. L. 99–93, title VIII, §801, Aug. 16, 1985, 99 Stat. 448.)

§1621. Declaration of national emergency by President; publication in Federal Register; effect on other laws; superseding legislation

(a)   With respect to Acts of Congress authorizing the exercise, during the period of a national emergency, of any special or extraordinary power, the President is authorized to declare such national emergency. Such proclamation shall immediately be transmitted to the Congress and published in the Federal Register.

(b)   Any provisions of law conferring powers and authorities to be exercised during a national emergency shall be effective and remain in effect (1) only when the President (in accordance with subsection (a) of this section), specifically declares a national emergency, and (2) only in accordance with this chapter. No law enacted after September 14, 1976, shall supersede this subchapter unless it does so in specific terms, referring to this subchapter, and declaring that the new law supersedes the provisions of this subchapter. (Pub. L. 94–412, title II, §201, Sept. 14, 1976, 90 Stat. 1255.)

§1601. Termination of existing declared emergencies

(a)   All powers and authorities possessed by the President, any other officer or employee of the Federal Government, or any executive agency, as defined in section 105 of title 5, as a result of the existence of any declaration of national emergency in effect on September 14, 1976, are terminated two years from September 14, 1976. Such termination shall not affect—

> (1) any action taken or proceeding pending not finally concluded or determined on such date;
> (2) any action or proceeding based on any act committed prior to such date; or
> (3) any rights or duties that matured or penalties that were incurred prior to such date.

(a)   For the purpose of this section, the words "any national emergency in effect" means a general declaration of emergency made by the President. (Pub. L. 94–412, title I, §101, Sept. 14, 1976, 90 Stat. 1255.)

§1631. Declaration of national emergency by Executive order; authority; publication in Federal Register; transmittal to Congress

When the President declares a national emergency, no powers or authorities made available by statute for use in the event of an emergency shall be exercised unless and until the President specifies the provisions of law under which he proposes that he, or other officers will act. Such specification may be made either in the declaration of a national emergency, or by one or more contemporaneous or subsequent Executive orders published in the Federal Register and transmitted to the Congress. (Pub. L. 94–412, title III, §301, Sept. 14, 1976, 90 Stat. 1257.)

§1641. Accountability and reporting requirements of President

(a)   Maintenance of file and index of Presidential orders, rules and regulations during national emergency

When the President declares a national emergency, or Congress declares war, the President shall be responsible for maintaining a file and index of all significant orders of the President, including Executive orders and proclamations, and each Executive agency shall maintain a file and index of all rules and regulations, issued during such emergency or war issued pursuant to such declarations.

(b)   Presidential orders, rules and regulations; transmittal to Congress

All such significant orders of the President, including Executive orders, and such rules and regulations shall be transmitted to the Congress promptly under means to assure confidentiality where appropriate.

(c)   Expenditures during national emergency; Presidential reports to Congress

When the President declares a national emergency or Congress declares war, the President shall transmit to Congress, within ninety days after the end of each six-month period after such declaration, a report on the total expenditures incurred by the United States Government during such six-month period which are directly attributable to the exercise of powers and authorities conferred by such declaration. Not later than ninety days after the termination of each such emergency or war, the President shall transmit a final report on all such expenditures. (Pub. L. 94–412, title IV, §401, Sept. 14, 1976, 90 Stat. 1257.)

50 U.S.C. 1541-1550:
https://uscode.house.gov/view.xhtml?path=/prelim@title50/chapter34&edition=prelim

Chapter 17: Military Uniforms

It's alarming, but more disappointing than any other term, that so many Americans claim to support Military, yet when a Veteran points out Military Laws, Orders, Regulations, Customs and Courtesies, that Civilians would say: *"I support and believe in our Military, but not sure about that."*

With the '*that*' being one of those being pointed out to the civilian. *That* is also why they didn't serve. What's even WORSE is when you show via actual Department of Defense, or the Branch of topic's actual Publication via an Official Military site… and one STILL refuses to acknowledge or believe. As an Army Veteran, we have the Department of the Army, Pamphlet 670-1.

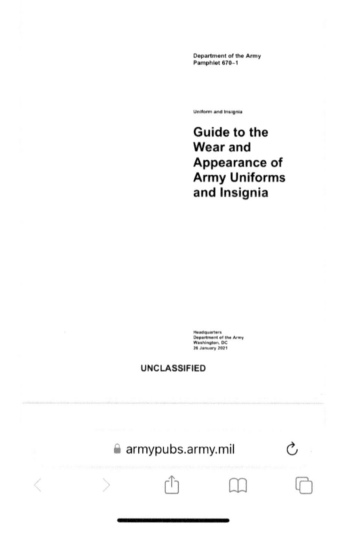

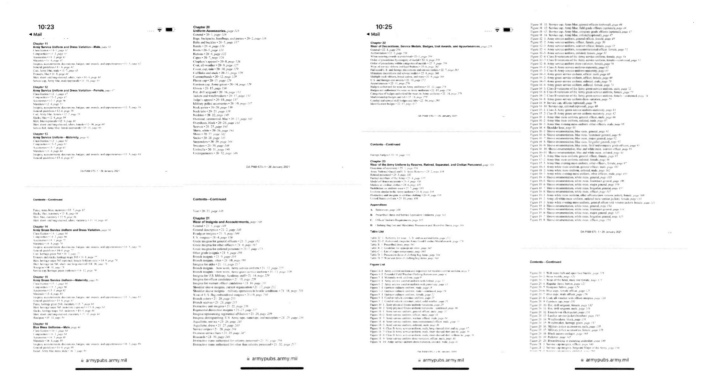

That's not '*chicken scratch*'… those are Uniform Regulations for the Army, alone.

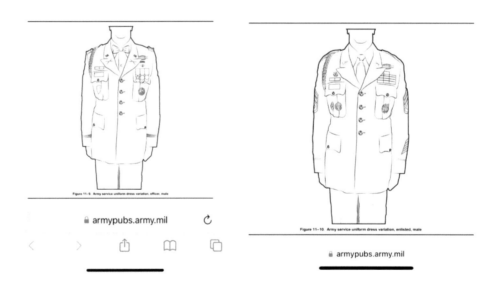

EVERY single Uniform around "Joe Biden" from January 20, 2021, to present day, has been a NON-REGULATION Uniform.

That means FAKE and NOT REAL. The worst part of this is how many Civilians who would not believe a Veteran for pointing out simple Military Regulations and Customs.

Ohhhhhhhhhh, but "we believe and support our Military," but won't listen to an honorably retired Veteran about Military Regs, Customs, Laws and Orders, aka Military life.

Let's look at Regulation Uniforms. We will go in the order of when each branch was founded.

Army

ARMY COMBAT UNIFORM

army.mil

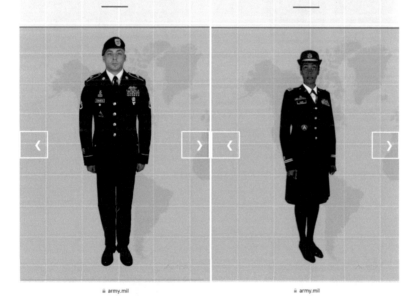

ARMY SERVICE UNIFORM   ARMY SERVICE UNIFORM

army.mil   army.mil

Navy

Marine Corps

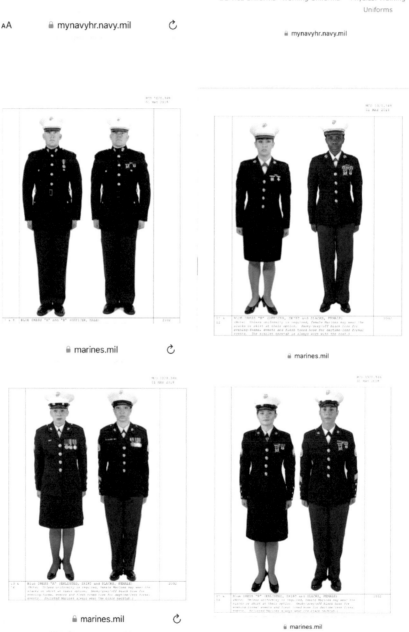

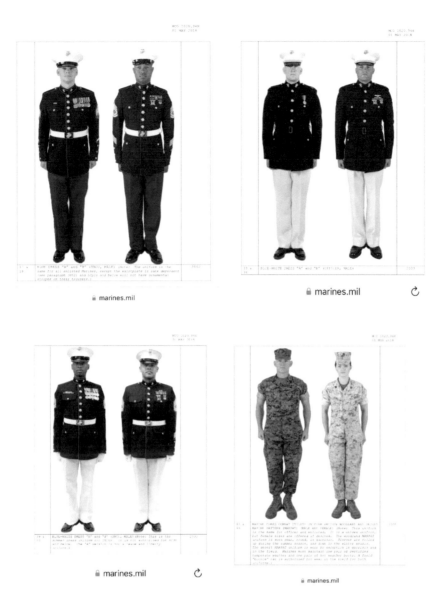

The Marines have more uniforms than the Oregon Ducks Football team. They claim to be the 'Men's Department' of the Navy… but I don't know with their closets…

Male Dress Coats

Men's Service Dress Blue (SDB) Coat

🔒 dcms.uscg.mil ↻

Female Dress Coats

Women's Service Dress Blue (SDB) Coat

🔒 dcms.uscg.mil ↻

Operational Uniforms:
Operational Tops & Bottoms, Coveralls, & T-Shirts

Male size numbers are even. Female size numbers are odd.

🔒 dcms.uscg.mil ↻

COMDTINST M1020.6K

3.B.10. Service Dress White (SDW)

Authorized Uniform Items	Additional Comments
SDW Coat	Men wear men's version. Women wear women's version.
White Trousers/Slacks	Women's slacks are unbelted with side zipper.
White Skirt (Women only)	Optional for women (unbelted).
White Shirt	Women: long or short sleeve.
Shoulder-boards	Hard shoulder boards.
Collar Insignia	No collar insignia.
Tie	Women: blue tab tie.
Nametag	Worn over wearer's right pocket.
Ribbons	Worn over wearer's left pocket.
Qualification Insignia	See Chapter 4.B.4 for proper wear instructions.
Miniature Devices	See Chapter 4.B.4 for proper wear instructions.
Full-Size Identification Badges	See Chapter 4.B.4 for proper wear instructions.
White Gloves	At prescribing officer's discretion.
White Socks or Hosiery	Socks are worn with oxfords; hosiery with pumps or flats.
White Oxford Shoes	Oxfords required for men. Optional high-gloss.
White Oxford Shoes, Pumps, or Flats	Oxfords, pumps, or flats are worn with the slacks. Pumps or flats may be worn with the skirt. Optional high-gloss.
White Belt with Brass Buckle	
Head Gear	Combination cap.
Occasions for Wear	Warm weather - official, business, social functions and ceremonies when senior officer wishes to pay special honor to the occasion, parades, reviews, evening socials.

🔒 media.defense.gov ↻

Air Force

DAFI36-2903 7 FEBRUARY 2020   121

Attachment 6

FLIGHT DUTY UNIFORM

A6.1. Flight Duty Uniform (FDU) and Desert Flight Duty Uniform (DFDU) Wear Guidance. The FDU and DFDU meet unique organizational and functional work requirements and are comprised of both distinctive and functional clothing items. Members will sew Velcro® on FDU/DFDU and equipment so they can remove any patches/accoutrements during contingencies. **(T-1).**

Figure A6.1. Flight Duty Uniform.

Space Force

The Space Force is a Department of the Air Force; therefore, their uniforms are a lot alike, and also why there's no uniform regulation handbook on the Operational Camouflage Pattern for the Space Force except via the Air Force Regulations.

Once you know Military Uniform Regulations, you'll be able to pick apart all the discrepancies and errors even though everything from January 20, 2021, and the Military Occupancy and Continuity of Operations Plan was planned. It's the same as finding those in uniforms stealing valor.

Chapter 18: 'The Blueprint'

June 12, 2015: Law of War Manual issued

The new Department of Defense, Law of War Manual, was issued and then updated again in December 2016. Federal and Military Lawyers took all the strengths from the Lieber Code of 1863, the Hague Conventions, the Nuremberg Trials, the Geneva Conventions, plus the Law of War Manuals from Canada, Germany, Australia and the United Kingdom, and combined those to strengthen United States Military Law, the Uniform Code of Military Justice.

Law of War Manual:

https://dod.defense.gov/Portals/1/Documents/pubs/DoD%20Law%20of%20War%20Manual%20-%20June%202015%20Updated%20Dec%202016.pdf?ver=2016-12-13-172036-190

A few examples of how it was used:

Chapter 12, 12.4, is the White Flag of Truce, that CIC Trump kept mentioning he gave Germany's Chancellor, Angela Merkel, the "white flag of surrender" in July 2021. How was he a former President giving the current Chancellor a white flag of truce?

Chapter 18 is very active removing Commanders from Leadership positions in which they violated or their superior's lost confidence in their ability to lead. There's been 140 plus Commanders relieved of duty since June 2017.

Law of War Manual
(FOREWORD)

The law of war is of fundamental importance to the Armed Forces of the United States.

The law of war is part of who we are. George Washington, as Commander in Chief of the Continental Army, agreed with his British adversary that the Revolutionary War would be "carried on agreeable to the rules which humanity formed" and "to prevent or punish every breach of the rules of war within the sphere of our respective commands." During the Civil War, President Lincoln approved a set of "Instructions for the Government of the Armies of the United States in the Field," which inspired other countries to adopt similar codes for their armed forces, and which served as a template for international codifications of the law of war.

After World War II, U.S. military lawyers, trying thousands of defendants before military commissions did, in the words of Justice Robert Jackson, "stay the hand of vengeance and voluntarily submit their captive enemies to the judgment of law" in "one of the most significant tributes that Power has ever paid to Reason." Reflecting on this distinctive history, one Chairman of the Joint Chiefs of Staff observed that "[t]he laws of war have a peculiarly American cast." And it is also true that the laws of war have shaped the U.S. Armed Forces as much as they have shaped any other armed force in the world.

The law of war is a part of our military heritage, and obeying it is the right thing to do. But we also know that the law of war poses no obstacle to fighting well and prevailing. Nations have developed the law of war to be fundamentally consistent with the military doctrines that are the basis for effective combat operations. For example, the self-control needed to refrain from violations of the law of war under the stresses of combat is the same good order and discipline necessary to operate cohesively and victoriously in battle. Similarly, the law of war's prohibitions on torture and unnecessary destruction are consistent with the practical insight that such actions ultimately frustrate rather than accomplish the mission.

This manual reflects many years of labor and expertise, on the part of civilian and military lawyers from every Military Service. It reflects the experience of this Department in applying the law of war in actual military operations, and it will help us remember the hard-learned lessons from the past. Understanding our duties imposed by the law of war and our rights under it is essential to our service in the nation's defense.

Stephen W. Preston
General Counsel of the Department of Defense

June 16, 2015: The Escalator Ride

The Boss rolls down the escalator to announce his 2016 Candidacy just four days after the Department of Defense's new Law of War Manual was issued.

February 23, 2016: Donald John Trump on Gitmo:

"*I want to make sure that if we have radical Islamic terrorists, we have a very safe place to keep 'em and we have a word, those are words our president won't even issue,*" he said. "*He's allowing people to get out that are terrible people. He's allowing a lot of people out of Guantanamo that should not be released.*"

Trump has come under fire for other comments he's made recently on the topic of terrorism -- namely his suggestion Wednesday night that President Obama is "*the founder of ISIS.*"

"*I will tell you that as far as Guantanamo is concerned I want to make sure, 100 percent sure, that if we're going to release people, number one they're going to be people that can be released and it's going to be safe to release them and there are plenty of bad ones out there and I'd use it for that,*" Trump continued

Donald Trump suggests he might try Americans at Gitmo:
https://www.cbsnews.com/news/donald-trump-suggests-he-might-try-americans-at-guantanamo-bay/

AP News:

> *"This morning, I watched President Obama talking about Gitmo, right, Guantanamo Bay, which by the way, which by the way, we are keeping open. Which we are keeping open ... and we're gonna load it up with some bad dudes, believe me, we're gonna load it up."*

This was 8 months before Election 2016… Can you name one thing that The Donald said that did not happen? <u>Nope</u>. You cannot. Not because it was all him, because it's all been planned.

October 20, 2016

Then Candidate Donald Trump roasting Hillary Rodham Clinton at the Al Smith Charity Dinner:
https://www.youtube.com/watch?v=Bmvxx_YbDsM

Everything he said, 100% came true. Despite the snickers, laughs, boos, animosity, bitterness, and hatred. He knew everything. He always knew. Now you know. And now you know, he already knew.

November 8, 2016

Hillary and team did not know how many votes to 'dump' in the 2016 Election… because if they'd added too many the first time versus DJT, they'd have been exposed from the start.

Hence why they lit right into Russia Collusion. It's a shame that politics got so dirty in this Country that Americans couldn't see right through it and treated this as just "dirty politics" and were willing to push that level of corruption under the rug and move on.

November 9, 2016

President Trump's picture on Fox News with Putin', it said, "ready for 'reset' and "I'll work with Trump." 4:56 AM CST.

Wed, Nov 09, 2016 · 4:56 AM

Add description...

PEOPLE
1 face available to add

Add name

DETAILS

IMG_0758.JPG
15.9MP 5312 x 2988 5.4 MB

SAMSUNG-SM-G920A

December 23, 2016

The Military Justice Act of 2016: was signed by Congress on December 23, 2016, in the National Defense Authorization Act of Fiscal Year 2017. Several concerns relating to military justice led Congress in 2016 to enact the Military Justice Act of 2016 (MJA), which made sweeping changes to the UCMJ. The UCMJ provides the basic framework for the military justice system and defines offenses subject to trial by court-martial. It includes the most sweeping changes to the Uniform Code of Military Justice in over 60 years and is effective Jan. 1, 2019.

And on December 23, 2016:

The Global Magnitsky Act of 2016 was the REAL "Durham Report"... Anytime with government and politics, one must always know the origin of an operation, laws, and orders. After November 8, 2016, the narrative was "Russia Collusion!" Take yourself back to the news those days, December 2016, January 2017 to the 'Durham Report' in May 2023...

"Russia! Russia! Russia!" and the fake dossier that Hillary and her cronies spent your taxpayer money on. Even though… It was all the perfect setup operation via the United States Military Generals and Commander-in-Chief.

The GMA is the real Durham Report because this is what the majority of Americans did not know anything about… because Americans have been conditioned to trust Politicians, the News, and stopped using critical thinking and common sense plus understanding how to keep Politicians in check… a very tiny percentage knew about this act.

Sergei Magnitsky was a Ukrainian-born Russian tax advisor responsible for exposing corruption and misconduct by Russian government officials while representing clients. His arrest in 2008 and subsequent death after eleven months in police custody generated international attention and triggered both official and unofficial inquiries into allegations of fraud, theft, and human rights violations in Russia. He died during the period from 2008-2012 that Vladmir Putin was not President.

The GMA's very important for what's happening in Ukraine as Putin worked with CIC Trump… the rest of 'news' was all optics and comms to play out the narrative to dismantle the globalists and deep state. The legal framework for the Global Magnitsky Sanctions consists of the following executive order, multiple public laws (statutes), and regulations:

Executive Order 13818
22 United States Code 2656
50 United States Code 35
31 Code of Federal Regulations 583

Executive Order 13818 ties in with the Global Fragility Act of 2019.

1). Executive Order 13818:
https://www.govinfo.gov/content/pkg/DCPD-201700923/pdf/DCPD-201700923.pdf

22 U.S. Code 2656 is the Management of Foreign Affairs:

2). 22 U.S. Code 2656:
https://uscode.house.gov/view.xhtml?req=(title:22%20section:2656%20edition:prelim)

Pretty amazing for the fact, the Executive Order 13818 is December 2017, and the Global Fragility Act is 2019… how they all tie in.

Global Fragility Act of 2019:
https://www.state.gov/2022-prologue-to-the-united-states-strategy-to-prevent-conflict-and-promote-stability/#:~:text=INTRODUCTION,more%20peaceful%20and%20stable%20world.

The 2019 Global Fragility Act ties in with the 2020 Strategy which is the 2017 National Security Strategy from December 2017.

The landmark 2019 Global Fragility Act ("the Act") presents a new and necessary opportunity for the U.S. Government to prioritize conflict prevention and transform how it partners with countries affected by fragility and conflict to foster a more peaceful and stable world. Learning from the United States' decades-long stabilization experiences conflict-affected settings such as Afghanistan and Iraq, and consistent with the Act, the 2020 U.S. Strategy to Prevent Conflict and Promote Stability ("the Strategy") conceives an integrated, evidence-based, prevention-focused, coherent and field-driven approach to address drivers of fragility that can threaten U.S. national security and ultimately cost millions of U.S. taxpayer dollars.

The purpose of this prologue to the 2020 Strategy is to reflect emerging threats and opportunities and outline guiding principles to inform our whole-of-government work, in partnership with other countries, institutions and organizations, as we implement the Strategy and its four goals. These principles fall into three categories: (1) we will challenge the U.S. Government status quo, (2) we will pursue meaningful partnership at all levels, and (3) we will exploit synergies with other Administration priorities. In executing these principles, we aim to fulfill the intent of the Act in a way that meets the catalytic vision of the expert civil society coalition and members of Congress who championed the Act and counters the emergent, challenging and historic trends the United States and international partners confront today.

The 2020 U.S. Strategy to Prevent Conflict and Promote Stability ("the Strategy"):
https://www.state.gov/wp-content/uploads/2022/03/2020-United-States-Strategy-to-Prevent-Conflict-and-Promote-Stability-2.pdf

The **2017 National Security Strategy** (NSS) affirms that the United States will work to strengthen fragile states "where state weakness or failure would magnify threats to the American homeland" and "empower reform-minded governments, people, and civil society" in these places. The President affirmed this commitment when he signed the **Global Fragility Act of 2019** (Title V of Div. J, P.L. 116-94) (GFA) into law in December 2019. This Strategy meets the law's requirement for a "Global Fragility Strategy."

This Strategy builds upon reforms initiated by the **2018 Stabilization Assistance Review, 2018 Elie Wiesel Genocide and Atrocities Prevention Act, 2018 National Strategy for Counterterrorism,** and **2019 U.S. Strategy on Women, Peace, and Security.**

Through this Strategy, the United States will pursue a different approach from previous efforts. Rather than externally driven nation-building, the United States will support locally driven political solutions that align with United States' national security interests. Rather than fragmented and broad-based efforts, the United States will target the political factors that drive fragility. Rather than diffuse and open-ended efforts, the United States will engage selectively based on national interests, host-nation political progress, and defined metrics. Rather than implementing a disparate set of activities, the United States will strategically integrate its policy, diplomatic, and programmatic response.

The United States government will pursue reforms to use taxpayer dollars judiciously and achieve measurable results. This Strategy prioritizes data-driven analysis, diplomacy, and information-sharing to understand local dynamics, target interventions, and hold actors accountable. It requires rigorous monitoring and evaluation and periodic reviews to assess policy outcomes, not just program outputs. The Strategy also requires greater insistence on host-nation political will, defining burden-sharing, leveraging a broader range of financing tools, and holding actors accountable. The United States will modify or end programs that are not producing sufficient results or where partners are not fulfilling their commitments.

Elie Wiesel Genocide and Atrocities Prevention Act of 2018:
https://www.govinfo.gov/content/pkg/PLAW-115publ441/pdf/PLAW-115publ441.pdf

This law directs the U.S. Department of State to provide additional training for Foreign Service Officers assigned to a country experiencing or at risk of mass atrocities, such as genocide or war crimes.

ELIE WIESEL GENOCIDE AND ATROCITIES PREVENTION REPORT

The Trump Administration has made a steadfast commitment to prevent, mitigate, and respond to mass atrocities, and has set up a whole-of-Government interagency structure to support this commitment. The 2017 National Security Strategy states: "We will hold perpetrators of genocide and mass atrocities accountable." President Trump further reiterated the United States Government's commitment in his remarks at the United States Holocaust Memorial Museum in 2017, where he stated, "We will never, ever be silent in the face of evil again . . . and we pledge: never again."

President Donald J. Trump also signed into law the Elie Wiesel Genocide and Atrocities Prevention Act of 2018 (Public Law (P.L.) 115-441), hereafter referred to as "the Act," on January 14, 2019. The Act requires a report to Congress within 180 days, and annually thereafter for the following 6 years. The President is pleased to provide the Congress with the first interagency report in response to the Act, which includes information on actions undertaken during the past 6 months. Future reports will provide information regarding United States Government efforts on atrocity prevention, mitigation, and response, within the 12-month reporting period, including an analysis of the effectiveness of tools used.

I. Global Assessment

The Act states that the President, in consultation with relevant departments and agencies, shall submit annual reports to Congress, including a global assessment of ongoing atrocities and countries at risk of atrocities. Please refer to the classified annex for an overview and analysis of current countries that are experiencing or at risk of mass atrocities.

II. Multilateral and Other Diplomatic Engagement: Sharing Responsibilities and Best Practices

The United States Government will continue to engage with multilateral institutions, international organizations, and key regional organizations to enhance their capacity and participation in efforts to prevent, mitigate, and respond to atrocities. The United States Government will urge the international community and multilateral institutions to share responsibility and information, and to build further capacity to prevent, mitigate, and respond to mass atrocities.

The United States Government continues to engage with the international community, including the United Nations (UN), to assist and strengthen the documentation of recent atrocities in places like Burma. For example, the United States Government 3 provided publicly available satellite imagery and pertinent information to the Independent International Fact-Finding Mission on Burma, which aided in the investigation of atrocities and human-rights violations and abuses committed by the Burmese security forces after 2011. The Fact-Finding Mission on Burma and its subsequent follow-on mechanism, the "Independent Investigative Mechanism for Myanmar," have focused on pursuing justice and promoting accountability for human-rights violations and abuses in Burma.

III. Consultations with Civil Society

In May and June of 2019, the Department of State, USAID, and the White House held meetings with civil society to brief on the United States Government's work on atrocity prevention to exchange information on efforts to improve and strengthen existing atrocity prevention and response efforts. The United States Government provided updates on its atrocity prevention training efforts for personnel. Civil society provided feedback on how the United States Government could improve and strengthen atrocity prevention efforts (see Section IV).

IV. United States Government and Civil Society Recommendations to Improve Atrocity Prevention and Mitigation Efforts

The United States Government continues to refine its toolset and build institutional capacity to prevent, mitigate, and respond to atrocities. The White House has met with key civil society groups to discuss how to implement the Act to effectively prevent and respond to atrocities and shape priorities. Civil Society discussions emphasized the importance of:

- Improved use of data analytics, qualitative analysis, and intelligence reporting to enhance early warning and forecasting of atrocity risks;
- Standardized atrocity prevention training for United States Government personnel;
- Regular information-sharing and consultations with civil society; and
- Streamlining efforts to prevent and mitigate atrocities within existing interagency policy processes.
- These recommendations will help inform the approach of the Atrocity Early Warning Task Force (mentioned below).

V. Efforts by the United States Government to Respond to Atrocities

VI. Atrocity Prevention Training for United States Government Personnel

PUBLIC LAW 115–441—JAN. 14, 2019

ELIE WIESEL GENOCIDE AND ATROCITIES PREVENTION ACT OF 2018
https://www.govinfo.gov/content/pkg/PLAW-115publ441/pdf/PLAW-115publ441.pdf

Genocide definition is found in 18 United States Code Section 1091:
https://www.justice.gov/archives/jm/criminal-resource-manual-19-genocide-18-usc-1091#:~:text=Section%201091%20of%20Title%2018,%2C%20racial%2C%20or%20religious%20group.

Prohibits genocide whether committed in time of peace or time of war. Genocide is defined in § 1091 and includes violent attacks with the specific intent to destroy, in whole or in part, a national, ethnic, racial, or religious group. There is Federal jurisdiction if the offense is committed within the United States. There is also Federal extraterritorial jurisdiction when the offender is a national of the United States.

3). 50 U.S. Code Chapter 35

CHAPTER 35—INTERNATIONAL EMERGENCY ECONOMIC POWERS
§1701. Unusual and extraordinary threat; declaration of national emergency; exercise of Presidential authorities

(1) Any authority granted to the President by section 1702 of this title may be exercised to deal with any unusual and extraordinary threat, which has its source in whole or substantial part outside the United States, to the national security, foreign policy, or economy of the United States, if the President declares a national emergency with respect to such threat.

(2) The authorities granted to the President by section 1702 of this title may only be exercised to deal with an unusual and extraordinary threat with respect to which a national emergency has been declared for purposes of this chapter and may not be exercised for any other purpose. Any exercise of such authorities to deal with any new threat shall be based on a new declaration of national emergency which must be with respect to such threat. (Pub. L. 95–223, title II, §202, Dec. 28, 1977, 91 Stat. 1626.)

50 USC Chapter 35:
https://uscode.house.gov/view.xhtml?path=/prelim@title50/chapter35&edition=prelim

4). 31 Code of Federal Regulations 583

PART 583—GLOBAL MAGNITSKY SANCTIONS REGULATIONS

January 17, 2017: Federal Continuity Directive 1

Issued January 17, 2017, with Operational Dates: 2018-2022.

Federal Continuity Directive 1:

https://www.gpo.gov/docs/default-source/accessibility-privacy-coop-files/January2017FCD1-2.pdf

The titles on the very front page were Department of Homeland Security and Federal Emergency Management Agency (FEMA).

It is 64 pages of how the 3 Branches of Government were under a Continuity of Government with key chapters: Reconstitution and Devolution. This outlined the Emergency Response Groups with Emergency Communications and Presidential Policy Directives which explained all the photos I took daily, weekly, monthly, and yearly to show the vast array of Aircraft in Operations that were taking place.

These FCD1 and 2 were very easy to read. And it was reads like this that shows how bad America reached where people didn't even know the simplicities of Government that they couldn't read a 68-page outline of how the Government was in a major clean out process with multiple people participating in the overhaul.

For example, read the policy of the FCD1.

A. Policy:

As established in PPD-40, "it is the policy of the United States to maintain a comprehensive and effective continuity capability through Continuity of Operations (COOP), Continuity of Government (COG), and Enduring Constitutional Government (ECG) programs, ensuring the resilience and preservation of government structure under the United States Constitution and the continuous performance of National Essential Functions (NEFs) under all conditions." National continuity programs are based on the continuous performance of NEFs through the sustainment of essential functions performed by D/As. NEFs are the focal point of all continuity programs and capabilities and represent the overarching responsibilities of the Federal Government to lead and sustain the Nation before, during, and in the aftermath of a catastrophic emergency.

The *NEFs* are:

1) Ensuring the continued functioning of our form of government under the United States Constitution, including the functioning of three separate branches of government;

2) Providing leadership visible to the Nation and the world and maintaining the trust and confidence of the American people;

3) Defending the United States against all enemies, foreign and domestic, and preventing or interdicting attacks against the United States or its people, property, or interests;

4) Maintaining and fostering effective relationships with foreign nations;

5) Protecting against threats to the homeland and bringing to justice perpetrators of crimes or attacks against the United States or its people, property, or interests;

6) Providing rapid and effective response to and recovery from the domestic consequences of an attack or other incident;

7) Protecting and stabilizing the Nation's economy and ensuring public confidence in its financial systems; and,

8) Providing for Federal Government services that address the national health, safety, and welfare needs of the United States.

Not a difficult read at all and would have provided so much relief and peace to many more had they simply taken initiative to read and apply.

January 20, 2017: President Donald John Trump Inauguration

Military Occupation and Continuity of Operations Plan goes into effect. There were two very key Optics standing behind him that day. Military Officers with headbands:

**President Donald Trump Inaugural Address
FULL SPEECH (C-SPAN)**

386K views 6y ago Shop ...**more**

Military Intelligence	**Judge Advocate Generals**

These were the Optics of what was about to come…

> *"We have it all. We've caught them all."* = **Military Intelligence.**

Who punishes crimes of those caught? = **JAG**.

January 25, 2017: **Border Security and Immigration Enforcement Improvements**

Executive Order 13767:
https://www.federalregister.gov/documents/2017/01/30/2017-02095/border-security-and-immigration-enforcement-improvements

Article IV of the Constitution is one of the most defined roles of the President in the Constitution. The number one role of the President is the protection of his people.

January 28, 2017: **Ethics Commitments by Executive Branch Appointees**

Executive Order 13770:
https://www.federalregister.gov/documents/2017/02/03/2017-02450/ethics-commitments-by-executive-branch-appointees

If you want to know how people kept quiet during the Operation and Continuity of Government… There are things called NDAs, but also Presidential Executive Orders such as this one which would have harsh punishment for signing and breaking.

As the Operation rolled along, this is why you heard CIC Trump in his speeches starting in November 2022 start addressing, we are going to end lobbying and defense contracts because "those are the key people who make excuses to stay in wars." Stupid and foolish wars as he noted elsewhere.

Keep in mind… this EO is 11 days after the issuing of the Federal Continuity Directive 1 on January 17, 2017. As you'll read below, January 2021, alone has a very specific title referencing this EO below to do with one of the three branches of governments.

February 9, 2017: **Enforcing Federal Law With Respect to Transnational Criminal Organizations and Preventing International Trafficking**

Executive Order 13773:
https://www.federalregister.gov/documents/2017/02/14/2017-03113/enforcing-federal-law-with-respect-to-transnational-criminal-organizations-and-preventing

This was the beginning of the war on trafficking. We should have NEVER let our Nation or any other Nation for that matter reach this depth of corruption with any kind of trafficking.

February 9, 2017: **Preventing Violence Against Federal, State, Tribal, and Local Law Enforcement Officers**

Executive Order 13774:
https://www.federalregister.gov/documents/2017/02/14/2017-03115/preventing-violence-against-federal-state-tribal-and-local-law-enforcement-officers

In conjunction with and correlation to the Federal Continuity Directives. Signing an Executive Order to prevent violence against all Law Enforcement Officers, sounds like a massive Operation taking place in order to prevent harm to those doing what's right by LAWS and ORDERS.

February 28, 2017: **Restoring the Rule of Law, Federalism, and Economic Growth by Reviewing the "Waters of the United States" Rule**

Executive Order 13778:
https://www.federalregister.gov/documents/2017/03/03/2017-04353/restoring-the-rule-of-law-federalism-and-economic-growth-by-reviewing-the-waters-of-the-united

Remember when all the news outlets kept showing articles and shows on pollution and chemicals in streams, rivers, lakes, etc.?

They were all Optics. He knew. He always knew. Now you know.

March 13, 2017: **Comprehensive Plan for Reorganizing the Executive Branch**

Executive Order 13781:
https://www.federalregister.gov/documents/2017/03/16/2017-05399/comprehensive-plan-for-reorganizing-the-executive-branch

This order feeds from the Executive Branch 8 days after Bossman took office. These all coincide with the Federal Continuity Directive 1, but more in particular what was coming in January 2021 that has its own title.

March 27, 2017: **Revocation of Federal Contracting Executive Orders**

Executive Order 13782:
https://www.federalregister.gov/documents/2017/03/30/2017-06382/revocation-of-federal-contracting-executive-orders

Also, very important immediately following the 13781 EO; this is to make sure all Executive Orders are promptly rescinded or enforcing the revoked orders.

March 29, 2017: **Establishing the President's Commission on Combating Drug Addiction and the Opioid Crisis**

Executive Order 13784:
https://www.federalregister.gov/documents/2017/04/03/2017-06716/establishing-the-presidents-commission-on-combating-drug-addiction-and-the-opioid-crisis

This is addressing the Drug Addiction and Opioid Crisis in America which would also lead to the cleaning up of the United States cities and streets.

May 11, 2017: **Establishment of Presidential Advisory Commission on Election Integrity**

Executive Order 13799:
https://www.federalregister.gov/documents/2017/05/16/2017-10003/establishment-of-presidential-advisory-commission-on-election-integrity

This would be the start of the ending of the 'stolen' Elections with the Committees in place to assure the Governors, Secretary of State's, Attorney Generals, Judges, and Lawyers are applying and upholding the Federal and State Election Laws.

May 11, 2017: Strengthening the Cybersecurity of Federal Networks and Critical Infrastructure

Executive Order 13800:
https://www.federalregister.gov/documents/2017/05/16/2017-10004/strengthening-the-cybersecurity-of-federal-networks-and-critical-infrastructure

This was yet another step to establishing the future of our Technology and Infrastructure as we moved closer to the establishment of the Space Force as the Space Council was about to be established two months from this order.

This Executive Order would also tie into the Cybersecurity section on page 12 of the 2017 National Security Strategy issued December 2017.

May 20, 2017: The Sword Dance, Saudi Arabia

CIC Donald John Trump is the only President to be involved in the traditional Saudi Arabia Sword Dance called the Najdi Ardah.

The history and significance of sword dancing is important to note. The most common Ardah in Saudi, called the Najdi Ardah, initially performed by Arav warriors in the Najda region of Saudi before meeting their enemies on the battlefield. Sword dancing was a way for the men to display their weaponry and show their heroic spirit.

For CIC Trump to be the only president to be involved in a Saudi Arabia Sword Dance is pure symbolism. This was symbolism was going to war together.

CIC Trump came to Saudi with folders displaying the Military had everything on their corruption the only way out of their heinous crimes was to bend the knee to the U.S. and capitulate a vow to bring down the New World Order together and what better way of showing their submission than with an honorable sword dance?

Saudi Arabia Dance:
https://www.cnn.com/2017/05/20/politics/trump-saudi-arabia-dance/index.html

CIC was given 83 gifts in this Historic trip:
https://www.independent.co.uk/news/world/americas/us-politics/saudi-arabia-donald-trump-83-gifts-us-president-portrait-meeting-swords-daggers-a7930496.html

President Trump Sword Dance:
Trump Welcomed with Sword Dance at Saudi Palace

June 13, 2017: Implementation Phase of the Federal Continuity Directives

This is the implementation of the Continuity of Operation Plan.

Federal Continuity Directive 2:
https://www.fema.gov/sites/default/files/2020-07/Federal_Continuity_Directive-2_June132017.pdf

Federal Continuity Directive 2 was issued on June 13, 2017, with Operational dates of 2020-2024.

I. Purpose

Federal Continuity Directive-2 (FCD-2) implements the requirements of FCD-1, Annex B (Essential Functions), and provides direction and guidance to Federal Executive Branch Departments and Agencies (D/As) to assist in validation of Mission Essential Functions (MEFs) and Primary Mission Essential Functions (PMEFs). The update and validation of essential functions includes conducting a comprehensive Business Process Analysis (BPA) to understand those processes necessary to the performance of organizational functions and requirements. It also includes conducting a Business Impact Analysis (BIA) to identify potential impacts on the performance of essential functions and the consequences of failure to sustain them. Further, it requires the application of organization-wide risk analysis to inform decision making and strengthen operations through effective risk management. FCD-2 outlines requirements and provides checklists and resources to assist D/As in identifying and assessing their essential functions through a risk-based process and in identifying candidate PMEFs that support the National Essential Functions (NEFs). This FCD provides guidance for conducting a BPA and BIA to identify essential function relationships, dependencies, time sensitivities, threats, vulnerabilities, consequences, and mitigation strategies related to the performance of the MEFs and PMEFs. This FCD also provides direction on the formalized process for submitting D/As' candidate PMEFs in support of the NEFs.

II. Applicability and Scope

The provisions of this FCD apply to the executive D/As enumerated in 5 United States Code (U.S.C.) § 101, including the U.S. Department of Homeland Security (DHS), independent establishments as defined by 5 U.S.C. § 104(1), government corporations as defined by 5 U.S.C. § 103(1), and the United States Postal Service. The D/As, commissions, bureaus, boards, and independent organizations are hereinafter referred to as "organizations" to better reflect the diverse organizational structures within the Federal Executive Branch. The provisions of this FCD are applicable at all levels of Federal Executive Branch organizations regardless of their location, including regional and field locations. Headquarters (HQ) elements are responsible for providing oversight and promulgating direction to their component, subcomponent, and field organizations. In this FCD, the term "headquarters" refers to the central, head offices of operations for organizations identified in Presidential Policy Directive (PPD)-40, Annex A, Categories of Departments and Agencies. The terms "component" or "subcomponent" refers to all organizational elements, whether at HQs or a regional, field, or satellite office. Though not a requirement, state, local, tribal, and territorial governments, non-government organizations, and private sector critical infrastructure owners and operators are strongly encouraged to adopt this approach, as there are many dependencies and interdependencies among various levels of government critical to ensuring the continued functioning of governments and the continued performance of essential functions. Specific guidance for non-federal organizations is available in the Continuity Guidance Circular.

IV. Policy and Background

PPD-40, National Continuity Policy, sets forth the policy of the United States to maintain a comprehensive and effective continuity capability through Continuity of Operations (COOP), Continuity of Government (COG), and Enduring Constitutional Government (ECG) programs ensuring the preservation of government structure under the United States Constitution and continuing performance of NEFs under all conditions.

As noted in FCD-1, national continuity programs are based on the continuous performance of NEFs through the sustainment of essential functions performed by D/As. NEFs are the foundation of all continuity programs and capabilities and represent the overarching responsibilities of the Federal Government to lead and sustain the Nation before, during, and in the aftermath of a catastrophic emergency. All D/As, regardless of size or location, are required to have a viable continuity capability to ensure organizational resilience and continued performance of essential functions under all conditions. The foundation of robust and viable continuity programs and capabilities is the understanding and commitment to the continued performance of the organization's essential functions. Organizations must consider and fully integrate continuity planning and procedures into all aspects of daily operations to create a culture of continuity that will ensure seamless continuation of essential functions under all conditions.

To preserve the government and sustain the NEFs, D/As must identify their MEFs and PMEFs and ensure that those functions can be continued during, or resumed rapidly after, a disruption to normal operations. While the Federal Government provides many services to the American people, Federal Executive Branch D/As must identify and prioritize those critical services that must continue during an emergency. D/As must set those priorities as part of their preparedness posture and not wait for a crisis or a continuity event to determine which activities must be sustained throughout the event. Only with a coordinated, organization-wide approach can D/As ensure resilience and the ability to continue to perform essential functions during both catastrophic emergencies and more routine disruptions to operations both planned and unplanned.

FCD-2 directs updates to and validation of essential functions, requiring the conduct of a comprehensive BPA, conduct of a BIA, and the application of agency-wide risk analysis in support of organizational resilience and continuity programs. This analytic approach defines how robust an organization's continuity program shall be and underscores that strengthening the continuity program will strengthen the enterprise, making the organization more resilient regardless of the challenges it may face. Risk analysis of a BPA, supported by a BIA, aids in the identification on non-obvious, emerging, and future risks or threats to an organization's operations. Structured and in-depth analysis enables organizations to consider and allocate resources to those areas of greatest risk and where the most benefit from investment may be achieved. Analytic findings and supporting documentation further enable justification of needed resources, as well as determinations on resource allocation throughout the organization. Investing in those areas critical to the performance of an organization's essential functions will further allow agencies to build resilience and more readily adapt to evolving threats. The use of analysis and related tools will maximize the organization's use of resources given dependency considerations for performance of both steady-state functions and essential functions during a catastrophic emergency.

June 21, 2017: Amending Executive Order 13597

Executive Order 13802:
https://www.federalregister.gov/documents/2017/06/26/2017-13458/amending-executive-order-13597

Prime example of an Executive Order from the Obama Era, that read well on paper, but one key little paragraph could affect the whole application and upholding of the Law, meaning it read and looked good on paper, but what was taking place in the action zone of a Law?

Many Laws read perfectly, but were not applied or upheld, or had a small clause that could negate the whole application plus more importantly, did it or does it support the Constitution hence *Marbury vs. Madison*, *1803*.

June 30, 2017: Reviving the National Space Council

Executive Order 13803:
https://www.federalregister.gov/documents/2017/07/07/2017-14378/reviving-the-national-space-council

Love the first word in this Executive Order… Reviving. Anyone who knows any history knows the Space Force was established by Donald John Trump, but was John F. Kennedy's baby.

This Executive Order is 3 years before the establishment of the Space Force, so, this Executive Order was the start to the vamping.

July 18, 2017: Trump Tower

The U.S. Military is reported to have rented $2.4 million dollars' worth of space at the Trump Tower. Documents released by the GSA have several redactions, including the name of who owns the government-rented space in Trump Tower. However, the GSA lease inventory records show that Joel R. Anderson, Mr. Trump's neighbor, is the owner, according to the Journal. Anderson is chairman of Anderson Media Corp., a DVD, CD, and book distributor, and is a member of the board of directors at Trump Tower.

The White House Military Office oversees the "nuclear football," which is the briefcase that constantly accompanies the president and would allow Mr. Trump to authorize a nuclear strike. The office is also required to be always near the president to provide support services relating to medical needs, transportation, communications and food.

July 22, 2017: USS Gerald Ford

President Trump commissions the aircraft carrier USS Gerald R. Ford (CVN-78) at Naval Station Norfolk, Virginia.

(*Fast Forward*) Now does the USS Gerald Ford in the Mediterranean Sea after the Israel Attack, on October 7, 2023, make sense? #Optic Everything ALWAYS stems back to CIC Trump.

July 25, 2017: Syria

President Trump holds a bilateral meeting and joint press conference with Lebanese Prime Minister Saad Hariri at the White House to discuss the humanitarian problem in Syria, Hezbollah, and anti-terrorism.

August 8, 2017: Warning to North Korea

"North Korea best not make any more threats to the United States," Mr. Trump told reporters at his golf club in Bedminster, N.J., where is spending much of the month on a working vacation.

> *"They will be met with fire and fury like the world has never seen."*

New York Times:
https://www.nytimes.com/2017/08/08/world/asia/north-korea-un-sanctions-nuclear-missile-united-nations.html#:~:text=Referring%20to%20North%20Korea's%20volatile,world%20has%20never%20seen%20before.%E2%80%9D

August 18, 2017: U.S. Cyber Command

Directs that the U.S. Cyber Command (USCYBERCOM) be elevated to the status of a Unified Combatant Command.
Unified Combatant Commands are organized either on a geographical basis (known as an "area of responsibility", AOR) or on a functional basis, e.g., special operations, force projection, transport, and cybersecurity.

There's 11 of those: https://www.defense.gov/About/combatant-commands/

August 24, 2017: **Imposing Additional Sanctions With Respect to the Situation in Venezuela**

Executive Order 13808:
https://www.federalregister.gov/documents/2017/08/29/2017-18468/imposing-additional-sanctions-with-respect-to-the-situation-in-venezuela

This is the first Executive Order where CIC Trump declared a National Emergency. There's a string of "taking additional steps to address the situation in Venezuela" Executive Orders

August 28, 2017: Finland

Holds a bilateral meeting and joint press conference with Finnish President Sauli Niinistö at the White House to discuss terrorism, Afghanistan, Russia, the Baltic Sea, and the Arctic.

August 28, 2017: **Restoring State, Tribal, and Local Law Enforcement's Access to Life-Saving Equipment and Resources**

Executive Order 13809:
https://www.federalregister.gov/documents/2017/08/31/2017-18679/restoring-state-tribal-and-local-law-enforcements-access-to-life-saving-equipment-and-resources

Here's a primary Executive Order that correlates and coincides with the Federal Continuity Directives as those outlines Local, State, Tribal, and Territorial Government and Law Enforcement outlines and guidelines.

September 8, 2017: Saudi Arabia and UAE

President Trump speaks by phone to Saudi Arabia's Crown Prince Mohammed bin Salman Al Saud, the United Arab Emirates Crown Prince Mohammed bin Zayed Al Nahyan and Qatar's Emir Tamim bin Hamad Al Thani concerning regional stability.

September 9, 2017: Turkey

President Trump speaks by phone to Turkish President Recep Tayyip Erdoğan, agreeing to further strengthen bilateral relations and increase stability in the Middle East.
September 12, 2017

President Trump holds a bilateral meeting with Malaysian Prime Minister Najib Razak at the White House focusing on trade, Islamic terrorism and Malaysian interest in Trump's infrastructure program.

September 15, 2017

President Trump in a phone call to Jewish leaders and rabbis reaffirms the administration's strong support for Israel and honors the upcoming celebration of High Holy Days such as Yom Kippur and Rosh Hashana.
September 17, 2017

President Trump, in a phone call to South Korean President Moon Jae-in, pledges to impose stronger sanctions on North Korea to counter its missile and nuclear programs.

September 18, 2017

Holds a bilateral meeting with Israeli Prime Minister Benjamin Netanyahu to discuss a possible future peace deal between the Israelis and Palestinians, and alleged Iranian aggression in the Middle East.
Holds a bilateral meeting with French President Emmanuel Macron to discuss the Paris Climate Change Agreement and the Iran nuclear deal.

Has dinner meeting with Latin American leaders such as Brazilian President Michel Temer, Colombian President Juan Manuel Santos, Panamanian President Juan Carlos Varela and Argentinian Vice President Gabriela Michetti to discuss the restoration of democracy in Venezuela.

September 19, 2017

In his maiden speech to the United Nations General Assembly, President Trump announces that if Kim Jong-un, dubbed "Rocket Man", forces the United States to defend itself or its allies, the United States will "totally destroy" North Korea.

He also indicates the possibility of further action against Venezuelan President Maduro's regime.
Denounces Iran as a "corrupt dictatorship" and describes the Iranian nuclear deal as an "embarrassment."

Attends a lunch meeting hosted by UN Secretary General António Guterres, seated with the leaders of Japan, South Korea, Turkey, and others.

Holds a bilateral meeting with Qatari Emir Tamim bin Hamad Al Thani to discuss solving the dispute between Qatar and the Arab states.

September 20, 2017

Holds a bilateral meeting with King Abdullah II of Jordan to discuss fighting terrorism in the Middle East and praises Jordan for taking refugees from Syria.

Holds a bilateral meeting with Palestinian President Mahmoud Abbas, promises to work on a peace deal between the Israelis and Palestinians.

Hosts a working lunch with African Union leader Alpha Conde and leaders from Nigeria, Côte d'Ivoire, Ethiopia, Ghana, Guinea, Namibia, Senegal, Uganda and South Africa, discussing economic opportunities in the African continent and the security situation South Sudan and Congo.

Holds a bilateral meeting with British Prime Minister Theresa May to discuss trade, North Korea, and Iran.

President Trump holds a bilateral meeting with Egyptian President Abdel Fattah el-Sisi and mentions he was considering the resumption of the foreign military aid to Egypt which was frozen over concerns of its human rights record.

September 20, 2017: **Imposing Additional Sanctions With Respect to North Korea**

Executive Order 13810:
https://www.federalregister.gov/documents/2017/09/25/2017-20647/imposing-additional-sanctions-with-respect-to-north-korea

Remember throughout 2016… "Donald Trump will get us in a Nuclear War with North Korea" about 27 times a day on every news outlet in America? Also remember "Donald Trump is going to lead us into World War 3?"

Yeah, everyone forgot that quick. They also forgot that he didn't lead us into ANY war for that matter. I should elaborate a lot more here just to drive the point home on his behalf, but I believe Mount Rushmore will someday do the talking for us.

September 21, 2017

Holds a bilateral meeting with Afghan President Ashraf Ghani to discuss the Afghanistan war strategy in combating Islamist terrorists.

Holds a bilateral meeting with Ukraine President Petro Poroshenko to discuss issues such as trade between both countries and the security situation in Ukraine.

Signs an executive order targeting individuals and companies trading with North Korea, including sanctions on foreign banks.

Holds a bilateral meeting with South Korean President Moon Jae-in to discuss recent provocations by North Korea.

Holds a bilateral meeting with Japanese Prime Minister Shinzō Abe and agree on their support for UN sanctions on North Korea.

Holds a bilateral meeting with Turkish President Recep Tayyip Erdoğan to discuss regional developments such as the Russian sale of S-400 missile system to Turkey and Northern Iraqi Kurdish independence referendum.

September 26, 2017

Holds a bilateral meeting and joint press conference with Spanish Prime Minister Mariano Rajoy at the White House to discuss both countries commitments in combating terrorism, the situations with North Korea and Venezuela and their opposition to Catalonia's independence from Spain.

October 6, 2017: 'Calm Before the Storm'

> *"Could be the calm before the storm…"* – "What storm Mr. President?"

NYT:
https://www.nytimes.com/2017/10/06/us/politics/trump-calls-meeting-with-military-leaders-the-calm-before-the-storm.html

October 20, 2017: Amending Executive Order 13223

Executive Order 13814:
https://www.federalregister.gov/documents/2017/10/24/2017-23270/amending-executive-order-13223

This is the very Executive Order that calls all Retired Members to Active-Duty.

"The authorities available for use during a national emergency under sections 688 and 690 of title 10, United States Code, are also invoked and made available, according to their terms, to the Secretary concerned, subject in the case of the Secretaries of the Army, Navy, and Air Force, to the direction of the Secretary of Defense."

There's that **Title 10** again... The same Title 10 all soldiers who take the Oath swear in under... **10 USC §502.** The same Title 10 that shows only the President can federalize the National Guard and Reserve Components to Active-Duty... **10 USC §12406.**

10 United States Code §688: Retired members: authority to order to active duty; duties

(a) AUTHORITY.-Under regulations prescribed by the Secretary of Defense, a member described in subsection (b) may be ordered to active duty by the Secretary of the military department concerned at any time.

(b) COVERED MEMBERS.-Except as provided in subsection (d), subsection (a) applies to the following members of the armed forces:

(1) A retired member of the Regular Army, Regular Navy, Regular Air Force, Regular Marine Corps, or Regular Space Force.
(2) A member of the Retired Reserve who was retired under section 1293, 7311, 7314, 8323, 9311, or 9314 of this title.
     (3) A member of the Fleet Reserve or Fleet Marine Corps Reserve.

10 United States Code 688: https://uscode.house.gov/view.xhtml?hl=false&edition=prelim&req=granuleid%3AUSC-prelim-title10-section688&num=0&saved=%7CZ3JhbnVsZWlkOlVTQy1wcmVsaW0tdGl0bGUxMC1zZWN0aW9uNjg4%7C%7C%7C0%7Cfalse%7Cprelim

10 United States Code §688a: Retired members: temporary authority to order to active duty in high-demand, low-density assignments

(a) AUTHORITY.-The Secretary of a military department may order to active duty a retired member who agrees to serve on active duty in an assignment intended to alleviate a high-demand, low-density military capability or in any other specialty designated by the Secretary as critical to meet wartime or peacetime requirements. Any such order may be made only with the consent of the member ordered to active duty and in accordance with an agreement between the Secretary and the member.

(b) DURATION.-The period of active duty of a member under an order to active duty under subsection (a) shall be specified in the agreement entered into under that subsection.

(c) LIMITATION.-No more than a total of 1,000 members may be on active duty at any time under subsection (a).

(d) RELATIONSHIP TO OTHER AUTHORITY.-The authority to order a retired member to active duty under this section is in addition to the authority under section 688 of this title or any other provision of law authorizing the Secretary concerned to order a retired member to active duty.

(e) INAPPLICABILITY OF CERTAIN PROVISIONS.-Retired members ordered to active duty under subsection (a) shall not be counted for purposes of section 688 or 690 of this title.

(f) EXPIRATION OF AUTHORITY.-A retired member may not be ordered to active duty under this section outside a period as follows:

(1) The period beginning on December 2, 2002, and ending on December 31, 2011.
(2) The period beginning on the date of the enactment of the National Defense Authorization Act for Fiscal Year 2018 and ending on December 31, 2022.

(g) EXCEPTIONS DURING PERIODS OF WAR OR NATIONAL EMERGENCY.-The limitations in subsections (c) and (f) shall not apply during a time of war or of national emergency declared by Congress or the President.

(h) HIGH-DEMAND, LOW-DENSITY MILITARY CAPABILITY DEFINED.-In this section, the term "high-demand, low-density military capability" means a combat, combat support or service support capability, unit, system, or occupational specialty that the Secretary of Defense determines has funding, equipment, or personnel levels that are substantially below the levels required to fully meet or sustain actual or expected operational requirements set by regional commanders.

10 United States Code 688a:
https://uscode.house.gov/view.xhtml?hl=false&edition=prelim&req=granuleid%3AUSC-prelim-title10-section688a&num=0&saved=%7CZ3JhbnVsZWlkOlVTQy1wcmVsaW0tdGl0bGUxMC1zZWN0aW9uNjg4a%7C%7C%7C0%7Cfalse%7Cprelim

10 United States Code §690: Retired members ordered to active duty: limitation on number

(a) GENERAL AND FLAG OFFICERS.-Not more than 15 retired general officers of the Army, Air Force, or Marine Corps, and not more than 15 retired flag officers of the Navy, may be on active duty at any one time. For the purposes of this subsection a retired officer ordered to active duty for a period of 60 days or less is not counted.

(b) LIMITATION BY SERVICE.-(1) Not more than 25 officers of any one armed force may be serving on active duty concurrently pursuant to orders to active duty issued under section 688 of this title.

(1) In the administration of paragraph (1), the following officers shall not be counted:

(A) A chaplain who is assigned to duty as a chaplain for the period of active duty to which ordered.

(B) A health care professional (as characterized by the Secretary concerned) who is assigned to duty as a health care professional for the period of the active duty to which ordered.

(C) Any officer assigned to duty with the American Battle Monuments Commission for the period of active duty to which ordered.

(D) Any member of the Retiree Council of the Army, Navy, or Air Force for the period on active duty to attend the annual meeting of the Retiree Council.

(E) An officer who is assigned to duty as a defense attaché or service attaché for the period of active duty to which ordered.

10 United States Code 690:
https://uscode.house.gov/view.xhtml?hl=false&edition=prelim&req=granuleid%3AUSC-prelim-title10-section690&num=0&saved=%7CZ3JhbnVsZWlkOlVTQy1wcmVsaW0tdGl0bGUxMC1zZWN0aW9uNjg4%7C%7C%7C0%7Cfalse%7Cprelim

November 21, 2017

President Trump and President Putin speak by telephone; Putin seeks support for his plan to end the Syrian civil war.

December 6, 2017: **CIC Trump declares Jerusalem capital of Israel.**

This was the turning point in the Bible and an early indicator of the Special Operation taking place.

The United States of America has always protected Israel. A lot of major deception took place during the take down of the RINOs and the Deep State. The far-left Democrats and Liberals have ALWAYS wanted to stop funding and protecting Israel… So, when "Biden" was shown in articles supporting Israel, everyone should have known this was all Optics.

CNN:
https://www.cnn.com/2017/12/06/politics/president-donald-trump-jerusalem/index.html

"The President's decision is an important step towards peace, for there is no peace that doesn't include Jerusalem as the capital of the State of Israel," Netanyahu said.

Chief Palestinian negotiator Saeb Erakat said Trump's decision "disqualified the United States of America to play any role in any peace process."

"President Trump just destroyed any policy of a two-state (solution)," Erakat said in a statement. "He has taken an action to recognize Jerusalem as the capital of Israel. This is in total contradiction of agreements signed between Palestinians and Israelis."

AP News:
https://apnews.com/article/north-america-donald-trump-ap-top-news-tel-aviv-jerusalem-1d4e1824283f41eaa8422227fa8e6ea7

Amazing how biased the media was; however, there's a reason in that as well. Everyone played a major role in making sure this Military Operation and Continuity of Government moved along until all was cleaned out all over the world. There's nobody that can stop God's watch and plan. God knows what He's doing and who He's using.

December 18, 2017: **National Security Strategy issued**

2017 National Security Strategy
https://trumpwhitehouse.archives.gov/wp-content/uploads/2017/12/NSS-Final-12-18-2017-0905.pdf

When one reads the 2017 NSS and applies the timestamps along with what was to come… keep in mind, this was issued December 18, 2017, two and a half years before the world would know "CoronaVirus 19" aka Covid.

There's a section in this titled Pandemic that describes what every American witnessed that was outlined in this Strategy 2.5 years before to the tee! Proving what I outlined throughout 2021 to 2023, that the Pandemic was a Strategic Plan to see how many Americans would sit at home at the command of the Government… especially the Government a whopping majority of those claimed they did not trust, but they sure sat their butts at home on a simple command.

A small peek into the NSS:

My fellow Americans:

The American people elected me to make America great again. I promised that my Administration would put the safety, interests, and well-being of our citizens first. I pledged that we would revitalize the American economy, rebuild our military, defend our borders, protect our sovereignty, and advance our values.

During my first year in office, you have witnessed my America First foreign policy in action. We are prioritizing the interests of our citizens and protecting our sovereign rights as a nation. America is leading again on the world stage. We are not hiding from the challenges we face. We are confronting them head-on and pursuing opportunities to promote the securities and prosperities of all Americans.

The United States faces an extraordinarily dangerous world, filled with a wide range of threats that have intensified in recent years. When I came into office, rogue regimes were developing nuclear weapons and missiles to threaten the entire planet. Radical Islamist terror groups were flourishing. Terrorists had taken control of vast swaths of the Middle East. Rival powers were aggressively undermining American interests around the globe. At home, porous borders and unenforced immigration laws had created a host of vulnerabilities. Criminal cartels were bringing drugs and danger into our communities. Unfair trade practices had weakened our economy and exported our jobs overseas. Unfair burden-sharing with our allies and inadequate investment in our own defense had invited danger from those who wish us harm. Too many Americans had lost trust in our government, faith in our future, and confidence in our values.

Nearly one year later, although serious challenges remain, we are charting a new and very different course.

We are rallying the world against the rogue regime in North Korea and confronting the danger posed by the dictatorship in Iran, which those determined to pursue a flawed nuclear deal had neglected. We have renewed our friendships in the Middle East and partnered with regional leaders to help drive out terrorists and extremists, cut off their financing, and discredit their wicked ideology. We crushed Islamic State of Iraq and Syria (ISIS) terrorists on the battlefields of Syria and Iraq, and will continue pursuing them until they are destroyed. America's allies are now contributing more to our common defense, strengthening even our strongest alliances. We have also continued to make clear that the United States will no longer tolerate economic aggression or unfair trading practices.

At home, we have restored confidence in America's purpose. We have recommitted ourselves to our founding principles and to the values that have made our families, communities, and society so successful. Jobs are coming back and our economy is growing. We are making historic investments in the United States military. We are enforcing our borders, building trade relationships based on fairness and reciprocity, and defending America's sovereignty without apology.

The whole world is lifted by America's renewal and the reemergence of American leadership. After one year, the world knows that America is prosperous, America is secure, and America is strong. We will bring about the better future we seek for our people and the world, by confronting the challenges and dangers posed by those who seek to destabilize the world and threaten America's people and interests.

My Administration's National Security Strategy lays out a strategic vision for protecting the American people and preserving our way of life, promoting our prosperity, preserving peace through strength, and advancing American influence in the world. We will pursue this beautiful vision—a world of strong, sovereign, and independent nations, each with its own cultures and dreams, thriving side-by-side in prosperity, freedom, and peace—throughout the upcoming year.

In pursuit of that future, we will look at the world with clear eyes and fresh thinking. We will promote a balance of power that favors the United States, our allies, and our partners. We will never lose sight of our values and their capacity to inspire, uplift, and renew.

Most of all, we will serve the American people and uphold their right to a government that prioritizes their security, their prosperity, and their interests. This National Security Strategy puts America First.

[SIGNED]

President Donald J. Trump
The White House
December 2017

Did you notice the infamous… '*My Fellow Americans*'?

December 20, 2017: **Blocking the Property of Persons Involved in Serious Human Rights Abuse or Corruption**

Executive Order 13818:
https://www.federalregister.gov/documents/2017/12/26/2017-27925/blocking-the-property-of-persons-involved-in-serious-human-rights-abuse-or-corruption

This would be the official declaration of WAR on all Trafficking: Drug, Human, Sex, and Children.

Notice all the Acts and United States Codes in the first paragraph as well, they all correlate and coincide. This blocked ALL assets and destroyed the 'dirty money' also known as Fiat Currency / the United States Dollar that wasn't worth anything after the U.S. left the gold standard in 1968.

Taking away Deep State/Cabal money = their destruction and death. They could not operate without the currency they controlled. This was the first National Emergency from those declared from December 2017 to March 2020 that allowed CIC DJT to initiate the 50 United States Code Laws in March 2020 as you'll read below.

January 2, 2018

Via Twitter, President Trump threatens to cut off U.S. aid to the Palestinian Authority, claiming the Palestinians were no longer willing to negotiate on a peace process with the Israelis—seemingly after his December 2017 decision to recognize Jerusalem as the capital of Israel.

January 8, 2018: Streamlining and Expediting Requests To Locate Broadband Facilities in Rural America

Executive Order 13821:
https://www.federalregister.gov/documents/2018/01/11/2018-00553/streamlining-and-expediting-requests-to-locate-broadband-facilities-in-rural-america

This Executive Order is as it reads:

Section 1. *Policy.* Americans need access to reliable, affordable broadband internet service to succeed in today's information-driven, global economy. Currently, too many American citizens and businesses still lack access to this basic tool of modern economic connectivity. This problem is particularly acute in rural America, and it hinders the ability of rural American communities to increase economic prosperity; attract new businesses; enhance job growth; extend the reach of affordable, high-quality healthcare; enrich student learning with digital tools; and facilitate access to the digital marketplace.

This is also tied into with the Federal Continuity Directives as well with the Emergency Communications along with the 1776 Commission on educating our children and people on the Foundation of America and our History.

January 9, 2018: Supporting Our Veterans During Their Transition From Uniformed Service to Civilian Life

Executive Order 13822:
https://www.federalregister.gov/documents/2018/01/12/2018-00630/supporting-our-veterans-during-their-transition-from-uniformed-service-to-civilian-life

It was CIC Donald John Trump who established more care for us Veterans than any other President. Everything everyone witnessed via "Biden" was a Continuity of Government stemming from Acts and Policies before him.

January 16, 2018

President Trump holds a bilateral meeting and joint press conference with Kazakhstani President Nursultan Nazarbayev at the White House

January 21, 2018

Long before CIC Donald John Trump said, "We have it all, we've caught them all" on the 2020 Campaign Trail, Q said, "we have it all."

"GUYS- email was sent out by NSA before election with some plausible deniability attached to it so people could say "FAKE"! HOWEVER, the main audience wasn't normies, it was the black hats, a shot across the bow to say, "*WE HAVE IT ALL*, YOUR'E RIGGING WON'T WORK". Q just brought it back up to speak directly to "THEM" again to show they are going to dump it all."

Q post 580:
https://qalerts.app/?n=580

January 25, 2018

Arrives in Davos, Switzerland to attend the 2018 Davos World Economic Forum. He is the first U.S. President to personally attend the annual Davos conference since President Bill Clinton in 2000.

January 30, 2018: Protecting America Through Lawful Detention of Terrorists

Executive Order 13823:
https://www.federalregister.gov/documents/2018/02/02/2018-02261/protecting-america-through-lawful-detention-of-terrorists

This Executive Order is the revoking of Obama's Executive Order that was issued to shut down the United States Naval Base and Guantanamo Bay Detainee Center aka Gitmo and "the Spa."

This Executive Order is very key, hence the fact "Biden" spent half of the 2020 Campaign championing to his lost minions he would close the facility.

Had those lost minions as well as Americans known about the Federal Continuity Directives and the new Law of War Manual, plus the significance of the Operations and Procedural Implementation and Application of those... everyone could have known from the start "Biden" was a WWII Commonwealth Act #671 history repeat of a Continuity of Government puppet actor.

This was issued just 29 days before CIC DJT changed the Courts Martial Manual.

February 5, 2018

At a speech in Cincinnati, Ohio, President Trump claims that Congressional Democrats, who "were like death and un-American" in not applauding during his State of the Union speech, were "treasonous" and that "we call that treason."

February 23, 2018

Holds a bilateral meeting and joint press conference with Australian Prime Minister Malcolm Turnbull at the White House.

February 27, 2018: Trump strikes $3.9 billion deal with Boeing for new Air Force One

WashingtonCNN —

President Donald Trump and Boeing have struck a deal over the development of two new Air Force One planes at a price tag of $3.9 billion, the White House and Boeing said Tuesday, and the President has asked for the planes to be ready by 2021.

CNN on the deal:
https://www.cnn.com/2018/02/27/politics/boeing-air-force-one-donald-trump/index.html

ABC News:
https://abcnews.go.com/Politics/president-trump-reaches-deal-boeing-air-force-planes/story?id=53391271

So, the tweet was December 6, 2016, which was after Election, but before Oath… and the deal was struck in February 2018, and expecting delivery by 2021…

For those who follow my Aircraft posts on my social media… You'd know that:

(1) Anyone can purchase decommissioned Military equipment and vehicles once weapons and technology are removed.
(2) "Joe Biden" didn't get the traditional flight into D.C. on Air Force One on January 20, 2021.
(3) Air Force One has flown with empty or no Call Sign 99.9% of the time since that day.
(4) All Air Force Two's have been flying with empty or no Call Signs since that day.

Ex-Military Aircraft:

Q: Do individuals actually own and fly ex-military jet aircraft?

A: Yes. In the United States, there are approximately one-thousand of privately owned vintage/classic jets, and there are many others elsewhere in the world. And the numbers are growing! In the US, the Federal Aviation Administration (FAA) closely regulates the ownership and operation of these aircraft. Many jets have restrictions placed on them which dictate where they may be flown and for what purpose. Most are licensed in the "Experimental, Exhibition" category, which means that they can only be flown to and from air shows and displays, for pilot proficiency and other specific activities. They may not be used as "personal transportation" machines. Presently, the CJAA is working closely with FAA officials to rewrite regulations affecting vintage/classic jet operations.

Q: Do SMTPA (Surplus Military Turbine Powered Aircraft) have their original guns and armament?

A: No, at least not in the USA. When an aircraft comes into the U.S., all weaponry has to be removed or made permanently inoperable. These aircraft are usually inspected by three government agencies: The US Customs, the Bureau of Alcohol Tobacco and Firearms (ATF) and the Federal Aviation Administration (FAA). These agencies ensure that jet warbird aircraft do not have any weapons. Additionally, most owners remove much of the wiring and equipment which once operated the aircraft's weaponry. This saves weight (and therefore fuel), and also makes the aircraft easier to maintain. If you see guns or bombs on an aircraft, they are almost always lightweight replicas, but some owners use original guns with their barrels welded closed.

Classic Jets Ownership:
https://classicjets.org/FAQ#:~:text=Q%3A%20Do%20individuals%20actually%20own,And%20the%20numbers%20are%20growing!

"If you really want to buy an old military jet, it is legal to do so if it has been de-militarized. However, it is incredibly expensive, so those that own an old military jet are typically celebrities or billionaires."

Owning Military Jets:

Now let's look at what the actual Government has to say about it:

PART 102–33—MANAGEMENT OF GOVERNMENT AIRCRAFT

Subpart B—Acquiring Government Aircraft and Aircraft Parts

§ 102-33.50 Under what circumstances may we acquire Government aircraft?

(a) When you meet the requirements for operating an in-house aviation program contained in OMB Circular A–76, "Performance of Commercial Activities" and OMB Circular A–11, "Preparation, Submission, and Execution of the Budget," Part 2, "Preparation and Submission of Budget Estimates," Section 25.5, "Summary of Requirements," Table 1, which refers to the Business Case for Acquisition and Maintenance of Aircraft, and Section 51.18, "Budgeting for the acquisition of capital assets," subparagraph (d) (Both circulars are available at *http://www.whitehouse.gov/omb*), you may—

(1) Acquire Federal aircraft when—
    (i) Aircraft are the optimum means of supporting your agency's official business;

    (ii) You do not have aircraft that can support your agency's official business safely (*e.g.,* in compliance with applicable safety standards and regulations) and cost-effectively;

    (iii) No commercial or other Governmental source is available to provide aviation services safely (*i.e.,* in compliance with applicable safety standards and regulations) and cost-effectively; and

    (iv) Congress has specifically authorized your agency to purchase, lease, or transfer aircraft and to maintain and operate those aircraft (see 31 U.S.C. 1343);

(2) Acquire Commercial Aviation Services (CAS) when—
    (i) Aircraft are the optimum means of supporting your agency's official business; and

    (ii) Using commercial aircraft and services is safe (*i.e.,* conforms to applicable laws, safety standards, and regulations) and is more cost effective than using Federal aircraft, aircraft from any other Governmental source, or scheduled air carriers.

(1) When acquiring aircraft, aircraft selection must be based on need, a strong business case, and life-cycle cost analysis, which conform to OMB Circular A–11, "Preparation, Submission, and Execution of the Budget," Part 2, "Preparation and Submission of Budget Estimates," Section 25.5, "Summary of Requirements," Table 1, which refers to the Business Case for Acquisition and Maintenance of Aircraft (available at http://www.whitehouse.gov/omb).

§ 102-33.60 What methods may we use to acquire Government aircraft?

Following the requirements of §§ 102–33.50 and 102–33.55, you (or an internal bureau or sub-agency within your agency) may acquire Government aircraft by means including, but not limited to—

(a) Purchase;
    (b) Borrowing from a non-Federal source;
    (c) Bailment from another executive agency;
    (d) Exchange/sale;
    (e) Reimbursable transfer from another executive agency (see §§ 102–36.75 and 102–36.80);
    (f) Transfer from another executive agency as approved by GSA;
    (g) Reassignment from one internal bureau or subagency to another within your agency;
    (h) Transfer of previously forfeited aircraft;
    (i) Insurance replacement (*i.e.,* receiving a replacement aircraft);
    (j) Capital lease;
    (k) Rent or charter;
    (l) Contract for full services (*i.e.,* aircraft plus crew and related aviation services) from a commercial source; or
    (m) Inter-service support agreements with other executive agencies for aircraft and services.

41 United States Code Chapter 102:
https://www.ecfr.gov/current/title-41/subtitle-C/chapter-102/subchapter-B/part-102-33

Are you going to believe that The Donald didn't make that deal and that the rest is all coincidence?

March 1, 2018: 2018 Amendments to the Manual for Courts-Martial, United States

Executive Order 13825:
https://www.federalregister.gov/documents/2018/03/08/2018-04860/2018-amendments-to-the-manual-for-courts-martial-united-states

Although other Presidents have amended the Courts-Martial Manual, it's very important to note that many Laws and Orders read beautifully on paper, but are they being applied and upheld and do they support the Constitution as *Marbury vs. Madison, 1803*, outlines and was ruled upon 200 plus years ago.

March 5, 2018

Holds a bilateral meeting with Israeli Prime Minister Benjamin Netanyahu at the White House.

March 6, 2018

President Trump holds a bilateral meeting and joint press conference with Swedish Prime Minister Stefan Löfven at the White House.

March 8, 2018

Accepts an invitation to meet with North Korean Leader Kim Jong-un by May 2018.

March 19, 2018: **Taking Additional Steps to Address the Situation in Venezuela**

Executive Order 13827:
https://www.federalregister.gov/documents/2018/03/21/2018-05916/taking-additional-steps-to-address-the-situation-in-venezuela
Further steps added to the National Emergency declared by President Trump with the Venezuelan government.

March 20, 2018

Meets with Crown Prince Mohammad bin Salman of Saudi Arabia in the Oval Office.

April 3, 2018

President Trump holds a joint press conference with the leaders of three Baltic states at the White House: Estonian President Kersti Kaljulaid, Latvian President Raimonds Vejonis and Lithuanian President Dalia Grybauskaite.

Never did anyone see "Biden" having these meetings. Now, the United States Military Aircraft movement in Estonia, Latvia, and Lithuania, in 2021, 2022, 2023 should make sense. Origin matters.

April 4, 2018

Signs a proclamation directing the deployment of the National Guard to the U.S.– Mexico border to fight illegal immigration.

The President is the only who can do so: 10 United States Code §12406.

§12406. National Guard in Federal service: call

Whenever-

(1) the United States, or any of the Commonwealths or possessions, is invaded or is in danger of invasion by a foreign nation;
(2) there is a rebellion or danger of a rebellion against the authority of the Government of the United States; or
(3) the President is unable with the regular forces to execute the laws of the United States;

The President may call into Federal service members and units of the National Guard of any State in such numbers as he considers necessary to repel the invasion, suppress the rebellion, or execute those laws. Orders for these purposes shall be issued through the governors of the States or, in the case of the District of Columbia, through the commanding general of the National Guard of the District of Columbia. (Added Pub. L. 103–337, div. A, title XVI, §1662(f)(1), Oct. 5, 1994, 108 Stat. 2994 ; amended Pub. L. 109–163, div. A, title X, §1057(a)(5), Jan. 6, 2006, 119 Stat. 3440.)

10 US Code §12406:
https://uscode.house.gov/view.xhtml?req=granuleid:USC-prelim-title10-section12406&num=0&edition=prelim

No one has EVER witnessed "Biden" directing the National Guard via Proclamation much less any other Military Law or Order. Because he's not president and it's all been planned.

April 10, 2018

Holds a bilateral meeting with Emir Tamim bin Hamad Al Thani of Qatar at the White House.

April 11, 2018

Signs a bill that reduces legal protections for websites that enable sex trafficking.

April 12, 2018

Launches a task force to "conduct a thorough evaluation of the operations and finances of the United States Postal System." This is how they found the "mules."

April 12, 2018: **Task Force on the United States Postal System**

Executive Order 13829:
https://www.federalregister.gov/documents/2018/04/18/2018-08272/task-force-on-the-united-states-postal-system

This Executive Order establishes the corruption the Deep State was using with the Postal Service and their mail-in voting corruption.

April 13, 2018

Friday the 13th was not a good day for Syria, as CIC Trump ordered missile strikes against Syria in retaliation for the chemical weapons attack on April 7 and challenged Iran and Russia to decide if they will continue to support the Assad regime.

In his address to the nation from the White House stated,

> *"A short time ago, I ordered the U.S. Armed Forces to launch precision strikes on targets associated with the chemical weapons capabilities of Syrian dictator, Bashar al-Assad, a combined operation with the armed forces of France and the United Kingdom is now under way."*

April 24, 2018

Holds a bilateral meeting and joint press conference with French President Emmanuel Macron at the White House.

President Trump and First Lady Melania Trump host their first state dinner in honor of French President Emmanuel Macron and his wife, Brigitte.

April 25, 2018

Macron addresses a joint meeting of the members of Congress.

April 27, 2018

Holds a bilateral meeting and joint press conference with German Chancellor Angela Merkel at the White House.

April 30, 2018

Holds a bilateral meeting and joint press conference with Nigerian President Muhammadu Buhari at the White House.

May 8, 2018

Announces in a speech that the U.S. will withdraw from the Obama-era Iran nuclear deal and reinstate sanctions.

May 21, 2018: **Prohibiting Certain Additional Transactions With Respect to Venezuela**

Executive Order 13835:
https://www.federalregister.gov/documents/2018/05/24/2018-11335/prohibiting-certain-additional-transactions-with-respect-to-venezuela

More punishments defined by the transactions related with the United States and the government of Venezuela. Notice the term: Central Bank of Venezuela.

May 22, 2018

Holds a bilateral meeting with South Korean President Moon Jae-in at the White House to discuss the denuclearization of North Korea.

June 7, 2018

Holds a bilateral meeting and joint press conference with Japanese Prime Minister Shinzō Abe at the White House.

June 8, 2018

Attends the 44th G7 summit with world leaders of G7 in La Malbaie, Canada.

Holds bilateral meetings with Canadian Prime Minister Justin Trudeau and French President Emmanuel Macron.

June 9, 2018

After President Trump leaves the 44th G7 summit early, he withdrew the United States' endorsement of a joint communique by the G7 and labeled Canadian Prime Minister Justin Trudeau "Very dishonest & meek."

He also addressed Trudeau by saying the Trump tariffs targeting Canada "are in response to his of 270% on dairy!"

June 11, 2018

Holds a bilateral meeting with Singaporean Prime Minister Lee Hsien Loong in the Istana Palace. Ever hear "Biden" talking to Singaporean Prime Minister? Now does the Singaporean Military Aircraft from the summer and early fall movement of 2023 in Idaho and Nevada from a National Guard Base make sense? #ItShould

June 12, 2018

President Trump and North Korean Leader Kim Jong-un participate in a summit at the Capella Hotel in Sentosa, Singapore.

President Trump and North Korean Leader Kim Jong-un sign a joint declaration titled "Joint Statement of President Donald J. Trump of the United States of America and Chairman Kim Jong Un of the Democratic People's Republic of Korea at the Singapore Summit."

June 19, 2018

Meets with King Felipe VI and Queen Letizia of Spain at the White House.

June 24, 2018

U.S. Army leaders say the next war will be fought in mega-cities, but the service has embarked on an ambitious effort to prepare most of its combat brigades to fight, not inside, but beneath them.

Late last year, the Army launched an accelerated effort that funnels some $572 million into training and equipping 26 of its 31 active combat brigades to fight in large-scale subterranean facilities that exist beneath dense urban areas around the world.

Military Daily News:
https://www.military.com/daily-news/2018/06/24/army-spending-half-billion-train-troops-fight-underground.html

June 25, 2018

Holds a bilateral meeting with King Abdullah II of Jordan at the White House.

June 27, 2018

Holds a bilateral meeting with Portuguese President Marcelo Rebelo de Sousa at the White House.
Senior Supreme Court Justice Anthony Kennedy announces his retirement from the Supreme Court, effective July 31, 2018.

July 2, 2018

Holds a bilateral meeting with Dutch Prime Minister Mark Rutte at the White House.

July 9, 2018

Nominates Brett Kavanaugh as an Associate Justice of the Supreme Court to fill the vacancy left by the impending retirement of Anthony Kennedy.

July 13, 2018: President Trump walks in front of Queen

President Trump and First Lady Melania Trump meet with Queen Elizabeth II at Windsor Castle for the first time since becoming president.

CIC Trump walks in front of Queen. This was NOT an error as the 47 U.S. Code 606 mainstream media implied at the time. The goal was to have the media smear Trump daily which is the ultimate distraction.

Now, look what the media said about Melania:

"Meyers also took a moment during his monologue to lampoon Melania Trump's instantly viral yellow dress, which she wore to attend a state dinner: "Yellow gowns," he quipped, "are, of course, the official uniform of women being held captive by beasts." Cut to a picture of Belle from Beauty and the Beast, *sporting the film's most famous—yellow—gown."*

"Trump Gaffes:"
https://www.vanityfair.com/hollywood/2018/07/trump-queen-elizabeth-meeting-gaffes-walk-in-front-royal-protocol

Not a gaffe at all. This is one tiny sliver of the dismantling of the Federal Corporation under the British Crown. She also placed CIC Trump in the center of their facing the press for pictures as a display to their submission. And insisted CIC Trump sit in Winston Churchills chair.

All part of the operation. Instead… it's a beautiful Optic. This has everything to do with Executive Order 13818 and the declaration on December 20, 2019, in the War Powers Resolution Act.

July 16, 2018

President Trump and President Vladimir Putin participate in the summit at the Presidential Palace in Helsinki, Finland.

At the joint press conference, Trump reiterates both his faulting of "U.S. foolishness and stupidity" and the Mueller investigation for the freeze in relations between Russia and the United States. Thank you, soccer ball.

July 22, 2018

CIC Trump tweets a threat to Iranian President Hassan Rouhani:

> *"NEVER, EVER THREATEN THE UNITED STATES AGAIN OR YOU WILL SUFFER CONSEQUENCES THE LIKES OF WHICH FEW THROUGHOUT HISTORY HAVE EVER SUFFERED BEFORE. WE ARE NO LONGER A COUNTRY THAT WILL STAND FOR YOUR DEMENTED WORDS OF VIOLENCE & DEATH. BE CAUTIOUS!"*

July 25, 2018

Holds a bilateral meeting and joint press conference with European Commission President Jean-Claude Juncker at the White House.

July 30, 2018

Holds a bilateral meeting and joint press conference with Italian Prime Minister Giuseppe Conte at the White House.

August 6, 2018: **Reimposing Certain Sanctions With Respect to Iran**

Executive Order 13846:
https://www.federalregister.gov/documents/2018/08/07/2018-17068/reimposing-certain-sanctions-with-respect-to-iran

Notice the term: ***Central Bank*** of Iran. All these Executive Orders all make up the Federal Laws of the outline of the Federal Continuity Directives plus the Military Occupancy of the cleanout of the Federal Corporation and their affiliates.

August 27, 2018

Holds a bilateral meeting with Kenyan President Uhuru Kenyatta at the White House.

September 5, 2018

Holds a bilateral meeting with Emir Sabah Al-Ahmad Al-Jaber Al-Sabah of Kuwait at the White House.

September 12, 2018: **Imposing Certain Sanctions in the Event of Foreign Interference in a United States Election**

Executive Order 13848:
https://www.federalregister.gov/documents/2018/09/14/2018-20203/imposing-certain-sanctions-in-the-event-of-foreign-interference-in-a-united-states-election

Probably the MOST important piece of paper in United States History since the Declaration of Independence. This Executive Order set the trap for all Governors, Secretary of State's, Attorney Generals, Judges, and Lawyers who did and do not apply, uphold, and enforce the Laws and Orders put into place around and with this Order to make ALL candidates participating in Elections, Fair and Reciprocal.

If you'll remember… on the 2016 Campaign Trail, CIC Trump said, "I do not agree with anything Bernie Sanders says, but his own people, screw him over." Little things like that… were comms the whole time. This is the MOST important line of the whole EO.

"…although there has been no evidence of a foreign power altering the outcome or vote tabulation in any United States election…"

This was written **TWO** months before ANY Election under President Trump's presidency… which means the only evidence of Election Interference was planned and known from 2016 and prior. Does not say no *Domestic*…

Altering the outcome = all votes from people and states…

Or vote tabulation = objections = which is what happened on January 6, 2021… this Executive Order which those key words "or vote tabulation" predicted the J6 plan and canceled out all events on that day as there were two objections in the Arizona State Electoral Vote count and the "insurrection" conveniently happened after those.

"*Or Vote Tabulation*" came 2.5 years before January 6, 2021, proving that day was a plan to expose and catch the Deep State all while they displayed their crimes to the public, whether the public knew and realized it or not.

   Note: *see grand final summary for this EO.*

September 24, 2018

Holds a bilateral meeting and dinner with Japanese Prime Minister Shinzō Abe at Trump Tower.

September 25, 2018

Attends the United Nations event on 'Global Drug Problem' at the Headquarters of the United Nations.
Holds a bilateral meeting with South Korean President Moon Jae-in to sign new revisions into their free trade agreement.

Holds bilateral meetings with Egyptian President Abdel Fattah el-Sisi and French President Emmanuel Macron at the UN General Assembly in New York City.

Holds a bilateral meeting with Colombian President Iván Duque Márquez at the UN General Assembly in New York City.

President Trump addressed the United Nations General Assembly at the Headquarters of the United Nations and drew laughter from international representatives when he said that the Trump "administration has accomplished more than almost any administration in the history of the United States—"so true." (remember those who laughed)

September 26, 2018

Holds bilateral meetings with Israeli Prime Minister Benjamin Netanyahu, Japanese Prime Minister Shinzō Abe, and British Prime Minister Theresa May at the UN General Assembly in New York City.

September 28, 2018

Holds a bilateral meeting with Chilean President Sebastián Piñera at the White House.
October 1, 2018

Announces the new USMCA trade agreement between the United States, Mexico, and Canada as a renegotiation of the former North American Trade Agreement.

November 1, 2018: Blocking Property of Additional Persons Contributing to the Situation in Venezuela

Executive Order 13850:
https://www.federalregister.gov/documents/2018/11/02/2018-24254/blocking-property-of-additional-persons-contributing-to-the-situation-in-venezuela

These Executive Orders with Venezuela also point out where a lot of the Deep State operatives had actors (no pun intended) who did their dirty work and exchanges.

November 10, 2018

Holds a bilateral meeting with French President Emmanuel Macron at the Élysée Palace.

November 11, 2018

Attends a ceremony at the Arc de Triomphe with 60 other world leaders marking the 100th anniversary of the end of World War I.

French President Emmanuel Macron delivers a speech in which he denounces nationalism as a betrayal of patriotism and warns against 'old demons coming back to wreak chaos and death'. This is seen as a rebuke of President Trump and Russian President Vladimir Putin, who is also in attendance. Clear evidence who was in charge and the Federal Corporation and Swamp didn't like it.

November 22, 2018

Authorizes troops stationed at the U.S.–Mexican border to use lethal force if deemed necessary and threatens to close the entire southern border with Mexico.

November 27, 2018: Blocking Property of Certain Persons Contributing to the Situation in Nicaragua

Executive Order 13851:
https://www.federalregister.gov/documents/2018/11/29/2018-26156/blocking-property-of-certain-persons-contributing-to-the-situation-in-nicaragua

One of the National Emergencies from December 2017 to March 2020 declared by President Trump. This Order along with Venezuela, Haiti, and Cuba, with the closest being 1,536 miles from Del Rio, Texas, and 98% of Americans believing there's 15 million flooding across the border…

CIC Donald John Trump's talks about the border has an operation outlining it and 99% of his speech revolves around policies, not actual crossing the border. We've got to do a LOT better job at critical thinking skills, Americans. Which starts with education of the right material.

This order addresses 'serious human rights abuse' = trafficking.

'Undermine democratic processes or institutions' = addressing interference with elections.

These are the dismantling of the Deep State operatives and their dirty money.

November 29, 2018

Travels to Buenos Aires, Argentina, ahead of the G20 summit.

November 29, 2018

Attends the G20 summit hosted by Argentine President Mauricio Macri.

President Trump signs the United States–Mexico–Canada Agreement (USMCA) along with Canadian Prime Minister Justin Trudeau and Mexican President Enrique Peña Nieto.

Holds bilateral meetings with Argentine President Mauricio Macri, Australian Prime Minister Scott Morrison, Indian Prime Minister Narendra Modi, Japanese Prime Minister Shinzō Abe and South Korean President Moon Jae-in.

November 30, 2018: George Herbert Walker Bush

This is the coffin of George H. W. Bush. The distraction was perfect, playing on everyone's emotions and heart strings with the dog, but the Flag is a *dead* giveaway, all pun intended.

(Photo Courtesy: USA Today, November 30, 2018)

One, the Flag is not placed correctly.
Two, the Flag is wrinkled.

From the Do's and Don'ts of the United States Flag straight from the Department of Defense dot Gov:

Other Do's and Don'ts:

-   Clean and damage-free flags should always be used. Dirty, ripped, wrinkled or frayed flags should not be used. Also, when flags are damaged, they should be destroyed in a dignified manner.

Department of Defense Displaying Old Glory:

December 1, 2018

Holds bilateral meetings with German Chancellor Angela Merkel and Turkish President Recep Tayyip Erdoğan.

Holds a bilateral meeting and dinner with Chinese President Xi Jinping, claiming they have reached an agreement to halt the escalating trade war between the United States and China.

December 12, 2018: **Establishing the White House Opportunity and Revitalization Council**

Executive Order 13853:
https://www.federalregister.gov/documents/2018/12/18/2018-27515/establishing-the-white-house-opportunity-and-revitalization-council

"This order establishes a White House Council to carry out my Administration's plan to encourage public and private investment in urban and economically distressed areas, including qualified opportunity zones. The Council shall lead joint efforts across executive departments and agencies (agencies) to engage with State, local, and tribal governments to find ways to better use public funds to revitalize urban and economically distressed communities."

The State, Local, and Tribal governments outlined in this Order coincide with the Federal Continuity Directives that led the Continuity of Government while trying to establish each American's individual responsibilities along with our communities at all levels.

December 21, 2018: **Abolish Human Trafficking Act of 2017**

This law strengthens and reauthorizes key programs supporting survivors of human trafficking and provides resources to law enforcement officials working to combat modern-day slavery.

An Act: To provide assistance in abolishing human trafficking in the United States.

Be it enacted by the Senate and House of Representatives of the United States of America in Congress assembled,

SECTION 1. SHORT TITLE; TABLE OF CONTENTS.

(a) SHORT TITLE.—This Act may be cited as the ''Abolish Human Trafficking Act of 2017''.

(b) TABLE OF CONTENTS.—The table of contents for this Act is as follows:

Sec. 1. Short title; table of contents.
Sec. 2. Preserving Domestic Trafficking Victims' Fund.
Sec. 3. Mandatory restitution for victims of commercial sexual exploitation.
Sec. 4. Victim-witness assistance in sexual exploitation cases.
Sec. 5. Victim protection training for the Department of Homeland Security.
Sec. 6. Direct services for child victims of human trafficking.
Sec. 7. Holistic training for Federal law enforcement officers and prosecutors.
Sec. 8. Best practices in delivering justice for victims of trafficking.
Sec. 9. Improving the national strategy to combat human trafficking.
Sec. 10. Specialized human trafficking training and technical assistance for service providers.
Sec. 11. Enhanced penalties for human trafficking, child exploitation, and repeat offenders.
Sec. 12. Targeting organized human trafficking perpetrators.
Sec. 13. Investigating complex human trafficking networks.
Sec. 14. Combating sex tourism.
Sec. 15. Human Trafficking Justice Coordinators.
Sec. 16. Interagency Task Force to Monitor and Combat Human Trafficking.
Sec. 17. Additional reporting on crime.
Sec. 18. Strengthening the national human trafficking hotline.
Sec. 19. Ending Government partnerships with the commercial sex industry.
Sec. 20. Understanding the effects of severe forms of trafficking in persons.
Sec. 21. Combating trafficking in persons.
Sec. 22. Grant accountability.
Sec. 23. HERO Act improvements.

S.1311 - 115th Congress 115-392
https://www.congress.gov/bill/115th-congress/senate-bill/1311

December 21, 2018: **Trafficking Victims Protection Act**

The President signed into law the Trafficking Victims Protection Act of 2017.

This law reauthorizes several grant programs within the Departments of Justice (DOJ), Health and Human Services (HHS), Labor (DOL), and State (DOS) that combat trafficking in persons.

Trafficking Victims Protection Act of 2017

TITLE I--FREDERICK DOUGLASS TRAFFICKING PREVENTION ACT OF 2017
TITLE II--JUSTICE FOR TRAFFICKING VICTIMS
TITLE III--SERVICES FOR TRAFFICKING SURVIVORS
TITLE IV--IMPROVED DATA COLLECTION AND INTERAGENCY COORDINATION
TITLE V--TRAINING AND TECHNICAL ASSISTANCE
TITLE VI--ACCOUNTABILITY
TITLE VII--PUBLIC-PRIVATE PARTNERSHIP ADVISORY COUNCIL TO END HUMAN TRAFFICKING

Public Law No: 115-393

S. 1312
https://www.congress.gov/bill/115th-congress/senate-bill/1312

Trafficking Victims Protection Act of 2017
https://www.coherentbabble.com/PublicLaws/PL115-393.pdf

December 21, 2018: Frederick Douglass Trafficking Victims Prevention and Protection Reauthorization Act of 2018

Frederick Douglass Act:
https://www.congress.gov/bill/115th-congress/house-bill/2200

This bill establishes programs to combat human trafficking, forced labor, and the use of child soldiers. It also modifies existing programs to address such issues.

The bill expands the definition of a "child soldier" as used in the Child Soldiers Prevention Act of 2008 to include minors who take part in hostilities as part of police forces or other security forces or recruited into such forces. It also modifies various reporting requirements on issues involving child soldiers.

The bill reauthorizes through FY2021 various programs for combatting human trafficking.

December 21, 2018: National Quantum Initiative Act

This bill directs the President to implement a National Quantum Initiative Program to, among other things, establish the goals and priorities for a 10-year plan to accelerate the development of quantum information science and technology applications. Quantum information science is the use of the laws of quantum physics for the storage, transmission, manipulation, or measurement of information.

And guess who carries out the basic research program on QIS? *Department of Energy*.

Public Law 115-368
https://www.congress.gov/bill/115th-congress/house-bill/6227

TITLE I--NATIONAL QUANTUM INITIATIVE
TITLE II--NATIONAL INSTITUTE OF STANDARDS AND TECHNOLOGY QUANTUM ACTIVITIES
TITLE III--NATIONAL SCIENCE FOUNDATION QUANTUM ACTIVITIES
TITLE IV--DEPARTMENT OF ENERGY QUANTUM ACTIVITIES

And the PDF via Government Information dot Gov:
https://www.govinfo.gov/content/pkg/COMPS-15322/pdf/COMPS-15322.pdf

December 24, 2018

Attacks the Federal Reserve via Twitter, saying they are the only problem in the economy, which is in a significant downturn.

January 9, 2019: Trafficking Victims Protection Reauthorization Act of 2017

To amend the Trafficking Victims Protection Act of 2000 to modify the criteria for determining whether countries are meeting the minimum standards for the elimination of human trafficking, and for other purposes.

Trafficking Victims Protection Reauthorization Act of 2017:
https://www.coherentbabble.com/PublicLaws/PL115-427.pdf

January 25, 2019: Taking Additional Steps To Address the National Emergency With Respect to Venezuela

Executive Order 13857:
https://www.federalregister.gov/documents/2019/01/30/2019-00615/taking-additional-steps-to-address-the-national-emergency-with-respect-to-venezuela

The title says it all.

"...particularly in light of actions by persons affiliated with the illegitimate Maduro regime, including **human rights violations and abuses** *in response to anti-Maduro protests, arbitrary arrest and detention of anti-Maduro protestors, curtailment of press freedom, harassment of political opponents, and continued attempts to undermine the Interim President of Venezuela and undermine the National Assembly, the only legitimate branch of government duly elected by the Venezuelan people, and to prevent the Interim President and the National Assembly from exercising legitimate authority in Venezuela"...*

February 1, 2019

Announces he is withdrawing the United States from the Intermediate-Range Nuclear Forces Treaty, accusing Russia of non-compliance.

Russia announced their suspension of the treaty the following day. It was an arms control treaty between the United States and the Soviet Union.

February 13, 2019

Holds a bilateral meeting with Colombian President Iván Duque Márquez at the White House.

February 15, 2019

Declares a national emergency to secure sufficient funds to construct a physical barrier along the Southern border. This was a verbal National Emergency.

February 20, 2019

Holds a bilateral meeting with Austrian Chancellor Sebastian Kurz at the White House.

February 27, 2019

Holds a bilateral meeting with Vietnamese President Nguyễn Phú Trọng and Vietnamese Prime Minister Nguyễn Xuân Phúc.

Participates in a summit at the Metropole Hotel in Hanoi, Vietnam, with North Korean Leader Kim Jong-un.

March 4, 2019: **Supporting the Transition of Active-Duty Service Members and Military Veterans Into the Merchant Marine**

Executive Order 13860:
https://www.federalregister.gov/documents/2019/03/07/2019-04298/supporting-the-transition-of-active-duty-service-members-and-military-veterans-into-the-merchant

Every aspect of the Military was activated during this Military Occupancy… in multiple Executive Orders: Retired Service members, Reserves, Individual Ready Reserves, Retired Coast Guard Officers, and Merchant Marines. Merchant Marines played a vital role during WWII. Yet another Comm for this Occupancy.

U.S. Marine Corps and Merchant Marines deepen ties:
https://gcaptain.com/us-marine-corps-and-us-merchant-marine-deepen-ties/

This 2023 article specifically talks about this Executive Order from 2019… all ties (all pun intended) with CIC Trump.

Continuous Note: In this article, as every other Military related article from 2021 to 2024, "Biden" was never mentioned… it was always a Commander or Secretary of Defense.

March 5, 2019: **National Roadmap to Empower Veterans and End Suicide**

Executive Order 13861:
https://www.federalregister.gov/documents/2019/03/08/2019-04437/national-roadmap-to-empower-veterans-and-end-suicide

If you'll remember in the news… "Biden" was displayed by the Military Occupancy, copying ALL of CIC Trump's policies, Laws, and Orders, such as this.

"Biden's" whole "presidency" has been claiming numbers from Republican Governed states and all of the Acts under his "presidency" were National Essential Functions as outlined in the Federal Continuity Directives under the Continuity of Operations Plan, but those were also added to Trump Acts.

Especially because these type subjects are sensitive and nerve strikers when discussed. It was CIC Trump who cared about Veterans and proved it in multiple ways that weren't "diplomatic speeches" for votes as "Biden" and his liberal cronies.

March 7, 2019

Holds a bilateral meeting with Czech Prime Minister Andrej Babiš at the White House.
Now does the Czechia Military movement in Israel in October 2023 make sense? You never saw "Biden" meet with ANY of these countries. There's a bigger reason, but for those who couldn't see that, the daily operations shown on "news" would still be enough to know, "he" never met with ANY of these Nations and Leaders.

March 14, 2019

Holds a bilateral meeting with Taoiseach Leo Varadkar of Ireland at the White House.

March 15, 2019: Taking Additional Steps to Address the National Emergency With Respect to Significant Transnational Criminal Organizations

Executive Order 13863:
https://www.federalregister.gov/documents/2019/03/19/2019-05370/taking-additional-steps-to-address-the-national-emergency-with-respect-to-significant-transnational

Although the Obama Administration passed this Law, it was CIC Trump who updated this EO and put it into action.

As stated before, there were many Laws that read perfectly on paper, but were not applied and upheld. They read that way as the Deep State operatives aka The Swamp worked behind the scenes for multiple years with their agendas. Their main agenda: *"create a problem there's already a solution to."*

March 19, 2019

Holds a bilateral meeting and joint press conference with Brazilian President Jair Bolsonaro at the White House.

March 22, 2019

Meets with the leaders of five Caribbean countries in Mar-a-Lago, Florida: Dominican President Danilo Medina, Haitian President Jovenel Moïse, Jamaican Prime Minister Andrew Holness, Saint Lucian Prime Minister Allen Chastanet and Bahamian Prime Minister Hubert Minnis.

March 25, 2019

Holds a bilateral meeting and joint press conference with Israeli Prime Minister Benjamin Netanyahu at the White House.

Signs a presidential proclamation to officially recognize Israel's sovereignty over the Golan Heights.

A Proclamation

The State of Israel took control of the Golan Heights in 1967 to safeguard its security from external threats. Today, aggressive acts by Iran and terrorist groups, including Hizballah, in southern Syria continue to make the Golan Heights a potential launching ground for attacks on Israel. Any possible future peace agreement in the region must account for Israel's need to protect itself from Syria and other regional threats. Based on these unique circumstances, it is therefore appropriate to recognize Israeli sovereignty over the Golan Heights.
Proclamation 9852:
https://www.federalregister.gov/documents/2019/03/28/2019-06199/recognizing-the-golan-heights-as-part-of-the-state-of-israel

9852, White House Archives:
https://trumpwhitehouse.archives.gov/presidential-actions/proclamation-recognizing-golan-heights-part-state-israel/

March 27, 2019

Meets with Fabiana Rosales, wife of Venezuelan Opposition Leader Juan Guaidó, at the White House.

April 2, 2019

Holds a bilateral meeting with NATO Secretary General Jens Stoltenberg at the White House.

April 9, 2019

Holds a bilateral meeting with Egyptian President Abdel Fattah el-Sisi at the White House.

April 11, 2019

Holds a bilateral meeting with South Korean President Moon Jae-in at the White House.

April 16, 2019

Uses the second veto of his Administration on a bipartisan resolution to end American involvement in the military campaign in Yemen. Congress priorly had voted to invoke the War Powers Act of 1973.

Amazing how the War Powers Act of 1973 is legit and authentic when mentioned by Congress, but when an honorably retired Veteran would tell and show people where it was invoked on December 20, 2019, what would be 8 months later… "*I don't know if I believe that.*" SMH

April 24, 2019: Transferring Responsibility for Background Investigations to the Department of Defense

Executive Order 13869:
https://www.federalregister.gov/documents/2019/04/29/2019-08797/transferring-responsibility-for-background-investigations-to-the-department-of-defense

This Order is one of the keys to what was to come in 2020… the Secretary of Defense to have equal authorization as the Commander-in-Chief with the Armed Forces, more particularly the National Guard.

It also outlines more specifics of the Military Occupancy without stating the obvious.

April 26, 2019

Holds a bilateral meeting with Japanese Prime Minister Shinzō Abe at the White House.

May 3, 2019

Holds a bilateral meeting with Slovak Prime Minister Peter Pellegrini at the White House.

May 13, 2019

Holds a bilateral meeting with Hungarian Prime Minister Viktor Orbán at the White House.

All the same countries that have been in and out of United States and Israel.

May 16, 2019

Holds a bilateral meeting with Swiss President Ueli Maurer at the White House.

May 23, 2019

Shaping the Deep Fight: Operational Implications for the 21st Century Subterranean Conflict (Pair this with October and November 2023 later)

Abstract:

Through historical analysis and the development of a subterranean typology, this study provides the operational planner with a better understanding of the operational implications of a subterranean fight. It allows the operational level planner to better understand the operating environment, estimate the enemy's capabilities, and provide the combatant commander with more suitable options. The subterranean threat is not an army problem, but a defense problem requiring combined resources and assets at all echelons. However, physical effects are only cogent when they are followed by deliberate cognitive design and virtual shaping effects. The United States must reshape their mental model and reframe the problem to shape the deep fight against an enemy whose subterranean networks make them impervious to our traditional, lethal, deep-fires effects. The answer to the subterranean threat is not in the next technological or tactical solution, rather in the operational artist's creative thinking and ability to reframe the problem, apply systematic thinking, and provide better solutions to the commander.

AD1:
https://apps.dtic.mil/sti/trecms/pdf/AD1083592.pdf

May 26, 2019

Meets with Japanese Prime Minister Shinzō Abe at Mobara Country Club and then attend a sumo tournament.

May 27, 2019

Holds a joint press conference with PM Shinzō Abe at the Akasaka Palace.
Meets with Emperor Naruhito and Empress Masako at the Tokyo Imperial Palace.

June 3, 2019

Arrives in London, United Kingdom.

President Trump and First Lady Melania Trump meet with Queen Elizabeth II at Buckingham Palace.

President Trump lays a wreath at the Tomb of the Unknown Warrior in Westminster Abbey.

President Trump and First Lady Melania Trump attends a state banquet hosted by Queen Elizabeth II at Buckingham Palace.

June 4, 2019

Holds a bilateral meeting and joint press conference with British Prime Minister Theresa May at 10 Downing Street.

June 5, 2019

Holds a bilateral meeting with German Chancellor Angela Merkel.
Arrives in Shannon, Ireland.

Holds a bilateral meeting with Irish Taoiseach Leo Varadkar.

June 6, 2019

Arrives in Caen, France.

Attends the 75th anniversary of D-Day memorial ceremonies in Normandy.

Holds a bilateral meeting with French President Emmanuel Macron at the Prefecture of Calvados.
Returns to Shannon, Ireland.

June 12, 2019

Holds a bilateral meeting and joint press conference with Polish President Andrzej Duda at the White House.

June 20, 2019

Holds a bilateral meeting with Canadian Prime Minister Justin Trudeau at the White House.

June 24, 2019: Imposing Sanctions With Respect to Iran

Executive Order 13876:
https://www.federalregister.gov/documents/2019/06/26/2019-13793/imposing-sanctions-with-respect-to-iran

Notice this is not a 'reimposing' sanctions with Iran Executive Order as the year previous. This is a whole new sanctions order with Iran. Notice the Secretary of State and U.S. Treasury mentioned... very key with the bankrupting the Federal Corporation and U.S. Dollar.

Notice these key terms and definitions:

(b) the term "entity" means a partnership, association, trust, joint venture, corporation, group, subgroup, or other organization;

(c) the term "foreign financial institution" means any foreign entity that is engaged in the business of accepting deposits, making, granting, transferring, holding, or brokering loans or credits, or purchasing or selling foreign exchange, securities, commodity futures or options, or procuring purchasers and sellers thereof, as principal or agent. The term includes, but is not limited to, depository institutions, banks, savings banks, money service businesses, trust companies, securities brokers and dealers, commodity futures and options brokers and dealers, forward contract and foreign exchange merchants, securities and commodities exchanges, clearing corporations, investment companies, employee benefit plans, dealers in precious metals, stones, or jewels, and holding companies, affiliates, or subsidiaries of any of the foregoing.

June 28, 2019

Attends the G20 summit hosted by Japanese Prime Minister Shinzō Abe.

Holds bilateral meetings with Brazilian President Jair Bolsonaro, Japanese Prime Minister Shinzō Abe, Indian Prime Minister Narendra Modi, German Chancellor Angela Merkel and Russian President Vladimir Putin.

June 29, 2019

Holds a bilateral meeting with Chinese President Xi Jinping, declaring a truce in the trade war.

Holds a bilateral meeting Turkish President Recep Tayyip Erdoğan.

Arrives in Seoul, South Korea.

June 30, 2019: **President Trump sets foot into North Korea**

This adds to the Sword Dance in Saudi Arabia from May 20, 2017, and stepping in front of the Queen on July 13, 2018. This is just another notch in the belt making World History.

CIC Trump becomes first President to step into North Korea:
https://www.youtube.com/watch?v=BB63oW_A1BI

Everyone forgets ALL throughout 2015 and 2016 after CIC Trump announced his 2016 campaign… Mainstream media, liberals, and democrats charged he would get us into Nuclear War with North Korea, yet not only did he not start ANY wars (thanks to the Military Occupancy Strategic Plan), but he became the first United States Leader to enter the territory. See how this was all building and adding up?

June 30, 2019

Holds a bilateral meeting and joint press conference with South Korean President Moon Jae-in at the Blue House.

Participates in a DMZ summit with South Korean President Moon Jae-in and North Korean Leader Kim Jong-un at the Inter-Korean Freedom House on the southern side of the Joint Security Area of the Korean Demilitarized Zone (DMZ).

Holds a bilateral meeting with North Korean Leader Kim Jong-un at the Inter-Korean Freedom House.

July 1, 2019: **The Taxpayer First Act**

Taxpayer First Act
https://www.congress.gov/bill/116th-congress/house-bill/3151

This bill revises provisions relating to the Internal Revenue Service (IRS) of 1986, its customer service, enforcement procedures, cybersecurity and identity protection, management of information technology, and use of electronic systems.

The Act - Public Law 116-25
https://www.congress.gov/116/plaws/publ25/PLAW-116publ25.pdf

July 9, 2019

Holds a bilateral meeting with Emir Tamim bin Hamad Al Thani of Qatar at the White House.

July 18, 2019

Holds a bilateral meeting with Dutch prime minister Mark Rutte at the White House.

July 22, 2019

Holds a bilateral meeting with Pakistani prime minister Imran Khan at the White House.

July 26, 2019

The Supreme Court rules in a 5–4 decision that President Trump may use military funding for construction of the border wall.

July 26, 2019: **Blocking Property and Suspending Entry of Certain Persons Contributing to the Situation in Mali**

Executive Order 13882:
https://www.federalregister.gov/documents/2019/07/30/2019-16383/blocking-property-and-suspending-entry-of-certain-persons-contributing-to-the-situation-in-mali

Another National Emergency added to the list of those declared from December 2017 to March 2020.

This EO puts a heavy emphasis on children and trafficking.

July 31, 2019

Holds a bilateral meeting with Mongolian president Khaltmaagiin Battulga at the White House.

August 1, 2019

The Washington Examiner is reporting the same report as Military.com from June 24, 2018, that the Army is spending a half billion training soldiers for underground warfare.

> *The Army is preparing soldiers for the wars of the future by training them to fight in subway tunnels and sewers common to big cities. Army leaders intend to spend $572 million to train and equip 26 of its 31 combat brigades to do battle in underground complexes, according to a report by Military.com.*

Washington Examiner:
https://www.washingtonexaminer.com/policy/defense-national-security/army-spending-a-half-billion-to-teach-soldiers-to-fight-in-sewers-and-subway-systems

August 20, 2019

Holds a bilateral meeting with Romanian president Klaus Iohannis at the White House.

August 21, 2019

Proclaims "I am the chosen one" to reporters at the White House.

August 24, 2019

Attends the 45th G7 summit in Biarritz and holds a bilateral meeting with French President Emmanuel Macron.

August 25, 2019

Holds bilateral meetings with Australian prime minister Scott Morrison, British prime minister Boris Johnson, Canadian prime minister Justin Trudeau and Japanese prime minister Shinzō Abe.

August 26, 2019

Holds bilateral meetings with Egyptian president Abdel Fattah el-Sisi, German chancellor Angela Merkel and Indian prime minister Narendra Modi.
Holds a joint press conference with French president Emmanuel Macron.

August 29, 2019

Establishes the U.S. Space Command. Notice this was 3 months before the Space Force was established.

August 30, 2019: **Establishing the National Quantum Initiative Advisory Committee**

Executive Order 13885:
https://www.federalregister.gov/documents/2019/09/05/2019-19367/establishing-the-national-quantum-initiative-advisory-committee

This EO is the introduction of what would become the Quantum Financial System that would be introduced 2 years and a month from this date with the launching of Quantum.gov.

> "Committee members must be qualified to provide advice and information on quantum information science and technology research, development, demonstrations, standards, education, technology transfers, commercial application, and national security economic concerns."

Stakeholders is a key term in this EO that's also mentioned in Federal Continuity Directives.

August 31, 2019: DARPA

DARPA seeks immediate access to tunnels under universities because the US Military thinks its next war will be underground.

DARPA on Business Insider:
https://www.businessinsider.in/slideshows/miscellaneous/darpa-is-asking-universities-for-access-to-their-tunnels-asap-and-its-because-the-us-military-thinks-its-next-war-will-go-underground/slidelist/70925373.cms

The day before… CNN (at the time still regular CNN in their big building before they were taken out) had a very condescending article (*go figure*) making fun of underground warfare.

> *"DARPA issued the request for information last week seeking university-owned or commercially managed underground urban tunnels and facilities, and yesterday's social media posts were a reminder of the upcoming deadline to respond," Jared B. Adams, DARPA's Chief of Communications, told CNN.*

> *"Complex urban underground infrastructure can present significant challenges for situational awareness in time-sensitive scenarios, such as active combat operations or disaster response," Adams explained.*

> *"So next time you find yourself exploring an abandoned tunnel deep under a US city and something scurries by, don't worry, that's an autonomous killer cave robot. Just move along. Quickly."*

These are the kind of sick individuals who 9/10 claim they 'believe' and 'support' the Military.

CNN on DARPA:
https://www.cnn.com/2019/08/29/us/darpa-tunnels-research-trnd/index.html

September 9, 2019: **Modernizing Sanctions To Combat Terrorism**

Executive Order 13886:
https://www.federalregister.gov/documents/2019/09/12/2019-19895/modernizing-sanctions-to-combat-terrorism

This Executive Order terminated a 1995 National Emergency declared by Bill Clinton and added additional steps to Executive Order 13224 from Bush Jr.

National Emergencies were not meant to be extended from one Administration to the next for 20 years. It's called a National Emergency for a *reason*.

Hard to believe because Americans have been duped for so long by Politicians on both sides of the aisle with agendas or could not defeat the corruption behind the scenes with the mafias and globalist puppet master's behind making sure these Politicians 'stayed in their lane'... but the line was drawn in the sand in 2016 and it's been a 7-year war to this point of this book.

September 19, 2019: **Modernizing Influenza Vaccines in the United States to Promote National Security and Public Health**

Executive Order 13887:
https://www.federalregister.gov/documents/2019/09/24/2019-20804/modernizing-influenza-vaccines-in-the-united-states-to-promote-national-security-and-public-health

Here's a great example of dismantling the Federal Corporation and smoking out the rats who were globalist funded by the Deep State cabal.

The Federal Continuity Directives clearly outline the Federal Government in a Continuity of Government starting on January 17, 2017, which means Military Occupancy via the Law of War Manual. Those FCDs, along with the 2017 National Security Strategy precisely, 2 and 3 years before 2020, painted a clear outline word for word of what was to come in 2020.

CIC Trump via the Military Occupancy gave everyone a chance to step across the line, give up, do the right thing for Humanity, and their punishment would be lesser. Notice the CDC is listed in this EO. The CDC had their opportunity to do right by Laws and Orders from the start of this Operation but chose the alternative.

September 20, 2019

Australian prime minister Scott Morrison, accompanied by his wife, begins a state visit, his second during the Trump presidency.
President Trump holds a bilateral meeting and joint press conference with Australian prime minister Scott Morrison at the White House.

September 23, 2019

Holds bilateral meetings with Pakistani prime minister Imran Khan, Polish president Andrzej Duda, New Zealand prime minister Jacinda Ardern, Singaporean prime minister Lee Hsien Loong, Egyptian president Abdel Fattah el-Sisi, and South Korean president Moon Jae-in at the UN General Assembly in New York City.

September 24, 2019

Addresses the United Nations General Assembly at the Headquarters of the United Nations. Holds bilateral meetings with British prime minister Boris Johnson and Indian prime minister Narendra Modi at the UN General Assembly in New York City.

While at the United Nations, President Trump tweets that he will release a memorandum of his July phone call to Ukrainian President Volodymyr Zelenskyy, in which they reportedly discussed Joe Biden, Hunter Biden, and the 2020 American election.

Speaker of the House Nancy Pelosi announces that the House of Representatives will launch a formal impeachment inquiry against President Trump.

September 25, 2019

Holds bilateral meetings with Japanese prime minister Shinzō Abe, Ukrainian president Volodymyr Zelenskyy, and Salvadoran president Nayib Bukele at the UN General Assembly in New York City.

October 2, 2019

Holds a bilateral meeting and joint press conference with Finnish president Sauli Niinistö at the White House.
While responding to reporters about the impeachment inquiry, President Trump calls Adam Schiff a "low life" and the whistle-blower's source a "spy."

October 7, 2019

Signs the U.S.–Japan trade agreement.

President Trump announces a Sunday night decision to withdraw U.S. special forces from northeastern Syria.

The House Intelligence, Foreign Affairs and Oversight committees subpoena the Department of Defense and the White House Office of Management and Budget for documents related to Ukraine.

The Trump administration announces it is adding 28 Chinese corporations to a blacklist over concerns of the role the companies played in human rights violations, barring American companies from doing business with these companies.

Federal Corporation subpoenas the DoD for doing what the Department of Defense is supposed to do? Remember, the Military is separate from Federal Government. The Military's supposed to remove anyone who violates the Constitution.

In November 2020, you'll see a very important Executive Order for the blacklist corporations.

October 14, 2019: **Blocking Property and Suspending Entry of Certain Persons Contributing to the Situation in Syria**

Executive Order 13894:
https://www.federalregister.gov/documents/2019/10/17/2019-22849/blocking-property-and-suspending-entry-of-certain-persons-contributing-to-the-situation-in-syria

Another National Emergency with a heavy emphasis on Human Rights Abuse. This also exposes the Obama Administration for their role in aiding the Syrian Arab Republic and their trafficking as defined and outlined in Obama's EOs.

October 16, 2019

Holds a bilateral meeting and joint press conference with Italian president Sergio Mattarella at the White House.

November 13, 2019

Holds a bilateral meeting and joint press conference with Turkish President Recep Tayyip Erdoğan at the White House.

November 14, 2019

Holds a bilateral meeting with NATO Secretary General Jens Stoltenberg at the White House.

November 16, 2019

Makes an unscheduled visit to Walter Reed National Military Medical Center to "begin portions of his routine annual physical exam" that included a "quick exam and labs", according to the White House.

November 25, 2019

Holds a bilateral meeting with Bulgarian prime minister Boyko Borisov at the White House.

All these bilateral meeting countries show up in United States and Israel Operations in 2021, 2022, and 2023.

December 3, 2019

Holds bilateral meetings with NATO secretary general Jens Stoltenberg, French president Emmanuel Macron and Canadian prime minister Justin Trudeau.

President Trump and First Lady Melania Trump attend a NATO dinner hosted by Queen Elizabeth II at Buckingham Palace.

December 4, 2019

Holds bilateral meetings with German chancellor Angela Merkel, Danish prime minister Mette Frederiksen and Italian prime minister Giuseppe Conte, cancels a scheduled press conference and leaves the NATO summit early.

December 10, 2019

Meets with Russian foreign minister Sergey Lavrov.

December 14, 2019

Holds a bilateral meeting with Paraguayan president Mario Abdo Benítez at the White House.

December 17, 2019

Holds a bilateral meeting with Guatemalan president Jimmy Morales at the White House.

December 20, 2019

President Donald John Trump establishes the 6th Branch of the United States Armed Forces, **the Space Force.**

Space Force - Defense.gov:
https://www.defense.gov/News/News-Stories/Article/Article/2046035/trump-signs-law-establishing-us-space-force/

Space Force Official Site:
https://www.spaceforce.mil/About-Us/About-Space-Force/History/

The U.S. Space Force was established Dec. 20, 2019, when the National Defense Authorization Act was signed into law (with bi-partisan support), creating the first new branch of the armed services in 73 years. The establishment of the USSF resulted from widespread recognition that Space was a national security imperative. When combined with the growing threat posed by near-peer competitors in space, it became clear there was a need for a military service focused solely on pursuing superiority in the space domain.

Library of Congress:
https://blogs.loc.gov/law/2022/12/u-s-space-force-the-sixth-branch-of-the-u-s-armed-forces/#:~:text=The%20U.S.%20Space%20Force%20was,of%20the%20U.S.%20Air%20Force.

December 20, 2019: Uniform Code of Military Justice overhauled / reissued

The first time since 1950, the UCMJ was reissued with new laws. Also, on the same day of the establishment of the Space Force, the UCMJ was modified, and a new Courts-Martial Manual reissued.

Appendix 2, Uniform Code of Military Justice reissued; Chapter 47.
https://jsc.defense.gov/Portals/99/Documents/UCMJ%20-%2020December2019.pdf

December 20, 2019: Manual for Courts-Martial

The same day as the UCMJ was overhauled and the Space Force was established, led to an all-new 772 page: **Manual for Courts-Martial 2019**

2019 Courts-Martial Manual:
https://jsc.defense.gov/Portals/99/Documents/2019%20MCM%20(Final)%20(20190108).pdf

Official Article posted on Army dot Mil:

A host of changes to the Uniform Code of Military Justice became effective Jan. 1, modernizing definitions for many offenses, adjusting maximum penalties, standardizing court-martial panels, creating new computer-crime laws, and much more.

The changes strike a balance between protecting the rights of the accused and empowering commanders to effect good order and discipline, said Col. Sara Root, chief of the Army's Military Justice Legislation Training Team.

"We're pretty excited," Root said. "It's a healthy growth of our military justice system."

Root and three members of her team spent the last year traveling to 48 installations to train 6,000 legal personnel and law-enforcement agents about the changes. Her two-day classes included everyone from judges to law clerks, and privates to generals, she said, and even 600 from other military services.

CODIFYING CHANGES

Many of the changes came about after a review by the Military Justice Review Group, consisting of military and criminal justice experts whose report made recommendations to Congress.

"We've had a lot of changes to our system [over the years], but piecemeal." Root said. She explained that the Review Group convened to take a thorough and holistic look at the system to standardize military law and update the Manual for Courts Martial.

Many of the MJRG's changes were incorporated into the Military Justice Act of 2016, the 2017 National Defense Authorization Act, and then Executive Order 13825 signed by the president March 8. Additionally, Secretary of the Army Mark Esper signed a directive Dec. 20 that clarifies definitions for dozens of offenses taking effect this week.

"We've really needed that much time," Root said, from 2017 to now, in order to train all members of the Army Judge Advocate General's Corps. Those attending her classes then needed time to train commanders and others on the installations, she added.

ADULTERY CHANGED

One of the changes replaces the offense of adultery with "extra-marital sexual conduct." The new offense broadens the definition of sexual intercourse, which now includes same-sex affairs. The amendments also now provide legal separation as a defense.

In the past, service members could be charged with adultery even if they had been legally separated for years but were not divorced. Now legal separation from a court of competent jurisdiction can be used as an affirmative defense, Root said.

Also in the past, prosecutors had to prove traditional intercourse to obtain a conviction for adultery, Root said. Now oral sex and other types of sexual intercourse are included.

PROTECTING JUNIOR SOLDIERS

UCMJ Article 93a provides stiffer penalties for recruiters, drill sergeants and others in "positions of special trust" convicted of abusing their authority over recruits or trainees.

The maximum sentence was increased from two years to five years of confinement for those in authority engaging in prohibited sexual activities with junior Soldiers. And it doesn't matter if the sex is consensual or not, Root said, it's still a crime.

Article 132 also protects victims and those reporting crimes from retaliation. An adverse personnel action -- such as a bad NCO Evaluation Report, if determined to be solely for reprisal --- can get the person in authority up to three years confinement without pay and a dishonorable discharge.

COMPUTER CRIMES

Article 123 provides stiff penalties for Soldiers who wrongfully access unauthorized information on government computers. Distributing classified information can earn a maximum sentence of 10 years confinement, but even wrongfully accessing it can get up to five years in jail. Unauthorized access of personally identifiable information, or PII, is also a crime. Intentionally damaging government computers or installing a virus can also bring five years in the clinker.

Article 121a updates offenses involving the fraudulent use of credit cards, debit cards or other access devices to acquire anything of value. The penalty for such crimes has been increased to a max of 15 years confinement if the theft is over $1,000.

If the theft is under $1,000 the maximum penalty was increased from five to 10 years confinement, and this crime also includes exceeding one's authorization to use the access device, for example, misusing a Government Travel Card.

Cyberstalking is also now included as a stalking offense under Article 130 of the UCMJ.

COURTS-MARTIAL

A "bench trial" by a judge alone can now determine guilt or innocence for many offenses. Almost any charge can be referred to such a forum, except for rape and sexual assault, which requires referral to a general court-martial. However, if the offense has a sentence of more than two years, the accused has a right to object to such charges being referred to a bench trial and could request a special or general court-martial.

If found guilty at a bench trial, Root said a Soldier cannot be given a punitive discharge and the max sentence would be limited to no more than six months forfeiture of pay and no more than six months confinement. The judge can still adjudge a reduction in rank.

"It's a great tool that we're really excited to see how commanders use it out in the formations," Root said.

More than half of the cases in the Army actually are settled by plea agreements in lieu of a contested trial, Root said. Commanders have always had the authority to limit the max sentence with a plea agreement, but she said now they can agree to a minimum sentence as well. This might result in a range for the judge to sentence within, for example, no less than one year confinement, but no more than five years confinement.

If a case goes to a non-capital general court-martial, the panel has now been standardized to eight members. In the past the size of the panel could vary from five to an unlimited number, but often around 10-12 members. Now each general court-martial must begin with eight panel members, she said, but could continue if one panel member must leave due to an emergency during trial.

Special courts-martial will now be set at four panel members. A court-martial convening authority can also authorize alternate members to be on a special or a general court-martial, she said.

Capital offenses such as murder require a 12-member panel. For a non-capital court-martial, three-fourths of the panel members must agree with the prosecution to convict the accused, she said. For instance, if only five members of an eight-member panel vote guilty, then the accused is acquitted. A conviction for a capital offense still requires a unanimous verdict.

EXPANDED AUTHORITY

Congress expanded judges' authorities to issue investigative subpoenas earlier in the process, for example, to obtain a surveillance video from a store. One of the most significant changes is that now military judges can issue warrants and orders to service providers to obtain electronic communications such as email correspondence.

In the past, trial counsel had to wait until preferring charges to issue investigative subpoenas. Now, with the approval of the general court-martial convening authority, trial counsel can issue subpoenas earlier to help determine whether charges are necessary. For electronic communications, the government previously had to rely on federal counterparts to assist with obtaining electronic communications.

"Being able to have these tools available earlier in the process is going to be helpful for overall justice," Root said.

The changes also call for more robust Article 32 hearings to help the commander determine if an accused should go to trial, she said. For instance, a preliminary hearing officer must now issue a more detailed report immediately after an Article 32 hearing's conclusion. In addition, both the accused and the victim now have the right to submit anything they deem relevant to the preliminary hearing officer within 24 hours after the hearing specifically for the court-martial convening authority to consider.

Aimed at speeding up the post-trial process, immediately following a court-martial, audio can now be provided to the accused, the victim, and the convening authority in lieu of a verbatim transcript which will be typed and provided later, but prior to appeal. A number of other procedural changes are aimed at making the military justice system even more efficient, Root said.

MORE CHANGES

More changes to punitive offenses also take effect this week. For instance, the definition of burglary has changed to include breaking and entering any building or structure of another, anytime, with the intent to commit any offense under the UCMJ. In the past, burglary was limited to breaking and entering the dwelling house of another in the nighttime.

The penalty for wearing unauthorized medals of valor has increased from 6 months to a max of one-year confinement along with forfeiture of pay and a bad-conduct discharge. This includes wearing an unauthorized Medal of Honor, Distinguished Service Cross, Silver Star, Purple Heart, or valor device. The maximum penalty for wearing any other unauthorized medal is still only six months.

Regarding misconduct that occurred prior to Jan. 1, the changes to the punitive articles are not retroactive, Root said. However, some of the procedural changes will apply to cases that were not referred to trial before Jan. 1. All members of the JAG Corps are trained in the changes and ready to go, Root said.

"We're pretty proud that our commanders are really at the center of this," she said, "and it just gives them some more tools for good order and discipline."

Article from Army dot Mil:
https://www.army.mil/article/215594/2019_brings_changes_to_military_justice_system

This all new UCMJ reissue coincides with the new Law of War Manual which was modified to be an umbrella to the UCMJ. That paired with what was to come in March 2020, makes the whole Military Occupancy shine like no other.

December 20, 2019: The Global Fragility Act of 2019

22 US Code 105:
https://uscode.house.gov/view.xhtml?path=/prelim@title22/chapter105&edition=prelim

Passed by the 116th Congress on the same day the Space Force was established, and the Uniform Code of Military Justice (Military Law) was reissued.

This Act presented a new and necessary opportunity for the U.S. Government to prioritize conflict prevention and transform how it partners with countries affected by fragility and conflict to foster a more peaceful and stable world.

Which coincides with ALL the Biblical, Historical, and Monumental peace treaties, deals, and trips CIC Trump made with multiple leaders who came aboard this multi-layered, massive Operation.

December 20, 2019: **War Powers Act amended**

Reports and briefings on use of military force and support of partner forces

Section 1550:

(a) In general

Not later than 180 days after December 20, 2019, and every 180 days thereafter, the President shall submit to the congressional defense committees, the Committee on Foreign Relations of the Senate, and the Committee on Foreign Affairs of the House of Representatives a report on actions taken pursuant to the Authorization for Use of Military Force (Public Law 107–40) against those countries or organizations described in such law, as well as any actions taken to command, coordinate, participate in the movement of, or accompany the regular or irregular military forces of any foreign country or government when such forces are engaged in hostilities or in situations where imminent involvement in hostilities is clearly indicated by the circumstances, during the preceding 180-day period.

*I'll use this below in the final summary.

January 2, 2020

Major General Qasem Soleimani, Iran's top security and intelligence commander, is killed in an airstrike at Baghdad International Airport. The Department of Defense issues a statement that the strike had been carried out "at the direction of the President."

> "*At my direction, the United States military successfully executed a flawless precision strike that killed the number-one terrorist anywhere in the world, Qasem Soleimani. Soleimani was plotting imminent and sinister attacks on American diplomats and military personnel, but we caught him in the act and terminated him.*" – CIC Trump

January 6, 2020

Holds a bilateral meeting with Saudi Arabian vice minister of defense Prince Khalid bin Salman.

January 7, 2020

Holds a bilateral meeting with Greek prime minister Kyriakos Mitsotakis at the White House.

January 9, 2020

The House votes to limit the president's ability to order military operations against Iran, unless explicitly authorized by Congress.

This should paint a small picture of the former Federal Corporate Congress. At this point, Congress is 3 years into a Military Occupancy and Continuity of Operations Plan. And just 20 days prior to this date, the Order to use Military Force and Support Partner Forces was placed in the War Powers Resolution Act of 1973 by the CIC.

The President can most certainly declare war. Congress decided that in 1973. Until that Act is amended, that's how it sits. Things like this should now show those who weren't following Legislation via Laws and Orders, the Deep State was running out of time as they were all trapped and just buying time, although to us who knew the Military Occupancy and COG, it was all planned.

January 10, 2020: **Imposing Sanctions With Respect to Additional Sectors of Iran**

Executive Order 13902:
https://www.federalregister.gov/documents/2020/01/14/2020-00534/imposing-sanctions-with-respect-to-additional-sectors-of-iran

Heavy emphasis on Section 7, (b), (c), and (d). And notice the terms: *Central Bank* of Iran and the terms of (b): the term "foreign financial institution" means any foreign entity that is engaged in the business of accepting deposits, making, granting, transferring, holding, or brokering loans or credits, or purchasing or selling foreign exchange, securities, commodity futures or options, or procuring purchasers and sellers thereof, as principal or agent. The term includes, but is not limited to, depository institutions, banks, savings banks, money service businesses, trust companies, securities brokers and dealers, commodity futures and options brokers and dealers, forward contract and foreign exchange merchants, securities and commodities exchanges, clearing corporations, investment companies, employee benefit plans, dealers in precious metals, stones, or jewels, and holding companies, affiliates, or subsidiaries of any of the foregoing.

January 21, 2020

Arrives in Switzerland to attend the 2020 Davos World Economic Forum.

January 27, 2020

Holds a bilateral meeting with Israeli prime minister Benjamin Netanyahu at the White House.

January 31, 2020: Combating Human Trafficking and Online Child Exploitation in the United States

Executive Order 13903:
https://www.federalregister.gov/documents/2020/02/05/2020-02438/combating-human-trafficking-and-online-child-exploitation-in-the-united-states

The War on Trafficking was outlined in Executive Order 13818, December 2017, paired with the 2017 National Security Strategy, and this Executive Order is more specific on Human and Child Trafficking.

Notice the term Homeland Security throughout this EO. It's the DHS who's on the front page as the leading authority on the Federal Continuity Directives.

February 2, 2020

The Trump administration announces travel restrictions on air traffic to and from China take effect. Secretary of Health and Human Services Alex Azar declares that COVID-19 "poses a public health emergency in the United States."

Keep in mind… the American Public has never heard of COVID at this point.

February 4, 2020: State of the Union Address

SOTU Address:
https://www.youtube.com/watch?v=Xb1xHhGJjJk

President Trump was the first to ever mention the word Corona-SARS virus in this delivery.

He also specifically said, "we will **never** be a Socialist nation."

> *"Our economy is the best it's ever been."*

> *"Our Military is completely rebuilt."*

> *"The vision I will lay out this evening demonstrates how we are building the world's most prosperous and inclusive society, one where every citizen can join in America's unparalleled success and where every community can take part in America's extraordinary rise."*

When one reads the Federal Continuity Directives and the 2017 National Security Strategy paired with this speech… It's very easy to see what was taking place, but also what was needed that would start a mere two weeks after this speech that made 2020 what we knew of it. But due to America and *many* Americans, they were too focused on and only remembered the drama of Nancy Pelosi ripping up the speech papers at the end, clearly did not remember or focus on the speech and actual policies, laws, and orders… proving my always continuous point throughout this operation.

February 5, 2020

Holds a bilateral meeting with Venezuelan opposition leader Juan Guaidó at the White House.

February 6, 2020

Holds a bilateral meeting with Kenyan president Uhuru Kenyatta at the White House.

February 12, 2020

Holds a bilateral meeting with Ecuadorian president Lenín Moreno at the White House.

February 24, 2020

Begins a two-day state visit to India.
Attends a "Namaste, Trump" rally in Gujarat and visits the Taj Mahal.

February 25, 2020

Holds a bilateral meeting and joint press conference with Indian prime minister Narendra Modi.
Attends a state dinner hosted by Indian president Ram Nath Kovind.

March 2, 2020

Holds a bilateral meeting with Colombian president Iván Duque Márquez at the White House.

March 2, 2020: Defense Production Act Amended

The Defense Production Act, 50 United States Code Chapter 55, was amended on this date to terminate on September 30, 2025. This meant when you saw the DPA "invoked" by "Biden" anywhere from January 21, 2021, to the end, was already appropriated and accounted for.

§4531. Presidential authorization for the national defense
(a) Expediting production and deliveries or services
(1) Authorized activities
To reduce current or projected shortfalls of industrial resources, critical technology items, or essential materials needed for national defense purposes, subject to such regulations as the President may prescribe, the President may authorize a guaranteeing agency to provide guarantees of loans by private institutions for the purpose of

financing any contractor, subcontractor, provider of critical infrastructure, or other person in support of production capabilities or supplies that are deemed by the guaranteeing agency to be necessary to create, maintain, expedite, expand, protect, or restore production and deliveries or services essential to the national defense.

(2) Presidential determinations required
Except during a period of national emergency declared by Congress or the President, a loan guarantee may be entered into under this section only if the President determines that—

§4564. Termination of chapter

(a) Termination
Subchapter I (except section 4514 of this title), subchapter II, and subchapter III (except sections 4557, 4558, and 4565 of this title) shall terminate on September 30, 2025, except that all authority extended under subchapter II shall be effective for any fiscal year only to such extent or in such amounts as are provided in advance in appropriations Acts.

50 United States Code Chapter 55:
https://uscode.house.gov/view.xhtml?path=/prelim@title50/chapter55&edition=prelim

March 7, 2020

Holds a working dinner with Brazilian president Jair Bolsonaro at Mar-a-Lago.

March 12, 2020

Holds a bilateral meeting with Taoiseach Leo Varadkar of Ireland at the White House.

March 13, 2020: Proclamation 9994

On March 13, 2020, a little over a month since the word 'Corona-virus' was first dropped to the public on the February 4, 2020, State of the Union address, this was issued. You'll notice this paragraph below:

This proclamation is not intended to, and does not, create any right or benefit, substantive, or procedural, enforceable at law or in equity by any party against the United States, its departments, agencies, or entities, its officers, employees, or agents, or any other person.

That means ANY company or corporation that sought their own interests - pharmaceuticals - that did not adhere to the Laws and Orders established, especially referring to health risks and death… which equals fraud, treason, and crimes against humanity… All these Proclamations and National Emergencies had to be displayed to the public and the people who were to enforce, apply, and uphold, all had opportunities to implement and do the right things, but chose otherwise and there's punishments for those via the Military and Federal Courts.

Because bullet point (b) before the above tells you:

(b) This proclamation shall be implemented consistent with applicable law and subject to the availability of appropriations.

The declaration opens access to $50 billion in emergency funding, lifts restrictions on doctors and hospitals, and waives student loan interest.

When challenged about the slow response to provide testing, CIC Trump blamed prior administrations saying, "I don't take responsibility at all."

And does not have to. This put all the responsibility on those 'experts' as Doctors, CEOs and their boards at hospitals, Governors, and other politicians.

March 18, 2020: **Prioritizing and Allocating Health and Medical Resources to Respond to the Spread of COVID-19**

Executive Order 13909:
https://www.federalregister.gov/documents/2020/03/23/2020-06161/prioritizing-and-allocating-health-and-medical-resources-to-respond-to-the-spread-of-covid-19

This would be following the 10th National Emergency under President Donald John Trump declared March 13, 2020, which was the first verbal National Emergency of the two verbal National Emergencies.

After one reads the Federal Continuity Directives from January 2017 to the most recent (at the time of this book: April 2023) plus the 2017 National Security Strategy, the Pandemic is clearly and definitively outlined as a planned event that would set the stage for the bigger event to clean up the filth and corruption of the U.S. streets and cities.

March 21, 2020

Announces in a press conference that he will invoke the Defense Production Act to increase production of hospital masks, saying he views the country as entering a wartime setting and that he is "a wartime president."

"*I view it – in a sense as a wartime president,*" Trump said after announcing he was invoking the Defense Production Act, which was established in 1950 in response to production needs during the Korean War.

CNN:
https://www.cnn.com/2020/03/18/politics/trump-defense-production-act-coronavirus/index.html

March 23, 2020: **Preventing Hoarding of Health and Medical Resources To Respond to the Spread of COVID-19**

Executive Order 13910:
https://www.federalregister.gov/documents/2020/03/26/2020-06478/preventing-hoarding-of-health-and-medical-resources-to-respond-to-the-spread-of-covid-19

Notice this line:

"*I also noted that while the Federal Government, along with State and local governments, have taken preventive and proactive measures to slow the spread of the virus and to treat those affected,*"

State and Local governments are defined throughout all Federal Continuity Directives issued long before this date plus the outline of multiple scenarios with a Pandemic to a tee.

March 27, 2020: **Delegating Additional Authority Under the Defense Production Act With Respect to Health and Medical Resources To Respond to the Spread of COVID-19**

Executive Order 13911:
https://www.federalregister.gov/documents/2020/04/01/2020-06969/delegating-additional-authority-under-the-defense-production-act-with-respect-to-health-and-medical

All these Covid-19 Executive Orders via National Emergencies tie in with the Federal Continuity Directives and National Security Strategies.

March 27, 2020: **National Emergency Authority To Order the Selected Reserve and Certain Members of the Individual Ready Reserve of the Armed Forces to Active Duty**

Executive Order 13912:
https://www.federalregister.gov/documents/2020/04/01/2020-06985/national-emergency-authority-to-order-the-selected-reserve-and-certain-members-of-the-individual

This is the Federal Order that accompanies the direct Military Order made by President Trump via Article II of the Constitution, 50 U.S. Code 33, Sections 1541 and 1550, making him a Wartime President.

This is the EO that called into service all Ready Reserves and Officers, Prior Service and Retirees of the Coast Guard.

Section 1. *Emergency Authority*. To provide additional authority to the Secretaries of Defense and Homeland Security to respond to the national emergency declared by Proclamation 9994, the authorities under section 12302 of title 10, United States Code, and sections 2127, 2308, 2314, and 3735 of title 14, United States Code, are invoked and made available, according to their terms, to the Secretaries of Defense and Homeland Security. The Secretaries of the Army, Navy, and Air Force, at the direction of the Secretary of Defense, and the Secretary of Homeland Security with respect to the Coast Guard when it is not operating as a service in the Navy, are authorized to order to active duty not to exceed 24 consecutive months, such units, and individual members of the Ready Reserve under the jurisdiction of the Secretary concerned, not to exceed 1,000,000 members on active duty at any one time, as the Secretary of Defense and, with respect to the Coast Guard when it is not operating as a service in the Navy, the Secretary of Homeland Security consider necessary. The Secretary of Defense or the Secretary of Homeland Security, as applicable, will ensure appropriate consultation is undertaken with relevant state officials with respect to the utilization of National Guard Reserve Component units activated under this authority.

Key lines:

> Not to exceed 24 consecutive months.
> Not to exceed 1,000,000 members on active duty at any one time.

Consecutive months means every 2 years, more units can be activated.

Reserves do <u>not</u> serve dual missions. Meaning, they do not serve State and Federal missions. They are Federal only.

Notice: 10 United States Code 12302.

And notice: Sections 2127, 2308, 2314, and 3735 of title 14, invoked and made available.

These actions clearly tipped the hat to the Military Occupancy.

See final summary for the continuation piece of this Executive Order.

March 30, 2020: **Donald Trump Press Conference where he tells what "jab" he supported…**

March 30, 2020, Press:
https://trumpwhitehouse.archives.gov/briefings-statements/remarks-president-trump-members-coronavirus-task-force-press-briefing/

This settles the whole malarkey about "President Trump endorsing the "jab"… Nobody ever wants to go back to the time and place aka ORIGIN of whatever the topic is. In this case, it was the "jab" topic.

In 2019, women who couldn't define a woman, yet wanted women's rights, filled the streets in MULTIPLE 'protests,' many wearing vajay-jay (the land down under) suits, chanting and holding up signs "my body, my choice"… Only to fast forward not even a full year later to "it's the President's fault" yet clearly couldn't even define a woman and have no clue what the President's actual role is defined by the Constitution.

The principle then must be health, and the topic must be the body if it's the President's responsibility on what you should or should not put in your body. The principle is what's the President's role according to the Constitution and the whole reason we even elect a President, and the topic is not the jab.

This was a multi-layered operation from the start. In 2019, you read above about the CDC being listed in a Influenza Vaccine Executive Order. In 2020, in another EO about Flu Vaccines, the CDC was not listed.

The CDC, FDA, and NIH did not uphold, apply, and enforce the Laws that were put into place. They pushed their jabs onto the public. That's not the President's role to tell you who, what and how to research, nor to tell what companies and people how to run their business.

There's a reason the quote 'hear to react' versus 'listen to respond' is so dynamic and potent AND another example of Americans believing what they want, hearing what they want, making their own assessments WITHOUT listening or paying attention to the origin. When actually…

This was all outlined in the National Security Strategy of 2017 and the February 2018 Continuity Directive LONG before 2020. Special Operations are titled Special Operations for a reason… They're very detailed, strategic, complex, and take time. And PS: The Military does NOT work on your time.

Origin matters. CIC Trump did not 'endorse' *the* jab. He endorsed **a** 'vaccine' and it wasn't 'the jab.' Here's President Trump's speech via the major Press Conference for "Covid."
March 30, 2020, Press Briefing by President Trump:

Rose Garden 5:12 P.M. EDT

THE PRESIDENT: Okay, thank you very much. Thank you. Very comfortable here. A lot of room. And we appreciate you being here.

Yesterday I announced that we would be extending our social distance guidelines through the end of April. This is based on modeling that shows the peak in fatalities will not arrive for another two weeks. The same modeling also shows that, by very vigorously following these guidelines, we could save more than 1 million American lives. Think of that: 1 million American lives.

Our future is in our own hands, and the choices and sacrifices we make will determine the fate of this virus and, really, the fate of our victory. We will have a great victory. We have no other choice. Every one of us has a role to play in winning this war. Every citizen, family, and business can make the difference in stopping the virus. This is our shared patriotic duty.

Challenging times are ahead for the next 30 days, and this is a very vital 30 days. We're sort of putting it all on the line, this 30 days. So important because we have to get back. But the more we dedicate ourselves today, the more quickly we will emerge on the other side of the crisis. And that's the time we're waiting for. The more we commit ourselves now, the sooner we can win the fight and return to our lives. And they will be great lives — maybe better than ever.

Today we reached a historic milestone in our war against the coronavirus. Over 1 million Americans have now been tested — more than any other country, by far; not even close — and tested accurately.

And I think what I'd like to do is ask Secretary Azar, who's done a fantastic job, to come up and just say a few words about the fact that we reached substantially now more than 1 million tests.

Please. Thank you, Alex.

SECRETARY AZAR: Well, thank you, Mr. President, for your leadership in marshaling all the resources that we have for this unprecedented testing effort. And thank you, Mr. Vice President, for leading a whole-of-economy approach to testing.

As the President mentioned, today the United States hit more than 1 million samples tested — a number that no other country has reached. We're now testing nearly 100,000 samples a day, also a level that no other country has reached.

I want to thank every partner that has been involved in this effort. That includes all of the men and women of the FDA and the CDC, including Director Redfield and Commissioner Hahn. Together, the FDA and CDC have worked to balance the need for testing on an aggressive scale with the scientific rigor that Americans expect.

Working with our testing coordinator, Admiral Giroir, they have now truly unleashed the ingenuity of the private sector and our state and local leaders, the centerpieces of America's historic approach to testing.

I want to thank those state and local leaders who have used their on-the-ground resources and knowledge to lead testing and make it much more easily accessible to the Americans who need it. I'm also grateful to FEMA, with whom we are now working closely to get state and local partners what they need.

I also want to thank CMS, where Administrator Verma has given healthcare providers unprecedented flexibility to scale up capacity for testing and treatment, and has ensured that tests will be paid for.

Finally, we would not be where we are today without the many American companies, entrepreneurs, and scientists who have worked day and night to develop, as of today, 20 different emergency testing options. With the FDA responding to request for authorization typically within 24 hours, the number of options is growing nearly every day.

FDA has also opened up new options for using the available tests, like self-swabbing and new options for reagents.

I also want to thank FDA and other components of HHS for incredibly rapid action on other tools that we need.

This weekend, we actually worked to secure 30 million tablets from Sandoz and **1 million tablets from Bayer of hydroxychloroquine and chloroquine**, which are potential COVID-19 treatments. And we authorized Battelle's new decontamination machines, which can each sterilize thousands of essential N95 masks for reuse every day.

So thank you, Mr. President, for your leadership and thank you to everybody who's played a part in getting us where we are today. Thank you.

THE PRESIDENT: Thank you very much. Thank you.

I'd like to ask Dr. Hahn to come up — FDA — because we have some really good stuff. First of all, the numbers have been incredible on testing, but in the days ahead, we're going to go even faster. And we have something from Abbott Labs, which is right here, and that's a five-minute test, highly accurate.

And I maybe can show that as we listen to our FDA Commissioner — the job he's done in the approval process. **We talked about the chloroquine and the hydroxychloroquine just now**.

I thought that I'd mention it, but Alex has already done that, but we have that now under test with 1,100 people in New York. And it was only the fast approval by FDA that allowed us to do that. It was a really rapid approval.

…… (Full Script available online)

THE PRESIDENT: Thank you, Doctor. Great job too. Really great job. Thank you, Steve.

So, the pharmaceutical company, **Sandoz, has been working with us very closely. And as Alex mentioned a little bit, 30 million doses of the hydroxychloroquine to the United States government has been given. And Bayer has donated 1 million doses of the chloroquine, which will soon be distributed to states and state health officials around the country. Teva Pharmaceuticals is also donating 6 million doses of hydroxychloroquine to U.S. hospitals. That's 6 million doses.**

…. (Full Script available online)

You should be saying congratulations to the men and women who have done this job, who have inherited a broken testing system, and who have made it great. And if you don't say it, I'll say it. I want to congratulate all of the people. You have done a fantastic job.

And we will see you all tomorrow. Thank you very much. Thank you. Thank you.

END 6:09 P.M. EDT

Keynote for those who keep and kept on and on and on about "the Jab"... had they been reading what mattered and paying attention versus ALL of the noise, drama and propaganda, they might would have read this:

> *"So, the pharmaceutical company, Sandoz, has been working with us very closely. And as Alex mentioned a little bit, 30 million doses of the hydroxychloroquine to the United States government has been given. And Bayer has donated 1 million doses of the chloroquine, which will soon be distributed to states and state health officials around the country. Teva Pharmaceuticals is also donating 6 million doses of hydroxychloroquine to U.S. hospitals. That's 6 million doses."*

Will you please read that out loud to yourself: **36 million doses of the hydroxychloroquine** *and* **1 million doses of the chloroquine.**

Did you notice the sentence about 'winning this war? 'Also, did you notice the question about masks being required? Did you notice the response to that question?

Outside of this being a well-defined Military Occupancy and Continuity of Operations Plan (Continuity of Government) ... Do you remember President Trump leaving it up to Governors and States to decide? Do you know what that signified? Governors and each official and down were to do what? Abide by, apply, uphold, and enforce the Laws and Orders set into place because the topic was a federal topic, not a one or multiple state emergency.

As President, he didn't give the power back to the Governors for them to become power tripping Nazi's to manipulate a massive portion of the population who cannot even name the three branches of government anymore, much less know their rights.

Mandatory = Not a Law
Required = Not a Law
Mandated = Not a Law
Requested = Not a Law
Ordered = Not a Law
Ordinance = Not a Law
Decree = Not a Law
Compulsory = Not a Law

He gave the power to the States and Governors to see what Governors were going up uphold the new historic Laws and Orders. To this date, how many people do you know still wearing masks? Wait till those sleepy Americans find out about the Special Operation to expose and take down the Swamp… that's **been** taking place.

Also, another keynote:

"So, it's been really pretty amazing what they've done, and the Army Corps of Engineers, what they've done. They've done — they just completed — think of it — a 2,900-bed hospital in New York in just about three days, maybe four days. And the whole city is talking about it.

On top of that, we floated in a great ship, which is going to be 1,000 rooms, which is being used for patients outside of what we're focused on. And that will free up a lot of rooms for what we're focused on. So, it's been great.

The Army Corps of Engineers has awarded contracts for the construction of alternate care facilities, also, at the State University at Stony Brook, State University Old Westbury, and the Westchester Community Center. We're sending 60 ambulances to New York City today. We have a total of 60. We're getting some additional ones, with up to 190 more to follow at different locations."

All the above outlines the Federal Continuity Directives from January 17, 2017, to April 2023 (most recent as of this book) to a tee of preparing for the cleanup of our streets and cities.

March 2020: Quotes about being a Wartime President:
Trump Says He's A 'Wartime President' Against Coronavirus Crisis | NBC Nightly News

Politico:

President Donald Trump on Wednesday began to invoke the rhetoric of "a wartime president" as he told reporters he views himself as one, while his administration fights to contain the spread of coronavirus and mitigate the economic fallout from the global pandemic.

"I do, I actually do, I'm looking at it that way," Trump told reporters during a press briefing at the White House when asked whether he considered the U.S. to be on a wartime footing. "I look at it, I view it as, in a sense, a wartime president. I mean, that's what we're fighting."

"To this day, nobody has ever seen like it, what they were able to do during World War II," he continued. "Now it's our time. We must sacrifice together, because we are all in this together, and we will come through together. It's the invisible enemy. That's always the toughest enemy, the invisible enemy."

"It's a very tough situation here. You have to do things," he explained later. "You have to close parts of an economy that six weeks ago were the best they've ever been. And then one day you have to close it down in order to defeat this enemy ... but we're doing it and we're doing it well."

Note: "And then one day you have to close it down in order to defeat this enemy… but we're doing it and we're doing it well" = Federal Continuity Directives as outlines what would come.

Politico, March 2020:
https://www.politico.com/news/2020/03/18/trump-administration-self-swab-coronavirus-tests-135590

The Guardian, March 2020:
https://www.theguardian.com/us-news/2020/mar/22/trump-coronavirus-election-november-2020

Reuters, March 2020:
https://www.reuters.com/article/us-health-coronavirus-usa-trump-act/trump-says-he-will-invoke-wartime-act-to-fight-enemy-coronavirus-idUSKBN2152XL

World War II reference:

"To this day nobody's seen anything like what they were able to do during World War II," Trump said. "And now it's our time. We must sacrifice together because we are all in this together and we'll come through together. It's the invisible enemy."

CNN, March 2020:
https://www.cnn.com/2020/03/18/politics/donald-trump-wartime-president-coronavirus/index.html

ABC, March 2020:
https://abcnews.go.com/Politics/trump-tweets-us-canada-closing-border-white-house/story?id=69660955

Fox News, March 2020:
https://www.foxnews.com/politics/trump-announces-he-is-invoking-defense-production-act-to-fight-coronavirus

March 30, 2020: Presidential Enhancement Act of 2019

The Presidential Transition Act of 1963 (PTA) authorizes funding for the General Services Administration (GSA) to provide suitable office space, staff compensation, and other services associated with the presidential transition process (3 U.S.C. §102 note). The act has since been amended in response to evolving understandings of the role of the government in the transition process. From enactment of the PTA in 1964 through the presidential transition of 2008-2009, most PTA-authorized support was provided after the election of the incoming President and Vice President. In the years since, Congress has expanded support for the presidential transition process to include authorization and funding for pre-election activities and support. Most recently, the act was amended by the Presidential Transition Enhancement Act of 2019 (P.L. 116-121), enacted on March 3, 2020.

PHA:
https://crsreports.congress.gov/product/pdf/R/R46602#:~:text=The%20Presidential%20Transition%20Enhancement%20Act%20of%202019%2C%20enacted%20on%20March,GSA%20and%20an%20ethics%20plan

April 4, 2020: Establishing the Committee for the Assessment of Foreign Participation in the United States Telecommunications Services Sector

This Executive Order coincides with the Federal Continuity Directives as they outline Emergency Communications via Emergency Radios plus the Telecommunications Act of 1996, the Federal Communications Commission, and the application of those for the events of cleaning up our Nation.

Executive Order 13923:
https://www.federalregister.gov/documents/2020/04/08/2020-07530/establishing-the-committee-for-the-assessment-of-foreign-participation-in-the-united-states

April 15, 2020

Announces that the US will stop funding the World Health Organization (WHO), after Trump criticized the WHO for being too lenient on China.

April 30, 2020: Delegating Authority Under the Defense Production Act With Respect to Food Supply Chain Resources During the National Emergency Caused by the Outbreak of COVID-19

Executive Order 13917:
https://www.federalregister.gov/documents/2020/05/01/2020-09536/delegating-authority-under-the-defense-production-act-with-respect-to-food-supply-chain-resources

As Americans witnessed the burning of facilities in 2021 and 2022, this was an early EO that would set the tone of what was to come. Most Americans know our processed foods are loaded with multiple preservatives and other chemical poisons that are not good for our health.

These type EO's were a declared war on the FDA in a legal kind of manner giving the proper authorities the legal manner prescribed a legal obligation and authority to assess and access these manufacturing and production facilities.

April 30, 2020: Ordering the Selected Reserve of the Armed Forces to Active Duty

Executive Order 13919:
https://www.federalregister.gov/documents/2020/05/04/2020-09645/ordering-the-selected-reserve-of-the-armed-forces-to-active-duty

This Executive Order is very iconic. The Commander-in-Chief augmenting the regular Armed Forces for Counternarcotic Operation in the Western Hemisphere (very broad) and giving equal authorization to the Secretary of Defense to Federalize the Selected Reservists to Active-Duty.

This EO was **not** revised or revoked, meaning active in 2021, 2022, and 2023.

See final summary for the continuation piece of this EO.

May 14, 2020: Delegating Authority Under the Defense Production Act to the Chief Executive Officer of the United States International Development Finance Corporation to Respond to the COVID-19 Outbreak

Which can actually be found in the Defense Production Act listed by President Donald J. Trump versus the 8 "invoking's" the "media" claimed "Biden" has that the DPA shows only two… and those two are one, an Act by Donald John Trump, and two, one authorized by the Secretary of Defense, which had already been given Orders by CIC Trump in the War Powers Resolution Act on December 20, 2019.

Executive Order 13922:
https://www.federalregister.gov/documents/2020/05/19/2020-10953/delegating-authority-under-the-defense-production-act-to-the-chief-executive-officer-of-the-united

May 19, 2020: Regulatory Relief to Support Economic Recovery

Executive Order 13924:
https://www.federalregister.gov/documents/2020/05/22/2020-11301/regulatory-relief-to-support-economic-recovery

In consistency with the Federal Continuity Directives.

Section 6 (a few key bullets):

(a) The Government should bear the burden of proving an alleged violation of law; the subject of enforcement should not bear the burden of proving compliance.
(d) Consistent with any executive branch confidentiality interests, the Government should provide favorable relevant evidence in possession of the agency to the subject of an administrative enforcement action.
(e) All rules of evidence and procedure should be public, clear, and effective.
(f) Penalties should be proportionate, transparent, and imposed in adherence to consistent standards and only as authorized by law.
(g) Administrative enforcement should be free of improper Government coercion.
(j) Agencies must be accountable for their administrative enforcement decisions.

When you read the FCDs, they clearly defined the Departments and Agencies, and this holds those accountable.

Notice the 'Applicable to Law.'

May 27, 2020

Threatens to close or impose regulation on social media after Twitter flags his post on mail-in ballots as inaccurate. Notice the date… "Conservatives" and "Republicans" did not start hearing or caring about Election Interference until AFTER November 2020.

At that point, Executive Order 13848 was in effect 1 year and 3 months.

June 1, 2020

Delivers a speech in the Rose Garden declaring that he was:

"Dispatching thousands and thousands of heavily armed soldiers, military personnel and law enforcement officers to stop the rioting, looting, vandalism, assaults and the wanton destruction of property," and,

"If a city or state refuses to take the actions that are necessary … then I'll deploy the United States military and quickly solve the problem for them."

June 2, 2020: Advancing International Religious Freedom

Executive Order 13926:
https://www.federalregister.gov/documents/2020/06/05/2020-12430/advancing-international-religious-freedom

Notice the International term for Religious Freedom, not just the United States. This also pairs with the declaration of naming Jerusalem capital of Israel that NO President has ever fulfilled, and it just so happened to be a crucial year of Jubilee.

It's also outlined in the 2017 National Security Strategy, and it was on full display with President Trump and prayer teams around him his whole visual Presidency.

June 1, 2020, the day after George Floyd protests… President Trump had the **National Guard** clear out the area in front the Ashburton House, the Parish House of "the Church of President's," St John's Episcopal Church, where he held a Bible up for the whole world to see, while the 'mainstream media' called it a photo op and insult. Imagine that… An 'insult' for holding a Bible up in front of a church that's supposed to teach that book.

June 11, 2020: **Blocking Property of Certain Persons Associated With the International Criminal Court**

Executive Order 13928:
https://www.federalregister.gov/documents/2020/06/15/2020-12953/blocking-property-of-certain-persons-associated-with-the-international-criminal-court

If the United States blocked the ICC and Russia did as well… How come Russia was the 'bad' guys to so many people?

Perhaps because they did not know anything about the recent Ukrainian history and events that took place with the Bush and Obama Administrations? Perhaps because they only go by ear say from the Soviet Union yet know nothing about it, just surface talk?

June 24, 2020

Holds a bilateral meeting and joint press conference with Polish president Andrzej Duda at the White House.

June 26, 2020: **Protecting American Monuments, Memorials, and Statues and Combating Recent Criminal Violence**

Executive Order 13933:
https://www.federalregister.gov/documents/2020/07/02/2020-14509/protecting-american-monuments-memorials-and-statues-and-combating-recent-criminal-violence

This Executive Order not only protects, but it also allows the National Guard and other forms of Law Enforcement to respond with full authority being a Federal Law.

July 1, 2020: **United States-Mexico-Canada-Agreement**

This ended NAFTA. The United States-Mexico-Canada Agreement (USMCA) entered into force on July 1, 2020. The USMCA, which substituted the North America Free Trade Agreement (NAFTA) is a mutually beneficial win for North American workers, farmers, ranchers, and businesses. The Agreement creates more balanced, reciprocal trade supporting high-paying jobs for Americans and grow the North American economy.

Agreement highlights include:

- Creating a more level playing field for American workers, including improved rules of origin for automobiles, trucks, other products, and disciplines on currency manipulation.
- Benefiting American farmers, ranchers, and agribusinesses by modernizing and strengthening food and agriculture trade in North America.
- Supporting a 21st Century economy through new protections for U.S. intellectual property and ensuring opportunities for trade in U.S. services.
- New chapters covering Digital Trade, Anticorruption, and Good Regulatory Practices, as well as a chapter devoted to ensuring that Small and Medium Sized Enterprises benefit from the Agreement.

USMCA Full:
https://ustr.gov/trade-agreements/free-trade-agreements/united-states-mexico-canada-agreement/agreement-between

USMCA Summary:
https://ustr.gov/trade-agreements/free-trade-agreements/united-states-mexico-canada-agreement

July 4, 2020

2020 Salute to America occurs on Independence Day in Washington, D.C., in addition to other events. This was the MASSIVE celebration with Military Aircraft seen on TV. And once again, already in a Military Occupancy and Continuity of Operations Plan aka Continuity of Government.

July 8, 2020

Holds a bilateral meeting and joint press conference with Mexican president Andrés Manuel López Obrador at the White House to discuss the new United States–Mexico–Canada Agreement.

July 14, 2020: The President's Executive Order on Hong Kong Normalization

Executive Order 13936:
https://www.federalregister.gov/documents/2020/07/17/2020-15646/the-presidents-executive-order-on-hong-kong-normalization

This is another National Emergency to add to the list of National Emergencies President Trump declared from December 2017 to March 2020 (10), this makes number 11.

July 31, 2020

Says he plans to use presidential authority to terminate the Chinese social media platform TikTok from operating in the U.S.

August 6, 2020: Addressing the Threat Posed by TikTok, and Taking Additional Steps To Address the National Emergency With Respect to the Information and Communications Technology and Services Supply Chain

Executive Order 13942:
https://www.federalregister.gov/documents/2020/08/11/2020-17699/addressing-the-threat-posed-by-tiktok-and-taking-additional-steps-to-address-the-national-emergency

This also ties into Section 230 in which CIC Trump addressed on December 15, 2022, in his Digital Bill of Rights speech.

"Biden" 'revoked' this Executive Order in 2022 which was the Military Occupancy and COG exposing his allegiance to the Communist Party of China. Congress under the COG passed the Bill in December 2022 to ban TikTok from Government Devices. The App 'WeChat' was also issued an Executive Order the same day, though the App is not as popular as TikTok, it was not just TikTok.

August 6, 2020: Combating Public Health Emergencies and Strengthening National Security by Ensuring Essential Medicines, Medical Countermeasures, and Critical Inputs Are Made in the United States

Executive Order 13944:
https://www.federalregister.gov/documents/2020/08/14/2020-18012/combating-public-health-emergencies-and-strengthening-national-security-by-ensuring-essential

Remember: "America First!" Americans should want to promote American Products first especially medicinal.

First paragraph:

"*The United States must protect our citizens, critical infrastructure, military forces, and economy against outbreaks of emerging infectious diseases and chemical, biological, radiological, and nuclear (CBRN) threats.*"

Another key paragraph:

*(d) combat the **trafficking of counterfeit** Essential Medicines, Medical Countermeasures, and Critical Inputs over e-commerce platforms and from third-party online sellers involved in the government procurement process.*

These coincide with the Federal Continuity Directives and 2017 National Security Strategy which clearly outline the "pandemic" to a very descriptive tee of what everyone witnessed in 2020… back in 2017.

This is also after the 2019 Influenza Vaccine Executive Orders which clearly defined the vaccines President Trump endorsed and supported were not the Pfizer, Johnson & Johnson, and Moderna vaccines that broke the law.

August 8, 2020: Fighting the Spread of COVID-19 by Providing Assistance to Renters and Homeowners

Executive Order 13945:
https://www.federalregister.gov/documents/2020/08/14/2020-18015/fighting-the-spread-of-covid-19-by-providing-assistance-to-renters-and-homeowners

Remember all the people who received "bailouts"? Remember what many of those people did with their bailout? Yeahhhhhhhhhhhhh.

Think how many of those dislike, whine, fuss, cuss, gripe, ridicule, mock, complain, moan, groan, and hate CIC Trump, but dang sure wanted that "bailout" money. Many said it was 'owed' to them. Think of all the people who feel like America, a country, owes them money. How did we get here Americans? How did we reach this mindset and attitude?

August 13, 2020

Brokers a peace agreement between United Arab Emirates and Israel, the first agreement between Israel and an Arab-Muslim nation.

August 20, 2020

Holds a bilateral meeting with Iraqi prime minister Mustafa Al-Kadhimi at the White House.

August 28, 2020: **Military Justice Act 2016**

MJA2016:
https://crsreports.congress.gov/product/pdf/R/R46503

The Military Justice Act was written by the United States Supreme Court in 2016 but was not signed into law until the 2017 National Defense Authorization Act. It is designed to improve the military justice system by enhancing efficiency and effectiveness while sustaining good order and discipline.

The major key behind this Act is the timeline of it. The United States Supreme Court wrote this in 2016, before the Federal Government went into Continuity of Government therefore leaving the other and only power in the United States in control, the United States Military.

Hence why the Supreme Court clarified in this act military justice, a system of justice separates from civilian courts, in 2016, before the Federal Continuity Directive 1 was issued January 17, 2017.

Let's look at some key lines in the MJA 2016:

The Supreme Court has called military justice a system of justice separate from jurisprudence in the civilian courts. Members of the Armed Forces are subject to rules, orders, proceedings, and consequences different from the rights and obligations of their civilian counterparts. Accordingly, it might be said that discipline is as important as liberty interests in the military justice system. The Constitution specifically exempts military members accused of a crime from the Fifth Amendment right to a grand jury indictment, from which the Supreme Court has inferred there is no right to a civil jury in courts-martial. However, in part because of the different standards provided in courts-martial, their jurisdiction is limited to those persons and offenses the military has a legitimate interest in regulating.

The Constitution, to provide for the common defense, gives Congress the power to raise, support, and regulate the Armed Forces, but makes the President Commander-in-Chief of the Armed Forces. Article III, which governs the federal judiciary, does not give it any explicit role in the military, and the Supreme Court has taken the view that Congress's power "To make Rules for the Government and Regulation of the land and naval Forces" is entirely separate from Article III. Therefore, courts-martial are not Article III courts and are not subject to the rules that apply in federal courts.

The timing of this both written, passed, and applied couldn't be any more precise, strategic, and lethal for all reasons morally, judicially, and the timeline of the Occupancy and Continuity of Government.

I'll explain in the summarization at the end of the Long Blueprint.

September 2, 2020

Urges North Carolina voters to cast two votes in the upcoming presidential election, once by mail and then again in person, to test his unsubstantiated claims that mail-in voting is prone to fraud.

Got to love CIC Trump! He's the ULTIMATE TROLL! There's only one way to test 'fair and reciprocal'… that's the put s statement out before it and what if those paying attention would have answered the call?

The Deep State and misinformed would have jumped all over that and been accusing him of 'cheating', but it would have been in writing as proof to prove. Reverse psychology.

September 4, 2020

Holds a trilateral meeting with Serbian president Aleksandar Vučić and Kosovan prime minister Avdullah Hoti at the White House.

September 15, 2020: **Abraham Accords**

The Abraham Accords is the Treaty of Peace, Diplomatic Relations and Full Normalization Between the United Arab Emirates and the State of Israel.

The Archived Agreement:

The Government of the United Arab Emirates and the Government of the State of Israel (hereinafter, the "Parties")

Aspiring to realize the vision of a Middle East region that is stable, peaceful and prosperous, for the benefit of all States and peoples in the region;

Desiring to establish peace, diplomatic and friendly relations, co-operation and full normalization of ties between them and their peoples, in accordance with this Treaty, and to chart together a new path to unlock the vast potential of their countries and of the region;

Reaffirming the "Joint Statement of the United States, the State of Israel, and the United Arab Emirates" (the "Abraham Accords"), dated 13 August 2020;

Believing that the further development of friendly relations meets the interests of lasting peace in the Middle East and that challenges can only be effectively addressed by cooperation and not by conflict;

Determined to ensure lasting peace, stability, security and prosperity for both their States and to develop and enhance their dynamic and innovative economies;

Reaffirming their shared commitment to normalize relations and promote stability through diplomatic engagement, increased economic cooperation and other close coordination;

Reaffirming also their shared belief that the establishment of peace and full normalization between them can help transform the Middle East by spurring economic growth, enhancing technological innovation and forging closer people-to-people relations;

Recognizing that the Arab and Jewish peoples are descendants of a common ancestor, Abraham, and *inspired*, in that spirit, to foster in the Middle East a reality in which Muslims, Jews, Christians and peoples of all faiths, denominations, beliefs and nationalities live in, and are committed to, a spirit of coexistence, mutual understanding and mutual respect;

Recalling the reception held on January 28, 2020, at which President Trump presented his Vision for Peace, and *committing* to continuing their efforts to achieve a just, comprehensive, realistic and enduring solution to the Israeli-Palestinian conflict;

Recalling the Treaties of Peace between the State of Israel and the Arab Republic of Egypt and between the State of Israel and the Hashemite Kingdom of Jordan, and committed to working together to realize a negotiated solution to the Israeli-Palestinian conflict that meets the legitimate needs and aspirations of both peoples, and to advance comprehensive Middle East peace, stability and prosperity;

Emphasizing the belief that the normalization of Israeli and Emirati relations is in the interest of both peoples and contributes to the cause of peace in the Middle East and the world;

Expressing deep appreciation to the United States for its profound contribution to this historic achievement;

Have agreed as follows:

- Establishment of Peace, Diplomatic Relations and Normalization: Peace, diplomatic relations and full normalization of bilateral ties are hereby established between the United Arab Emirates and the State of Israel.

- General Principles: The Parties shall be guided in their relations by the provisions of the Charter of the United Nations and the principles of international law governing relations among States. In particular, they shall recognize and respect each other's sovereignty and right to live in peace and security, develop friendly relations of cooperation between them and their peoples, and settle all disputes between them by peaceful means.

- Establishment of Embassies: The Parties shall exchange resident ambassadors as soon as practicable after the signing of this Treaty, and shall conduct diplomatic and consular relations in accordance with the applicable rules of international law.

- Peace and Stability: The Parties shall attach profound importance to mutual understanding, cooperation and coordination between them in the spheres of peace and stability, as a fundamental pillar of their relations and as a means for enhancing those spheres in the Middle East as a whole. They undertake to take the necessary steps to prevent any terrorist or hostile activities against each other on or from their respective territories, as well as deny any support for such activities abroad or allowing such support on or from their respective territories. Recognizing the new era of peace and friendly relations between them, as well as the centrality of stability to the well-being of their respective peoples and of the region, the Parties undertake to consider and discuss these matters regularly, and to conclude detailed agreements and arrangements on coordination and cooperation.

- Cooperation and Agreements in Other Spheres: As an integral part of their commitment to peace, prosperity, diplomatic and friendly relations, cooperation and full normalization, the Parties shall work to advance the cause of peace, stability and prosperity throughout the Middle East, and to unlock the great potential of their countries and of the region. For such purposes, the Parties shall conclude bilateral agreements in the following spheres at the earliest practicable date, as well as in other spheres of mutual interest as may be agreed:- Finance and Investment- Civil Aviation- Visas and Consular Services- Innovation, Trade and Economic Relations

- – Healthcare
  – Science, Technology and Peaceful Uses of Outer-Space
  – Tourism, Culture and Sport
  – Energy
  – Environment
  – Education

– Maritime Arrangements
– Telecommunications and Post
– Agriculture and Food Security
– Water
– Legal Cooperation

- Any such agreements concluded before the entry into force of this Treaty shall enter into effect with the entry into force of this Treaty unless otherwise stipulated therein. Agreed principles for cooperation in specific spheres are annexed to this Treaty and form an integral part thereof.

- Mutual Understanding and Co-existence: The Parties undertake to foster mutual understanding, respect, co-existence and a culture of peace between their societies in the spirit of their common ancestor, Abraham, and the new era of peace and friendly relations ushered in by this Treaty, including by cultivating people-to-people programs, interfaith dialogue and cultural, academic, youth, scientific, and other exchanges between their peoples. They shall conclude and implement the necessary visa and consular services agreements and arrangements so as to facilitate efficient and secure travel for their respective nationals to the territory of each other. The Parties shall work together to counter extremism, which promotes hatred and division, and terrorism and its justifications, including by preventing radicalization and recruitment and by combating incitement and discrimination. They shall work towards establishing a High-Level Joint Forum for Peace and Co-Existence dedicated to advancing these goals.

- Strategic Agenda for the Middle East: Further to the Abraham Accords, the Parties stand ready to join with the United States to develop and launch a "Strategic Agenda for the Middle East" in order to expand regional diplomatic, trade, stability and other cooperation. They are committed to work together, and with the United States and others, as appropriate, in order to advance the cause of peace, stability and prosperity in the relations between them and for the Middle East as a whole, including by seeking to advance regional security and stability; pursue regional economic opportunities; promote a culture of peace across the region; and consider joint aid and development programs.

- Other Rights and Obligations: This Treaty does not affect and shall not be interpreted as affecting, in any way, the rights and obligations of the Parties under the Charter of the United Nations. The Parties shall take all necessary measures for the application in their bilateral relations of the provisions of the multilateral conventions of which they are both parties, including the submission of appropriate notification to the depositaries of such conventions.

- Respect for Obligations: The Parties undertake to fulfill in good faith their obligations under this Treaty, without regard to action or inaction of any other party and independently of any instrument inconsistent with this Treaty. For the purposes of this paragraph each Party represents to the other that in its opinion and interpretation there is no inconsistency between their existing treaty obligations and this Treaty. The Parties undertake not to enter into any obligation in conflict with this Treaty. Subject to Article 103 of the Charter of the United Nations, in the event of a conflict between the obligations of the Parties under the present Treaty and any of their other obligations, the obligations under this Treaty shall be binding and implemented. The Parties further undertake to adopt any legislation or other internal legal procedure necessary in order to implement this Treaty, and to repeal any national legislation or official publications inconsistent with this Treaty.

- Ratification and Entry into Force: This Treaty shall be ratified by both Parties as soon as practicable in conformity with their respective national procedures and will enter into force following the exchange of instruments of ratification.

- Settlement of Disputes: Disputes arising out of the application or interpretation of this Treaty shall be resolved by negotiation. Any such dispute which cannot be settled by negotiation may be referred to conciliation or arbitration subject to the agreement of the Parties.

- Registration: This Treaty shall be transmitted to the Secretary-General of the United Nations for registration in accordance with the provisions of Article 102 of the Charter of the United Nations.

Department of State:
https://www.state.gov/the-abraham-accords/

Abraham Accords:
https://trumpwhitehouse.archives.gov/briefings-statements/abraham-accords-peace-agreement-treaty-of-peace-diplomatic-relations-and-full-normalization-between-the-united-arab-emirates-and-the-state-of-israel/

September 21, 2020: Blocking Property of Certain Persons With Respect to the Conventional Arms Activities of Iran

Executive Order 13949:
https://www.federalregister.gov/documents/2020/09/23/2020-21160/blocking-property-of-certain-persons-with-respect-to-the-conventional-arms-activities-of-iran

More actions against Iran. Blocking Properties. Just a couple key sections:

(d) The prohibitions in subsection (a) of this section apply except to the extent provided by statutes, or in regulations, orders, directives, or licenses that may be issued pursuant to this order, and notwithstanding any contract entered into or any license or permit granted before the date of this order.

(e) The prohibitions in subsection (a) of this section do not apply to property and interests in property of the Government of Iran that were blocked pursuant to Executive Order 12170 of November 14, 1979 (Blocking Iranian Government Property), and thereafter made subject to the transfer directives set forth in Executive Order 12281 of January 19, 1981 (Direction to Transfer Certain Iranian Government Assets), and implementing regulations thereunder.

September 23, 2020

Holds a news conference in the James S. Brady Press Briefing Room. In response to a question about if he would commit to a peaceful transfer of power he says, "Well, we'll have to see what happens. You know that. I've been complaining very strongly about the ballots. And the ballots are a disaster,"

One, why did the "Biden" "Administration" build a replica of the James S. Brady Press Room?

Two, why are they asking CIC Trump in September, two months before election, if he would commit to a peaceful transfer of power, long before any kind of results?

Keep in mind, Executive Order 13848, was in place 2 years and 5 days at this point.

September 24, 2020: An America-First Healthcare Plan

Executive Order 13951:
https://www.federalregister.gov/documents/2020/10/01/2020-21914/an-america-first-healthcare-plan

This is one of the most definitive Healthcare revelations one can read. No one can walk away from reading this saying anything negative about CIC Donald John Trump and the Military who's been a part of this Biblical, Historical, Monumental Covert Special Operation for quite a while.

The intro to this… very keen on mentioning dates and exposing past Presidents on hopium and promises never delivered.

Section 1. *Purpose.* Since January 20, 2017, my Administration has been committed to the goal of bringing great healthcare to the American people and putting patients first. To that end, my Administration has taken monumental steps to improve the efficiency and quality of healthcare in the United States.

(a)   My Administration has been committed to restoring choice and control to the American patient. On December 22, 2017, I signed into law the repeal of the burdensome individual-mandate penalty, liberating millions of low-income Americans from a tax that penalized them for not purchasing health-insurance coverage they did not want or could not afford. (Read Full Order online)

October 3, 2020: Saving Lives Through Increased Support for Mental- and Behavioral-Health Needs

Executive Order 13954:
https://www.federalregister.gov/documents/2020/10/08/2020-22510/saving-lives-through-increased-support-for-mental--and-behavioral-health-needs

It was CIC Donald John Trump who gives and cared about the Military and Veterans. There's a huge difference in someone who's child serves to utilize that as a tool for candidacy and office such as people like Joe Biden and Ron DeSantis etc.

"Biden" is very well known in his past for *Plagiarism*. This is a simple yet key strategy by the Military Generals to have "Biden" claim all of CIC Trump's successes as his. This is what happens when people stop following current events and simply reading.

October 7, 2020

Launching of Quantum.gov

October 23, 2020

Brokers a peace agreement between Sudan and Israel, the third agreement between Israel and an Arab-Muslim nation in less than three months.

November 2, 2020: **Establishing the President's Advisory 1776 Commission**

Executive Order 13958:
https://www.federalregister.gov/documents/2020/11/05/2020-24793/establishing-the-presidents-advisory-1776-commission

This is another Biblical and Monumental moment in our Nation's history. However, the only unfortunate part of it is, our Nation had to come to reestablish our Foundation just a short 244 years to this date.

May we NEVER reach this place again. This also became the 1776 Report published in January 2021… imagine that. January 2021… and to think that it died right there?

I don't think so…………! CIC Trump has said MULTIPLE times, we're going to stop funding schools and colleges who do not teach our Foundation and History.

Best BELIEVE everything that man says and has said has come to fruition… What makes you think this won't? And WHY would anyone not want our history taught?

November 3, 2020: 2020 Presidential Election

4-Star General Nakasone tweets:

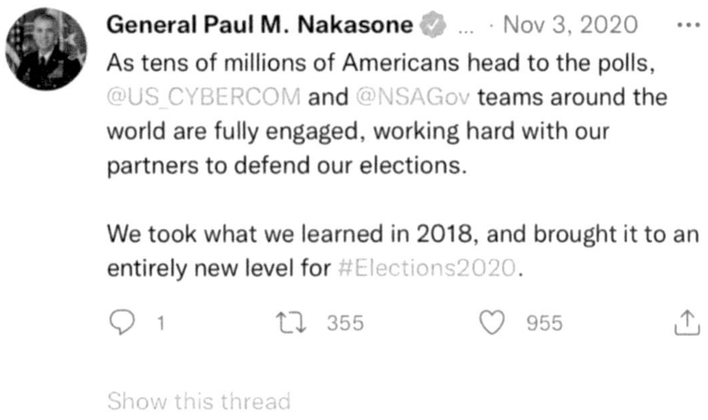
General Paul M. Nakasone
· Nov 3, 2020
As tens of millions of Americans head to the polls, @US_CYBERCOM and @NSAGov teams around the world are fully engaged, working hard with our partners to defend our elections.
We took what we learned in 2018, and brought it to an entirely new level for #Elections2020.
1
355
955
Show this thread

National Security Agency and ***United States Cyber Command*** with joint partners all over the world…

Now why would the greatest Nation of all with the greatest Military (Military Intelligence and Technology) need partners all over the world watching our Election? Perhaps Support of Partner Forces in 50 U.S.C Section 1550?

Maybe perhaps they weren't just watching our Election? Perhaps the Deep State who aren't just in the United States… We were watching along with our Support Partners whose Elections were also 'stolen'?

Executive Order 13848 set the trap for the United States… It was other Military and Federal Laws that set the traps to help our partners.

Also note: Executive Order 13912 from March 2020 and Section 1550 of the War Powers Resolution Act, the word ***PARTNERS***.

November 9, 2020: Christopher Miller to Secretary of Defense

CIC Trump fires SECDEF Mark Esper and appoints Chris Miller, 6 days after he "lost" the Election… makes a lot of sense, doesn't it?

The way it makes PERFECT sense is the Military Occupancy and Federal Continuity Directives that CLEARLY paint a perfect picture of a Continuity of Government which means the Military's operating via an Occupancy.

November 12, 2020: Addressing the Threat From Securities Investments That Finance Communist Chinese Military Companies

Executive Order 13959:
https://www.federalregister.gov/documents/2020/11/17/2020-25459/addressing-the-threat-from-securities-investments-that-finance-communist-chinese-military-companies

This added to the National Emergencies CIC Trump declared.

I, DONALD J. TRUMP, President of the United States of America, find that the People's Republic of China (PRC) is increasingly exploiting United States capital to resource and to enable the development and modernization of its military, intelligence, and other security apparatuses, which continues to allow the PRC to directly threaten the United States homeland and United States forces overseas, including by developing and deploying weapons of mass destruction, advanced conventional weapons, and malicious cyber-enabled actions against the United States and its people.

I therefore further find that the PRC's military-industrial complex, by directly supporting the efforts of the PRC's military, intelligence, and other security apparatuses, constitutes an unusual and extraordinary threat, which has its source in substantial part outside the United States, to the national security, foreign policy, and economy of the United States. To protect the United States homeland and the American people, I hereby declare a national emergency with respect to this threat.

(i) beginning 9:30 a.m. eastern standard time on January 11, 2021, any transaction in publicly traded securities, or any securities that are derivative of, or are designed to provide investment exposure to such securities, of any

Communist Chinese military company as defined in section 4(a)(i) of this order, by any United States person; and… (Read full order online)

This Executive Order was epic and so very specific… effective immediately after January 11, 2021, 9:30 EST.

This calls out the People's Republic of China and anyone funding the Chinese communist military.

For some unknown reason nobody saw the 2,000 plus Presidents and CEOs stepping down or being removed starting immediately after this date.

For some unknown reason nobody saw multiple Congressmen and women not re-running for positions they were locks in – in the old swamp system.

For some unknown reason nobody remembered Jeff Bezos suddenly stepping down from Amazon for "philanthropy" reasons.

For some unknown reason nobody remembered Warren Buffett leaving the Bill Gates Foundation and donated HALF his fortune, June 23, 2021.

For some unknown reason nobody remembered Bill Gates and his wife announcing divorce.

For some unknown reason nobody remembered Mark Zuckerburg dumping $25 million in stocks every single day.

For some unknown reason nobody remembered GameStop and many companies in short squeezes causing major financial consequences for certain hedge funds and large losses for short sellers.

This is also one of those Executive Orders extended via "Biden" which was the COG and Military Occupancy as "Biden" was not real.

This Executive Order amongst many others extended would have not benefited "Biden" or Joe Biden in ANY capacity in a normal situation. See 'why' origin matters?

December 3, 2020: Promoting the Use of Trustworthy Artificial Intelligence in the Federal Government

Executive Order 13960:
https://www.federalregister.gov/documents/2020/12/08/2020-27065/promoting-the-use-of-trustworthy-artificial-intelligence-in-the-federal-government

Legislation and Executive Orders:
https://www.ai.gov/legislation-and-executive-orders/

National Institute of Standards and Technology:
https://www.nist.gov/artificial-intelligence/EO13960

Artificial Intelligence is where we are in technology. The National AI Initiative provides an overarching framework to strengthen and coordinate AI research, development, demonstration, and education activities across all U.S. Departments and Agencies, in cooperation with academia, industry, non-profits, and civil society organizations.

December 7, 2020: Governance and Integration of Federal Mission Resilience

Executive Order 13961:
https://www.federalregister.gov/documents/2020/12/10/2020-27353/governance-and-integration-of-federal-mission-resilience

Amazing how the Continuity of Government was right in front of everyone, not only in the Federal Continuity Directives, but also placed in this Federal Resilience Act as you'll read the terms below:

> **Presidential Policy Directive-40 (PPD-40)**
> **National Essential Functions (NEFs)**

All in consistency with the Federal Continuity Directives issued January 17 and June 13, 2017.

December 7, 2020: State of Texas versus Commonwealth of Pennsylvania, State of Georgia, State of Michigan and State of Wisconsin

United States Supreme Court docket:
https://www.supremecourt.gov/docketpdf/22/22o155/163234/20201209155327055_no.%2022o155%20original%20motion%20to%20intervene.pdf

CIC Trump filed through the United States Supreme Court via the State of Texas (whom he was not a resident of - there was your Optic) versus the Commonwealth of Pennsylvania, state of Georgia, state of Michigan, and state of Wisconsin.

President Trump as President had to do everything by the Law in more than one way.

One, we are a Nation of Laws and Orders… in MULTIPLE years past, the Laws and Orders read perfectly on paper, but MULTIPLE lawmakers, legislators, and officials did not apply or uphold those, many blatantly breaking those.

Many of those violated Laws and Orders simply because Americans stopped holding them accountable, mainly because the majority of Americans stopped caring and understanding how the Government and Congress works.

Two, President Trump and the Military Occupancy chose this way as a way to expose the Federal Corporation and the Deep State to the public as this exposed Governors, Attorney Generals, Secretary of States, Judges and Lawyers for blatantly breaking and not upholding Federal Laws in place.

December 8, 2020: Ensuring Access to United States Government COVID-19 Vaccines

Executive Order 13962:
https://www.federalregister.gov/documents/2020/12/11/2020-27455/ensuring-access-to-united-states-government-covid-19-vaccines

This coincides with the 2019 Influenza Vaccine Executive Orders, President Trump's Press Conference on March 30, 2020, and the Executive Order about American Medicines.

Nowhere does it mention the CDC as the 2019 Executive Order. The CDC, NIH, and FDA plus Johnson and Johnson, Moderna, and Pfizer, all broke Laws put into place.

President Trump's Executive Orders (Laws) plus Operation Warp Speed were under Military Occupancy and Continuity of Government and he made it loud and clear what vaccines were safe in the March 30, 2020, speech.

How come Americans whined, griped, cussed, fussed, and then turned those into hate saying and asking, "how come President Trump endorsed the jab?" How come those same Americans didn't listen to any of his speeches or read any of his Laws, Orders, and Press Conferences?

December 10, 2020

Brokers a normalization agreement between Morocco and Israel, the fourth agreement between Israel and an Arab nation since August. The White House said the U.S. would recognize Morocco's claim over Western Sahara as part of the deal.

December 12, 2020: Army versus Navy Football Game

Did President Trump look like a "defeated" President on that day? The same game where the Cadets were in unison jumping up and down yelling "USA! USA! USA!" when he walked out?

Might want to watch again, it's a day that will go down in History since this was post November 3, 2020, the Election Day.

President Donald J. Trump Attends the 2020 Army Navy Game
117K views 2y ago ...more

President Donald J. Trump Attends the 2020 Army Navy Game
117K views 2y ago ...more
Trump White House Archived 72.7K   Subscribe

Have you ever seen "Joe Biden" at the Army-Navy game? Did you know he was a standout football player in high school?

January 5, 2021: Addressing the Threat Posed by Applications and Other Software Developed or Controlled by Chinese Companies

Executive Order 13971:
https://www.federalregister.gov/documents/2021/01/08/2021-00305/addressing-the-threat-posed-by-applications-and-other-software-developed-or-controlled-by-chinese

Signed the day before January 6, 2021. Because J6 was all planned and the Executive Order 13848 from September 12, 2018, held all those answers two years before.

One of the key lines in this Executive Order:

This data collection threatens to provide the Government of the People's Republic of China (PRC) and the Chinese Communist Party (CCP) with access to Americans' personal and proprietary information—which would permit China to track the locations of Federal employees and contractors, and build dossiers of personal information.

January 6, 2021: The "Insurrection"

With the signing of Executive Order 13848, September 12, 2018, two months before any Election under CIC Trump… the key line in that EO saying:

*'Although no foreign power has altered the outcome <u>or</u> **vote tabulation** in any United States election…'*

The first portion means ALL votes from we the people… hence it doesn't say domestic, and outcome means overall…

'Vote Tabulation' is the key for this section… because after 2 objections in the Arizona count, ironically and "conveniently" the "Insurrection" took place.

And… Just so "conveniently" (although all part of the dismantling of the Deep State)… The most secure place on the planet… 2,000-pound rotunda doors which open from the inside out, were 'compromised' by "Trump Supporters" from the outside in… LOL

Here's what was supposed to happen after the two Objections:

(B) Requirements for objections or questions.-

   (i) Objections.- No objection or other question arising in the matter shall be in order unless the objection or question-
   (I) is made in writing;
   (II) is signed by at least one-fifth of the Senators duly chosen and sworn and one-fifth of the Members of the House of Representatives duly chosen and sworn; and
   (III) in the case of an objection, states clearly and concisely, without argument, one of the grounds listed under clause (ii).

   (ii) Grounds for objections.-The only grounds for objections shall be as follows:
   (I) The electors of the State were not lawfully certified under a certificate of ascertainment of appointment of electors according to section 5(a)(1).
   (II) The vote of one or more electors has not been regularly given.

(C) Consideration of objections and questions.-

   (i) In general.-When all objections so made to any vote or paper from a State, or other question arising in the matter, shall have been received and read, the Senate shall thereupon withdraw, and such objections and questions shall be submitted to the Senate for its decision; and the Speaker of the House of Representatives shall, in like manner, submit such objections and questions to the House of Representatives for its decision.

   (ii) DETERMINATION.-No objection or any other question arising in the matter may be sustained unless such objection or question is sustained by separate concurring votes of each House.

(D) RECONVENING.-When the two Houses have voted, they shall immediately again meet, and the presiding officer shall then announce the decision of the questions submitted. No vote or paper from any other State shall be acted upon until the objections previously made to any vote or paper from any State, and other questions arising in the matter, shall have been finally disposed of.

Also reads:

"…but in case there shall arise the question which of two or more of such State authorities determining what electors have been appointed, as mentioned in section 5 of this title, is the lawful tribunal of such State, the votes regularly given of those electors, and those only, of such State shall be counted whose title as electors the two Houses, acting separately, shall concurrently decide is supported by the decision of such State so authorized by its law; and in such case of more than one return or paper purporting to be a return from a State, if there shall have been no such determination of the question in the State aforesaid, then those votes, and those only, shall be counted which the two Houses shall concurrently decide were cast by lawful electors appointed in accordance with the laws of the State, unless the two Houses, acting separately, shall concurrently decide such votes not to be the lawful votes of the legally appointed electors of such State. But if the two Houses shall disagree in respect of the counting of such votes, then, and in that case, the votes of the electors whose appointment shall have been certified by the executive of the State, under the seal thereof, shall be counted. When the two Houses have voted, they shall immediately again meet, and the presiding officer shall then announce the decision of the questions submitted. No votes or papers from any other State shall be acted upon until the objections previously made to the votes or papers from any State shall have been finally disposed of."

That would be two portions of: **3 United States Code 15**.

3 US Code 15 from the House dot Gov:
https://uscode.house.gov/view.xhtml?req=granuleid:USC-prelim-title3-section15&num=0&edition=prelim

3 US Code 15:
https://www.govinfo.gov/content/pkg/USCODE-2014-title3/pdf/USCODE-2014-title3-chap1-sec15.pdf

Instead, Pelosi and the gang (Remember: Military Occupancy / COOP / all planned) shuffle back in quickly, without protocol and measures of addressing the Objections, and begin counting the 47 remaining states… all of which broke:

18 US Code §2381:
https://uscode.house.gov/view.xhtml?path=/prelim@title18/part1/chapter115&edition=prelim

§2381. Treason
Whoever, owing allegiance to the United States, levies war against them or adheres to their enemies, giving them aid and comfort within the United States or elsewhere, is guilty of treason and shall suffer death, or shall be imprisoned not less than five years and fined under this title but not less than $10,000; and shall be incapable of holding any office under the United States. (June 25, 1948, ch. 645, 62 Stat. 807; Pub. L. 103–322, title XXXIII, §330016(2)(J), Sept. 13, 1994, 108 Stat. 2148.)

18 US Code §2384:
https://uscode.house.gov/view.xhtml?req=granuleid:USC-1999-title18-section2384&num=0&edition=1999#:~:text=Conspiracy%20to%20commit%20offense%20or,5%2C%20Government%20Organization%20and%20Employees.

§2384. Seditious conspiracy

If two or more persons in any State or Territory, or in any place subject to the jurisdiction of the United States, conspire to overthrow, put down, or to destroy by force the Government of the United States, or to levy war against them, or to oppose by force the authority thereof, or by force to prevent, hinder, or delay the execution of any law of the United States, or by force to seize, take, or possess any property of the United States contrary to the authority thereof, they shall each be fined under this title or imprisoned not more than twenty years, or both. (June 25, 1948, ch. 645, 62 Stat. 808; July 24, 1956, ch. 678, §1, 70 Stat. 623; Pub. L. 103–322, title XXXIII, §330016(1)(N), Sept. 13, 1994, 108 Stat. 2148.)

18 US Code §2385:
https://uscode.house.gov/view.xhtml?path=/prelim@title18/part1/chapter115&edition=prelim#:~:text=%C2%A72385.,Advocating%20overthrow%20of%20Government&text=the%20purposes%20thereof%E2%80%94-,Shall%20be%20fined%20under%20this%20title%20or%20imprisoned%20not%20more,years%20next%20following%20his%20conviction.

§2385. Advocating overthrow of Government

Whoever knowingly or willfully advocates, abets, advises, or teaches the duty, necessity, desirability, or propriety of overthrowing or destroying the government of the United States or the government of any State, Territory, District or Possession thereof, or the government of any political subdivision therein, by force or violence, or by the assassination of any officer of any such government; or

Whoever, with intent to cause the overthrow or destruction of any such government, prints, publishes, edits, issues, circulates, sells, distributes, or publicly displays any written or printed matter advocating, advising, or teaching the duty, necessity, desirability, or propriety of overthrowing or destroying any government in the United States by force or violence, or attempts to do so; or

Whoever organizes or helps or attempts to organize any society, group, or assembly of persons who teach, advocate, or encourage the overthrow or destruction of any such government by force or violence; or becomes or is a member of, or affiliates with, any such society, group, or assembly of persons, knowing the purposes thereof—

Shall be fined under this title or imprisoned not more than twenty years, or both, and shall be ineligible for employment by the United States or any department or agency thereof, for the five years next following his conviction.

If two or more persons conspire to commit any offense named in this section, each shall be fined under this title or imprisoned not more than twenty years, or both, and shall be ineligible for employment by the United States or any department or agency thereof, for the five years next following his conviction.

As used in this section, the terms "organizes" and "organize", with respect to any society, group, or assembly of persons, include the recruiting of new members, the forming of new units, and the regrouping or expansion of existing clubs, classes, and other units of such society, group, or assembly of persons. (June 25, 1948, ch. 645, 62 Stat. 808; July 24, 1956, ch. 678, §2, 70 Stat. 623; Pub. L. 87–486, June 19, 1962, 76 Stat. 103; Pub. L. 103–322, title XXXIII, §330016(1)(N), Sept. 13, 1994, 108 Stat. 2148.)

52 US Code §20511:
https://uscode.house.gov/view.xhtml?req=(title:52%20section:20511%20edition:prelim)

§20511. Criminal penalties

A person, including an election official, who in any election for Federal office-

(1) knowingly and willfully intimidates, threatens, or coerces, or attempts to intimidate, threaten, or coerce, any person for-
    (A) registering to vote, or voting, or attempting to register or vote;
    (B) urging or aiding any person to register to vote, to vote, or to attempt to register or vote; or
    (C) exercising any right under this chapter; or

(2) knowingly and willfully deprives, defrauds, or attempts to deprive or defraud the residents of a State of a fair and impartially conducted election process, by-

> (A) the procurement or submission of voter registration applications that are known by the person to be materially false, fictitious, or fraudulent under the laws of the State in which the election is held; or

> (B) the procurement, casting, or tabulation of ballots that are known by the person to be materially false, fictitious, or fraudulent under the laws of the State in which the election is held, shall be fined in accordance with title 18 (which fines shall be paid into the general fund of the Treasury, miscellaneous receipts (pursuant to section 3302 of title 31), notwithstanding any other law), or imprisoned not more than 5 years, or both. (Pub. L. 103–31, §12, May 20, 1993, 107 Stat. 88 .)

This was all very well strategically planned via the United States Military Generals and the Commander-in-Chief long before 2016. Every intricate detail from Laws, Orders, Statutes, Acts, Codes, Military Regulations, Optics and Comms. That's why the line in Executive Order 13848 is so very important… that very line canceled out ALL votes from the people's perspectives, as it did not say domestic, which applied to the Dominion System and those who added or deleted votes, and it canceled out the narrative of the "Insurrection" on January 6, 2021, as it's outlined in our Statutes and Codes what was to happen via protocol with Objections.

According to the Declaration of Independence, there is NO SUCH THING as an Insurrection as it clearly states:

> *That to secure these rights, Governments are instituted among Men, deriving their just powers from the consent of the governed, --That whenever any Form of Government becomes destructive of these ends, it is the Right of the People to alter or to abolish it, and to institute new Government, laying its foundation on such principles and organizing its powers in such form, as to them shall seem most likely to effect their Safety and Happiness.*

Look at this key line: *"it is the Right of the People to alter or to abolish it."*

> *But when a long train of abuses and usurpations, pursuing invariably the same Object evinces a design to reduce them under absolute Despotism, it is their right, it is their duty, to throw off such Government, and to provide new Guards for their future security.*

Look at this key line: *"to throw off such Government."* It pays to know your Foundation, History, Laws, and Orders.

January 6, 2021: The first components of the National Guard move into D.C.
The Mainstream Media told you from day one who is and was in charge without saying: *"Donald John Trump is your Commander-in-Chief."*

There's only ONE person who can Federalize the National Guard to Active-Duty and there's only ONE person who the National Guard of the District of Columbia DIRECTLY answers to period…

10 United States Code §12302:

Ready Reserve

(a) In time of national emergency declared by the President after January 1, 1953, or when otherwise authorized by law, an authority designated by the Secretary concerned may, without the consent of the persons concerned, order any unit, and any member not assigned to a unit organized to serve as a unit, in the Ready Reserve under the jurisdiction of that Secretary to active duty for not more than 24 consecutive months.

(b) To achieve fair treatment as between members in the Ready Reserve who are being considered for recall to duty without their consent, consideration shall be given to-

(1) the length and nature of previous service, to assure such sharing of exposure to hazards as the national security and military requirements will reasonably allow;
(2) family responsibilities; and
(3) employment necessary to maintain the national health, safety, or interest.

The **Secretary of Defense** shall prescribe such policies and procedures as he considers necessary to carry out this subsection.

(c) Not more than 1,000,000 members of the Ready Reserve may be on active duty, without their consent, under this section at any one time.

10 United States Code §12302:
https://uscode.house.gov/view.xhtml?req=granuleid:USC-prelim-title10-section12302&num=0&edition=prelim#:~:text=13223.-,Ordering%20the%20Ready%20Reserve%20of%20the%20Armed%20Forces%20To%20Active,the%20Secretary%20of%20Homeland%20Security

10 United States Code §12304: Selected Reserve and certain Individual Ready Reserve members; order to active duty other than during war or national emergency

(a) AUTHORITY.-Notwithstanding the provisions of section 12302(a) or any other provision of law, when the **President** determines that it is necessary to augment the active forces for any named operational mission or that it is necessary to provide assistance referred to in subsection (b), he may authorize the Secretary of Defense and the Secretary of Homeland Security with respect to the Coast Guard when it is not operating as a service in the Navy, without the consent of the members concerned, to order any unit, and any member not assigned to a unit organized to serve as a unit of the Selected Reserve (as defined in section 10143(a) of this title), or any member in the Individual Ready Reserve mobilization category and designated as essential under regulations prescribed by the Secretary concerned, under their respective jurisdictions, to active duty for not more than 365 consecutive days.

(b) SUPPORT FOR RESPONSES TO **CERTAIN EMERGENCIES**.-The authority under subsection (a) includes authority to order a unit or member to active duty to provide assistance in responding to an emergency involving-

> (1) a use or threatened use of a weapon of mass destruction; or
> (2) a terrorist attack or threatened terrorist attack in the United States that results, or could result, in significant loss of life or property.

10 U.S. Code §12304:
https://uscode.house.gov/view.xhtml?req=granuleid:USC-prelim-title10-section12304&num=0&edition=prelim#:~:text=10%20USC%2012304%3A%20Selected%20Reserve,during%20war%20or%20national%20emergency

10 United States Code §12406: National Guard in Federal service: call

Whenever-
(1) the United States, or any of the Commonwealths or possessions, is invaded or is in danger of invasion by a foreign nation;
(2) there is a rebellion or danger of a rebellion against the authority of the Government of the United States; or
(3) the President is unable with the regular forces to execute the laws of the United States;

The President may call into Federal service members and units of the National Guard of any State in such numbers as he considers necessary to repel the invasion, suppress the rebellion, or execute those laws. Orders for these purposes shall be issued through the governors of the States or, in the case of the District of Columbia, through the commanding general of the National Guard of the District of Columbia.

10 U.S. Code §12406:
https://uscode.house.gov/view.xhtml?req=granuleid:USC-prelim-title10-section12406&num=0&edition=prelim

The same Oath all of us Veterans take when swearing in the United States Armed Forces… is found in *10 United States Code §502*…

Yeah, *same* Title 10. Which should tell ANYONE, one cannot believe in the Military, but not the Laws, Orders, Regulations that 'govern' the Military.

The first time in United States History, all 50 states' National Guard and Reserve Components were in one location at one time… and the Order came from December 20, 2019, in 50 U.S.C. §1550, the War Powers Resolution Act, where the President declared a certain kind of war, in which PEADs would have also been signed, along with the proof we were already under a Military Occupancy and Continuity of Operations Plan due to the issuing of Federal Continuity Directives 1 and 2 with the Operational Dates posted in the Federal Register.

This is why it is VERY IMPORTANT to comprehend the Military is separate from the Federal Government and Politics.

January 8, 2021

Announces he would not be attending Biden's inauguration, making him the first outgoing President not to attend his elected successor's inauguration since the 1869 inauguration of Ulysses S. Grant.

What are the odds that Ulysses S. Grant was the President to sign the Organic Act of 1871? That led to the signing of the Organic Act of 1878 establishing the Federal Corporation?

January 12, 2021

Travels to Alamo, Texas, near the U.S.–Mexico border to examine progress on the US–Mexico border wall and meets with Border Patrol personnel.

Asserted the 25th Amendment is of "zero risk" to him and claimed it will "come back to haunt the Biden administration" adding "be careful what you wish for".

January 13, 2021: Amending Executive Order 13959—Addressing the Threat From Securities Investments That Finance Communist Chinese Military Companies

Executive Order 13974:
https://www.federalregister.gov/documents/2021/01/19/2021-01228/amending-executive-order-13959addressing-the-threat-from-securities-investments-that-finance

"(b) Notwithstanding subsection (a)(i) of this section, any transaction entered into on or before 11:59 p.m. eastern standard time on November 11, 2021, solely to divest, in whole or in part, from securities that any United States person held as of 9:30 a.m. eastern standard time on January 11, 2021, in a Communist Chinese military company as defined in section 4(a)(i) of this order, is permitted. Effective at 11:59 p.m. eastern standard time on November 11, 2021, possession of any such securities by a United States person is prohibited.

(c) Notwithstanding subsection (a)(ii) of this section, for a person determined to be a Communist Chinese military company pursuant to section 4(a)(ii) or (iii) of this order, any transaction entered into on or before 365 days from the date of such determination, solely to divest, in whole or in part, from securities that any United States person held in such person, as of the date 60 days from the date of such determination, is permitted. Effective at 11:59 p.m. eastern standard time on the date 365 days after the date of such determination, possession of any such securities by a United States person is prohibited." (Read full order online)

There's no secret "Biden" and Democrats love them some China… So, why would "Biden" extend this CIC Trump Executive Order past November 11, 2022, for one year?

"I hereby expand the scope of the national emergency declared in Executive Order 13959 to address those threats."

Expanding:
https://www.whitehouse.gov/briefing-room/presidential-actions/2021/06/03/executive-order-on-addressing-the-threat-from-securities-investments-that-finance-certain-companies-of-the-peoples-republic-of-china/

For this reason, the national emergency declared in Executive Order 13959 of November 12, 2020, expanded in scope by Executive Order 14032 of June 3, 2021, must continue in effect beyond November 12, 2022. Therefore, in accordance with section 202(d) of the National Emergencies Act (50 U.S.C. 1622(d)), I am continuing for 1 year the national emergency declared in Executive Order 13959 with respect to the threat from securities investments that finance certain companies of the PRC and expanded in Executive Order 14032.

Notice of Continuation:
https://www.whitehouse.gov/briefing-room/presidential-actions/2022/11/08/notice-on-the-continuation-of-the-national-emergency-with-respect-to-the-threat-from-securities-investments-that-finance-certain-companies-of-the-peoples-republic-of-china-2/

"Biden's Executive Order 14032" amended Executive Order 13959 and revoked Executive Order 13974 in its entirety. Notice the Original Executive Order by CIC DJT was not revoked.

January 13, 2021

January 14, 2021: **Encouraging Buy American Policies for the United States Postal Service**

Executive Order 13975:
https://www.federalregister.gov/documents/2021/01/21/2021-01469/encouraging-buy-american-policies-for-the-united-states-postal-service

Definitions. *As used in this order:*

(a) "Buy American" means all policies that require, or provide a preference for, the purchase or acquisition of goods, products, or materials produced in the United States, including iron, steel, and manufactured goods; and

(b) "Buy American Laws" means all statutes, regulations, rules, and Executive Orders relating to Federal procurement or Federal grants—including those that refer to "Buy America" or "Buy American"—that require, or provide a preference for, the purchase or acquisition of goods, products, or materials produced in the United States, including iron, steel, and manufactured goods.

Because… who wants to buy American and support America? SMH. HAHA!

January 14, 2021

Vice President Pence makes an unscheduled stop at the United States Capitol to meet with United States National Guard troops ahead of Biden's inauguration.

The ONLY person who could Federalize National Guard to Active-Duty is the President found in 10 United States Code 12406. 6 days before January 20, who's your President?

January 18, 2021: Protecting Law Enforcement Officers, Judges, Prosecutors, and Their Families
No coincidence. No coincidences AT ALL. All the Laws and Orders that have been in place for years suddenly being applied and enforced, along with the new Laws and Orders given and passed, being applied, and enforced… would require protection of these people demonstrating their integrity and spine to start standing up for the way laws and orders were supposed to be administered for the people not against us.

Fair and reciprocal. One of CIC Trump's mottos in everything. As CIC Trump said in a speech in… "I've pissed off a lot of rich people and I'm going to have to go away for a while, but I'll be back."

Those rich people are the agenda-based swamp. The agenda-based swamp who plays on the emotions of all people with party affiliations while they're all buddies in the background.

Executive Order 13977:
https://www.federalregister.gov/documents/2021/01/22/2021-01635/protecting-law-enforcement-officers-judges-prosecutors-and-their-families

Section 1. *Purpose.* Under the Constitution and Federal law, our government vests in judges, prosecutors, and law enforcement officers the power to make decisions of enormous consequence. Because of the importance of their work, these public servants face unique risks to their safety and the safety of their families. Some who face or have received an adverse judicial decision have sought to intimidate or punish judges and prosecutors with threats of harm.

Judges, prosecutors, and law enforcement officers should not have to choose between public service and subjecting themselves and their families to danger. My Administration has no higher priorities than preserving the rule of law in our country and protecting the men and women who serve under its flag.

January 17, 2021: More National Guard to D.C.

More troops arrive adding up to over 30,000 National Guard members from all 50 states in the District of Columbia for the "Inauguration."

Now… Why suddenly after ALL the Democrat and Republican Presidential Inaugurations… would we need 30,000 plus Troops for an "Inauguration" that was pre-planned not allowing any spectators?

Where was the threat if no public were allowed to attend? Makes ZERO sense, yet perfect sense for what I knew and know. One article says they came as far as Guam… IF there was NO EVIDENCE of a Continuity of Operations Plan and Military Occupancy, and this was simply a regular 4 years to an inauguration, the National Guard coming from Guam… makes zero sense or at least to us Vets.

Why were ALL 50 states' National Guard PLUS Guam needed for an "inauguration?" That makes a LOT of $$$$ense. SMH lol.

Guam:
https://www.nationalguard.mil/News/Article/2474814/national-guard-troops-head-to-dc-from-as-far-away-as-guam/

Remember from above… The War Powers Act which is 50 U.S. Code Section 1550, Title 10 Sections 12302, 12304 and 12406 plus Executive Orders 13912 and 13919?

ALL those were already in place from December 20, 2019, March 27, 2020, and April 30, 2020. Hence why it pays to understand Military Laws and Orders and how they operate and function with the Commander-in-Chief and Chain of Commands. Military's separate from everything else. If you don't like it, we don't care.

There were two different on looks that day with the Reserves and National Guard.

One, there were Troops there on CIC Donald John Trump's orders who the 47 U.S. Code 606 "mainstream media" did not show which were pulling guard at points that did not allow public access to the usual areas the public would view the Inauguration hence why there were also zero leaks that day.

His Troops were also shown turning their backs on the "motorcade" of "Bidens." There's one thing an enlisted soldier will ALWAYS do… Salute the President.

Two, there were "Troops" the 47 U.S. Code 606 "mainstream media" showed who were NOT real Troops… the pictures are still available on CBS' website.

ANY Veteran who served honorably and for the right reasons, who had their eyes open that day, or looks at pictures today, can tell you they were all kinds of "jacked-up" in which other colorful language would generally be applied.

The January 20, 2021, "Inauguration" was a perfect opportunity to dupe all Americans who watched, because 99% of that number has no clue what Military Uniform Regs are and watch they were watching. And the Veterans of the U.S. should be ashamed they let such a magnificent act play in front of them without seeing all the jacked-up uniforms and non-regulation pieces.

You must ask yourself, why were the blockades and perimeters so far out? There had to be a "celebration" that actual day for those who were used to seeing the "motorcade" and celebrations around the White House and Capitol Building or that would have been a dead give-away. We will discuss the "Inauguration" more on the January 20 tab. When you know the bigger picture… the 40,000 feet aircraft view and work your way in… it's obvious:

Blocking traffic

Heavy security

National Guard troops block traffic near the U.S. Capitol on January 19 in Washington, D.C. Tens of thousands of National Guard troops were deployed as additional security for President-elect Joe Biden's inauguration following the January 6 attack on the U.S. Capitol.

A National Guard member mans a security checkpoint near the U.S. Capitol on January 19 in Washington, D.C. About 25,000 National Guard troops were deployed as additional security for President-elect Joe Biden's inauguration following the January 6 attack on the Capitol.

cbsnews.com

Notice the distractions right off the bat…

One… it's CBS News official page.
Two… if you're not a Veteran or in the Military, you don't know what to look for.
Three… "Because it's CBS," plus the fancy write-up, why not trust them?

The uniform is all kinds of jacked up as NCO's would say in the Military. Let's look how:

Those patches wouldn't be the same patch. And they also wouldn't be different colors and look like they came from 1847. These are NOT regulation gloves. The ONLY Flag on the United States Army uniform is on the shoulder.

One, soldiers would not have different camo patterns. This "soldier" is wearing a MultiCam uniform with an ACU Kevlar Vest. Two, it's not an Army patch for rank at all. A rank patch would be there. But that's not a regulation piece of uniform, plus it's brown, which makes 3 different type patterns. Not regulation. Military uniforms do not have brand names displayed.

That Kevlar helmet cover is all jacked up. The NVG mount is correct, but many surplus stores already have these mounted, OR using Vets for a staged event, this would be a no brainer. But there wouldn't be a need for night missions in D.C. that would require night vision.

Three, the GatorNeck is RARELY authorized for wear even in very windy and sandy desert conditions, but especially in regular duty in a region that not that cold. But what a PERFECT place to use it when you don't want a family member recognized on National TV… *"Hey! That's my cousin Coolio! Wait, he's not in the military!"*

You wouldn't have some wearing PC's and others not. They'd be in unison aka uniform. And once again, all the patterns are different. The water bottle… No. We have canteens for that. I can't even… this is all kinds of jacked up everywhere.

Their head cover is not unified. One wouldn't be wearing brown, black, and others wearing PC's.

One has a green backpack, the other has a black, NO. One has a black faceguard, another has a blue medical guard, NO.

OCP and MultiCam, NO. OCP and ACU, NO. The green piece, whatever that is on thigh, NO.

The first "soldier" has eye cover hanging, no case. The second "soldier" has protective case. NO.

Those are just a FEW of the atrocities that day. See more on the January 20th Tab. Once again, "Covid" was all part of the plan, where hundreds of soldiers in those jacked-up uniforms could not be recognized in person or at home by friends and family members who knows the person is NOT actually in the military as majority of those were actors.

The Pharmaceutical CEO's and Boards plus Hospital CEO's and Boards took things into their hands and retaliated during the Military's usage of the tactic to get people to stay at home and move about more effectively and efficiently doing their tunnel operations. Biological Chemical Threats and Pandemics were already outlined in certain issues of the Federal Continuity Directives and the December 2017 National Security Strategy to the tee.

You don't have to believe me now, but you will. This Operation has many suave pieces and plans.

January 18, 2021: Ensuring Democratic Accountability in Agency Rulemaking

Executive Order 13979:
https://www.federalregister.gov/documents/2021/01/22/2021-01644/ensuring-democratic-accountability-in-agency-rulemaking

Notice the date of this Order and pair the terminology below with the COOP and Military Occupancy.

This coincides with the Federal Continuity Directives about Departments and Agencies. Notice Section 1 below, Purpose, *the consent of the governed* which equals we the people.

Notice the dates when you read the EO… "within 180 days and 90 days of this order."

Notice the paragraph talking about: "consistent with public safety, security, and privacy interests, in the *Federal Register*." There's that Federal Register that ALL Executive Orders for public access. The FCD1 and FCD2 clearly outlined the President has a Presidential Policy Directive (PPD-40) in place for all the 3 Branches of Government in a Continuity of Government…

Which means it was a Military Occupancy from the start… and this EO on January 18, 2021, is consistent with the FCDs published January 17, 2017, June 13, 2017, February 2018, May 2020, January 2021, July 2021, and April 2023, as it states below:

The President chooses Federal agency heads who exercise executive authority and implement his regulatory agenda. Who was the President on January 18, 2021? And why was President Trump writing Executive Orders consistent with the FCDs and Military Occupancy especially if January 6, 2021, was real, not staged and he "lost" the 2020 Election?

January 18, 2021: Protecting the United States From Certain Unmanned Aircraft Systems

Executive Order 13981:
https://www.federalregister.gov/documents/2021/01/22/2021-01646/protecting-the-united-states-from-certain-unmanned-aircraft-systems

Notice these specific terms:

*(e) The term **"Intelligence Community"** has the same meaning set forth for that term in section 3003(4) of title 50, United States Code.*

*(f) The term "National Airspace System" (NAS) means the common network of United States airspace; air navigation facilities, equipment, and services; airports or landing areas; aeronautical charts, information, and services; related rules, regulations, and procedures; technical information; and manpower and material. The term also includes system components shared jointly by the **Departments of Defense, Transportation, and Homeland Security.***

January 18, 2021: 1776 Commission Report

1776 Report:
https://trumpwhitehouse.archives.gov/wp-content/uploads/2021/01/The-Presidents-Advisory-1776-Commission-Final-Report.pdf

No coincidence it was 45 pages long… this is the follow up to the 1776 Commission Executive Order.

January 19, 2021: Taking Additional Steps To Address the National Emergency With Respect to Significant Malicious Cyber-Enabled Activities

Executive Order 13984:
https://www.federalregister.gov/documents/2021/01/25/2021-01714/taking-additional-steps-to-address-the-national-emergency-with-respect-to-significant-malicious

To address these threats, to deter foreign malicious cyber actors' use of United States IaaS products, and to assist in the investigation of transactions involving foreign malicious cyber actors, the United States must ensure that providers offering United States IaaS products verify the identity of persons obtaining an IaaS account ("Account") for the provision of these products and maintain records of those transactions.

In appropriate circumstances, to further protect against malicious cyber-enabled activities, the United States must also limit certain foreign actors' access to United States IaaS products. Further, the United States must encourage more robust cooperation among United States IaaS providers, including by increasing voluntary information sharing, to bolster efforts to thwart the actions of foreign malicious cyber actors.

As CIC Trump said on December 15, 2022, we need to establish a Digital Bill of Rights as technology is never going away therefore, we must have a foundation with a criterion for the many facets of Cybersecurity and the threats against this vast topic as well.

January 20, 2021: **Joseph Robinette Biden Jr. and the "Inauguration"**

"Inauguration" pictures from CBS News dot com:

Stage is set

The West Front of the U.S. Capitol is draped in flags in preparations for the 59th inaugural ceremony for President-elect Joe Biden and Vice President-elect Kamala Harris on January 20, 2021.

≡ cbsnews.com

Yes… yes it was. Let's look at more little details and kick it off with this epic Optic. Let's start with **William "Bill" Clinton's Inauguration, George W. Bush's, and Barack Obama's**:

Now let's look at **Donald John Trump's Inauguration**:

Now let's look at the **"Joe Biden" "Inauguration"**:

Now, let's look at the first major Optic of January 20, 2021:

Details, Details, Details

Bullis, woodcrafter with the Capitol Carpentry Division, heads a team that hangs five huge 22-foot by 12-foot flags and bunting behind the podium. This project begins about two weeks prior to the ceremony with the installation of wooden supports the length of the flags. Scaffolding is hung off the top of the building, and Bullis and his team attach background white sheets the length of the flags. The current American flag hangs in the center, and it is flanked on either side by the American flag in use at the time the President's home state entered the union. The first American flag with 13 stars hangs on either side of those flags.

≈ aoc.gov

Notice the description about the two Flags representing the President's home state and when they entered the union?

Architect of the Capitol:
https://www.aoc.gov/explore-capitol-campus/blog/one-team-one-mission-one-day

So, if you'll go back to previous pages and look at the two inside flags in slots 2 and 4 from left to right.

Clinton: 25 Stars = Arkansas
Bush Jr.: 28 Stars = Texas
Obama: 21 Stars = Illinois

So, if this was not a 'movie' but more specifically a Military Occupancy and Continuity of Operations Plan which includes Devolution and Reconstitution, found in those Federal Continuity Directives, then…

So, why does "Biden" have 13 Stars?

13 Stars = Rhode Island.

You want absolute proof Donald John Trump is your Commander-in-Chief in a Military Occupation and Continuity of Operations Plan? Or how about some Optics and *Paying Attention to Details.*

13 Stars = Original 13 Colonies = Revolutionary Foundation

How come Clinton, Bush Jr., and Obama's State Flags were accurate, but CIC DJT had 13 Stars, Rhode Island, and "Biden" had the same? Perhaps because it's a Military Occupancy and Continuity of Operations Plan?

Right in front of ya!

Now let's look at the jacked up Military Uniforms on January 20 for "Biden."

"Can someone please open the door." LOL

Reviewing the troops

President Joe Biden, first lady Dr. Jill Biden, Vice President Kamala Harris and her husband Douglas Emhoff attend the Pass in Review ceremony, hosted by the Joint Task Force-National Capital Region, on the East Front of the U.S. Capitol after the inauguration on January 20, 2021.

cbsnews.com

Paying respects

President Joe Biden and Vice President Kamala Harris participate in a wreath-laying ceremony at the Tomb of the Unknown Soldier at the Arlington National Cemetery following the 59th presidential inauguration on January 20, 2021.

Not ONLY are these not Regulation Uniforms… but look at this gem, Vets. What in the pushups for life is going on here? If Civilians only knew what kind of 'ass-chewing' and counseling statement this would be.

Another angle shows this "soldiers" cover on the ground. Anyone can argue that he cannot break form to pick his cover up, that's also true, however, it does not take away that these are still non-regulation uniforms. Plus, there's other soldiers elsewhere from January 20, 2021, to present day, who have not worn a cover where they should have, not to mention all the uniforms being non-regulation and all jacked up. One mistake doesn't cancel out ALL the visuals you've seen since January 20, 2021. And how come no one picked his cover up like CIC Trump does to soldiers?

"Formal uniform hats, or "covers," must be worn outside and carried indoors."

Military Traditions and Customs:
https://www.militaryonesource.mil/relationships/support-community/common-military-traditions-and-customs/

"The President's Own" United States Marine Band

"The President's Own" United States Marine Band performs for the inauguration of Joe Biden on the West Front of the U.S. Capitol on January 20, 2021 in Washington, D.C.

What in the "oh, you almost had it" is going on here? Wrong cap. Wrong stripe on pants. Wrong service shirt.

I'm not sure what the cat on the left is… except all kinds of jacked-up and not regulation anything. And where's his cover? You can look at multiple photos of the bands indoors with headsets, but not outside.

And this one:

What in the AARP Subscription is going on here? That one takes the cake, candles, gifts, and Grandma's dentures right there… SMH. HAHA!

The Marine Band is the band of the President and serves the office of the presidency in a **non-partisan** fashion. So, why would they not have Uniform correct if "Biden" was actually inaugurated?

YouTube: "The President's Own" Marine Corps band.

Marine Corps Official Band:
https://www.marineband.marines.mil/About/Marine-Band-Uniform/

Ohhh, it gets better for you Devil Dogs:

Marine Band rehearsal

Master Gunnery Sargent Matthew Harding, a trumpet player with "The President's Own" United States Marine Band, during a rehearsal for the inauguration of President-elect Joe Biden on January 19, 2021

cbsnews.com

Sergeant is misspelled. And this is CBS News. Two, look at the Uniform: ***Battle Dress Uniform***. You don't wear a Field-Grade Officer Service Cap with Combat Uniform. Two, article says he's a Master Gunnery Sergeant, so, why would he be wearing an Officer's cap?

And drum roll, the last time the Marine Corps wore BDU's was April 1, 2005. No April Fools there. The new MARPAT uniform was approved June 2001, and was approved for wear in 2002, and changeover took place, October 1, 2004.

COMBAT UTILITY UNIFORM AND BOOT GUIDANCE:
https://www.marines.mil/News/Messages/Messages-Display/Article/887056/combat-utility-uniform-and-boot-guidance/

They also said that the U.S. Army Band aka Pershing's Own was there:

U.S. Army Band member

A member of the U.S. Army Band ahead of the inauguration of President-elect Joe Biden on the West Front of the U.S. Capitol on January 20, 2021 in Washington, D.C.

cbsnews.com

cbsnews.com

For the average civilian… they look very real. But they're not.

Here's the **Official "The President's Own" Marine Corps Band**:

Remember those Marine Corps Uniform Regulations?

When you go to their official YouTube page, how come there's not any Inaugural Footage for January 20, 2021?

Go ahead, *go look*.

The **Official U.S. Army Band**:

When you go to their official YouTube page, how come there's not any Inaugural Footage for January 20, 2021?

U.S. Army Band Official page:
https://www.bands.army.mil/musicandvideo

Army Band:
https://usarmyband.com/ensembles/the-u-s-army-concert-band

Army Band Live Webcasts:
https://usarmyband.com/live-webcasts

Let's look at the **ONE thing** that's remained consistent with the Military Occupancy since **January 20, 2017**:

The Military Intelligence Headband at "Biden's Inauguration" on January 20, 2021, which was what's leading to this next point below.

Emotional farewell

One day before being inaugurated as the 46th president of the United States, Joe Biden becomes emotional as he delivers farewell remarks to his home state at the Major Joseph R. "Beau" Biden III National Guard/Reserve Center January 19, 2021 in New Castle, Delaware.

The reserve center is named for his late son Beau Biden, who served as the state's attorney general and as a major in the National Guard before dying of brain cancer at age 46 in 2015.

⊞ cbsnews.com

Why would "Biden" have an emotional FAREWELL delivering remarks to "his" home state? Why?

The "Mainstream Media" told all the sleepy Americans "he's" been at home in Delaware more than anywhere. So, why did he have to bid an emotional farewell?

Farewell *definition*: 'used to express good wishes on parting.'

What did he part?

Parting *definition*: 'the act of leaving or being separated from someone. The act of dividing into parts.'

Oh, that's right! A little thing called a 21 Gun Salute, but this one with a little twist.

Let's look at **Presidential Inauguration 21 Gun Salutes** starting with:

Richard M. Nixon

President Richard M. Nixon
Inauguration Day 1969

Ronald Reagan

President Ronald W. Reagan
Inauguration Day 1981

George Herbert Walker Bush

President George H.W. Bush
Inauguration Day 1989

President's First Hail To The Chief | From Nixon (1969) To Biden (2021)

William "Bill" Clinton

"Hail to the Chief" | US Presidential Anthem | President Bill Clinton Inauguration 1993 Edi...

"Hail to the Chief" | US Presidential Anthem | President Bill Clinton Inauguration 1997 Edi...

George W. Bush

President's First Hail To The Chief | From Nixon (1969) To Biden (2021)

Barack Obama

Barack Obama Oath of Office / Sworn In - President Obama: The Inauguration - BBC...

634K views 14y ago #bbc ...more

Watch President Barack Obama Get Sworn-in for Second Term

46K views 10y ago ...more

Donald John Trump

21 Gun Battery Salute To President Trump

100K views 6y ago ...more

▶ Answer one question
YouTube advertiser survey   ⌄

U.S: Donald Trump arrives at Joint Base Andrews, will receive a 21-Gun salute | Worl...

The last photo is January 20, 2021, at Joint Base Andrews. Outside of the fact that every President before Donald John Trump received 4 Cannons and 21 Rounds Fired which are 21 Gun Salutes by definition, Presidents do **NOT** receive 21 Gun Salute farewells. At Inauguration services the 21 Gun Salute starts after the President takes his Oath. There are four flourishes and as soon as 'Hail to the Chief' starts playing, the 21 Gun Salute starts firing.

There's 21 Gun Salutes at Inaugurations and there's 21 Gun Salutes at Funerals when a President dies. A U.S. presidential death also involves 21-gun salutes and other military traditions. On the day after the death of the president, a former president or president-elect—unless this day falls on a Sunday or holiday, in which case the honor will be rendered the following day—the commanders of Army installations with the necessary personnel and material traditionally order that one gun be fired every half-hour, beginning at reveille, and ending at retreat.

On the day of burial, a 21-minute gun salute traditionally is fired starting at noon at all military installations with the necessary personnel and material. Guns will be fired at one-minute intervals. Also, on the day of burial, those installations will fire a 50-gun salute—one round for each state—at five-second intervals immediately following lowering of the flag.

Donald John Trump clearly walked off Marine One on a Red-Carpet rollout (High Honor) with the Official Presidential Salute Battery aka the Old Guard = 3rd IR firing a 21 Gun Salute with 4 Cannons. The whole world witnessed Donald John Trump receive a Presidential Inauguration and it does not matter that it was not a traditional service… the plan was already in place and the finale of this Military Occupancy and Continuity of Operations Plan has much more impact on History than a brief service.

Four Cannons and 21 Guns is a 21 Gun Salute. 21 Gun Salutes are fired in honor of a national flag, the sovereign or chief of state of a foreign nation, a member of a reigning royal family, and the president, ex-presidents, and president-elect of the United States. The 21-gun salute is also fired at noon on George Washington's birthday, President's Day, Memorial Day, Independence Day, and the day of the funeral of a president, ex-president, or president-elect.

There needs to be a heavy emphasis on 21 Guns versus a *21 Gun Salute*. This is why terminology matters. In layman's terms, if you want to look at it this way… guns = rounds fired.

A 3 Volley with 21 Guns means 3 cannons with 21 rounds fired. That's why it's key to separate the 4 Cannons from the 3 Cannons… notice this key line found in the same article from Arlington National Cemetery website:

*The 21-gun salute is **not** to be confused with the three-volley salute (or three-rifle volley) rendered at military honors funerals, which you might see or hear at Arlington National Cemetery.*

21-Gun Salute

Salute by cannon or artillery is a military tradition that originated in the 14th century. The 21-gun salute, commonly recognized by many nations, is the highest honor rendered. The custom stems from naval tradition, when a warship would signify its lack of hostile intent by firing its cannons out to sea until all ammunition was spent. The British navy developed the custom of a seven-gun salute because naval vessels typically had seven guns (and possibly also due to the number seven's Biblical and mystical significance). Because greater quantities of gunpowder could be stored on dry land, forts could fire three rounds for every one fired at sea — hence the number 21. With the improvement of naval gunpowder, honors rendered at sea increased to 21, as well. The 21-gun salute eventually became the international standard.

In the United States, the custom has changed over time. In 1810, the War Department defined the "national salute" as equal to the number of states in the Union (at the time, 17). This salute was fired by all U.S. military installations on Independence Day and whenever the president visited a military

≜ arlingtoncemetery.mil

Today, the U.S. military fires a 21-gun salute in honor of a national flag, the sovereign or chief of state of a foreign nation, a member of a reigning royal family, and the president, ex-presidents and president-elect of the United States. The 21-gun salute is also fired at noon on George Washington's birthday, President's Day, Memorial Day, Independence Day, and the day of the funeral of a president, ex-president or president-elect.

Gun salutes for other U.S. and foreign military and civilian leaders vary in number, based on protocol and the honoree's rank. These salutes are always in odd numbers.

The 21-gun salute is not to be confused with the three-volley salute (or three-rifle volley) rendered at military honors funerals, which you might see or hear at Arlington National Cemetery.

≜ arlingtoncemetery.mil

Arlington Cemetery dot Mil:
https://www.arlingtoncemetery.mil/Visit/Events-and-Ceremonies/Ceremonies/21-Gun-Salute

On the Air Force Honor Guard page, their definition of a 3 Volley Salute is the best:

The 3 Volley Salute is Commonly, BUT INCORRECTLY, referred to as the 21-Gun Salute…

   Man, I love punctuation, grammar, and terminology!

Air Force Honor Guard Official:
https://www.honorguard.af.mil/About-Us/

The ***21-gun salute*** is sometimes confused with the tradition of firing three volleys of rifle fire at a military funeral. This technically is NOT a *21-Gun Salute*, but instead refers to a different tradition established during the European dynastic wars from 1688 to 1748.

During these conflicts, fighting was commonly halted on the battlefield to clear the dead. Once the dead were removed, three rounds would be fired to indicate that fighting should resume.

The tradition became part of military funerals to honor the nation's war dead, but it should not be confused with the higher honor of the 21-gun salute, which has evolved into a category similar to honors like the Purple Heart.

It is not offered to all who die in service to the country but is reserved for those who earned higher honors through exemplary service. In contemporary times, some military funerals may feature the three-gun salute, while the funerals of flag officers, current and former presidents, presidents-elect, cabinet secretaries, and other dignitaries may feature 21 guns.

3 Volley:
https://veteran.com/21-gun-salute/

Anyone who's ever taken the Oath of Enlistment... that's **10 United States Code 502** which specifically says:

"I, _____, do solemnly swear (or affirm) that I will support and defend the Constitution of the United States against all enemies, foreign and domestic; that I will bear true faith and allegiance to the same; and that I will obey the orders of the President of the United States and the orders of the officers appointed over me, according to regulations and the Uniform Code of Military Justice. So help me God."

10 US Code 502:
https://uscode.house.gov/view.xhtml?req=granuleid:USC-prelim-title10-section502&num=0&edition=prelim

Notice the line: *According to regulations and the Uniform Code of Military Justice.* That Oath is from the same Title 10 outlines the President is the ONLY who can Federalize the Reserves to Active-Duty which is 10 United States Codes 12302 and 12304 and the National Guard to Active-Duty in 10 United States Code 12406.

The point of bringing those together in this example... is if you 'believe' and 'support' the Military... you cannot have one of those without the other. The same thing applies to Customs... Military Customs are not party or religious affiliated.

<u>Location</u> is the key. January 20th, 2021, is the ONLY "Inauguration" that's shown cannons at Arlington National Cemetery and that was for a great reason.

So, if we're not in a Military Occupancy and Continuity of Government, though they're VERY written out in Legislation, Laws, and Orders, then how come Joseph Robinette Biden Jr. had **3 Cannons** on January 20, 2021?

That's right. On January 20, 2021, when the whole WORLD <u>thought</u> they saw Joseph Robinette Biden Jr. celebrate an Inauguration ceremony, he in fact received a full grade by Military Customs **FUNERAL SERVICE**.

It does NOT matter what the media says, this is NOT a 21 Gun Salute by Military Regulations and Customs... This only "salute" that was shown on January 20, 2021, with "Biden" by Military Customs is a Military Funeral Honors.

There's a key reason the Mainstream Media's delivering what someone would call 'false information' or slangily call it a *lie*... Wartime Presidency comes with Wartime Powers: **47 US Code §606** which is titled "War Powers of the President."

§ 606. War powers of President

(a) Priority communications During the continuance of a war in which the United States is engaged, the President is authorized, if he finds it necessary for the national defense and security, to direct that such communications as in his judgment may be essential to the national defense and security shall have preference or priority with any carrier subject to this chapter. He may give these directions at and for such times as he may determine, and may modify, change, suspend, or annul them and for any such purpose he is authorized to issue orders directly, or through such person or persons as he designates for the purpose, or through the Commission. Any carrier complying with any such order or direction for preference or priority herein authorized shall be exempt from any and all provisions in existing law imposing civil or criminal penalties, obligations, or liabilities upon carriers by reason of giving preference or priority in compliance with such order or direction.

47 United States Code §606:
https://www.govinfo.gov/content/pkg/USCODE-2011-title47/pdf/USCODE-2011-title47-chap5-subchapVI-sec606.pdf

Because this is a Military Occupancy that was meant to be a controlled Operation, meaning a long period of time, there would need to be ***distractions***. Hence the terms: Devolution and Reconstitution in the Federal Continuity Directives. Checkmate. 99% of Americans even Veterans did not see what was "*hidden*" in plain sight. Even though, it was NOT hidden!

January 20, 2021: Donald John Trump at Joint Base Andrews

When the WHOLE world thought "orange-man bad" rode off into the sunset on January 20, 2021, they _all_ thought wrong. CIC Donald John Trump walks off Marine One on a Red-Carpet rollout. The Red-Carpet equals high honor and royalty. It's the United States Army, 3rd Infantry Regiment, known as the Old Guard, the Official Presidential Salute Battery who performs all Inaugurations for the President.

They use 4 Cannons with 21 rounds fired, called a "21 Gun Salute." A 21 Gun Salute is for the President of the United States, Former Presidents, President-Elects, Foreign heads of states, heads of government, and reigning monarchs. There's also 19, 17, 15, 13, 11, 7, and 5-gun salutes. Military Customs and Bearings are outlined very well. On the 4th ruffle of Hail to the Chief, the 21 Gun Salute is to start - simultaneously.

On January 20, 2021, CIC DJT walked off Marine One on a Red-Carpet rollout and on the 4th ruffle / flourish of Hail to the Chief, a 21 Gun Salute started with 4 cannons which is THE full-grade Presidential Inauguration by Constitutional and Military Regulations and Customs.

January 21, 2021: Fake Press Rooms, White House, and Capitol Building

Why does the Mainstream Media only show you the same locations with "Biden?"

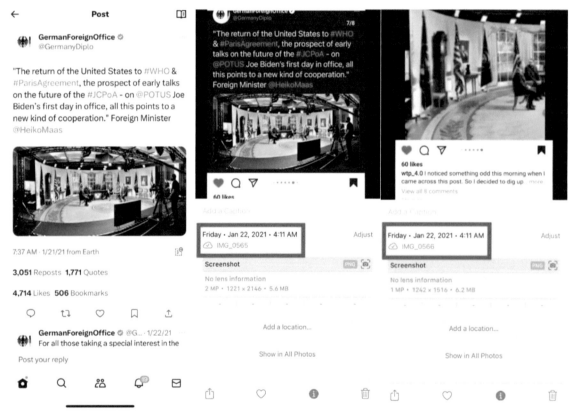

Official Twitter Post:
https://x.com/GermanyDiplo/status/1352249084497813507?s=20

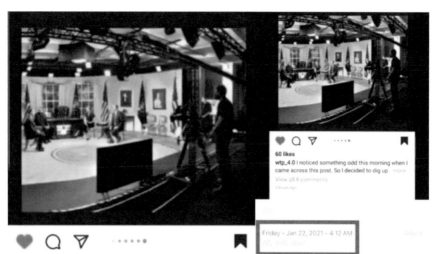

60 likes

wtp_4.0 I noticed something odd this morning when I
came across this post. So I decided to dig up … more

View all 8 comments

2 hours ago

Charlie Spiering ✓
@charliespiering

The digital projection window of
Biden's White House set shows
flowers in bloom in the Rose Garden.

The set was constructed across the
street from the actual WH in the
Executive Office Building

10:13 AM · 06 Oct 21 · TweetDeck

President Biden ✓
@POTUS
🏳 United States government official

We're facing an inflection point
with the climate crisis — and the
time to act is now. This morning, I
reconvened the Major Economies
Forum on Energy and Climate to
discuss our progress here at home
and how we can rally the world to
tackle this crisis with the urgency
it demands.

10:43 pm · 17 Sep 2021 · The White House

Suddenly, skyscrapers, cranes, and freight boxes? LOL This looks like Long Beach, California.

Ohhhhhhhhhhhhhhh, because it's on the INTERNET, it's true. That's rightttttt. The hell with a Veteran showing current, bipartisan Legislation plus Military Laws, Orders, Regulations, Customs and Courtesies, our Foundation, and how they all coincide.

The mainstream media have not been lying to you from January 20, 2017, to the present day, reading this… they're under the code above, 47 U.S. Code 606.

The more visual Continuity of Government by definition:

July 19, 2021: 50 United States Code Chapter 33 Section 1550:

In the 50 United States Code Chapter 33, titled War Powers Resolution, this outlines how a President has power and authority of the Armed Forces and how to declare war.

The very bottom of the code page is the last amendment to the code.

50 USC Chapter 33:
https://uscode.house.gov/view.xhtml?path=/prelim@title50/chapter33&edition=prelim

This is the last filing in the 50 USC 33 Section 1550:

<h1 style="text-align:center">Executive Documents</h1>

Delegation of Authority Under Section 1285 of the National Defense Authorization Act for Fiscal Year 2020 Memorandum of President of the United States, July 19, 2021, 86 F.R. 39939, provided: Memorandum for the Secretary of Defense

By the authority vested in me as President by the Constitution and the laws of the United States of America, including section 301 of title 3, United States Code, I hereby delegate to the Secretary of Defense the authority and functions vested in the President by section 1285(a) through (e) of Public Law 116–92 [50 U.S.C. 1550(a) to (e)] on the use of military force and support of partner forces to the Congress.

Keys from that paragraph to dissect:

3 USC §301
50 USC §1550(a) to (e)

Section 301 of Title 3:

§301. General authorization to delegate functions; publication of delegations

The President of the United States is authorized to designate and empower the head of any department or agency in the executive branch, or any official thereof who is required to be appointed by and with the advice and consent of the Senate, to perform without approval, ratification, or other action by the President (1) any function which is vested in the President by law, or (2) any function which such officer is required or authorized by law to perform only with or subject to the approval, ratification, or other action of the President: *Provided*, That nothing contained herein shall relieve the President of his responsibility in office for the acts of any such head or other official designated by him to perform such functions. Such designation and authorization shall be in writing, shall be published in the Federal Register, shall be subject to such terms, conditions, and limitations as the President may deem advisable, and shall be revocable at any time by the President in whole or in part. (Added Oct. 31, 1951, ch. 655, §10, 65 Stat. 712 .)

Now let's take a gander at **50 USC 1550(a) and (b):**

(a) In general

Not later than 180 days after December 20, 2019, and every 180 days thereafter, the President shall submit to the congressional defense committees, the Committee on Foreign Relations of the Senate, and the Committee on Foreign Affairs of the House of Representatives a report on actions taken pursuant to the Authorization for Use of Military Force (Public Law 107–40) against those countries or organizations described in such law, as well as any actions taken to command, coordinate, participate in the movement of, or accompany the regular or irregular military forces of any foreign country or government when such forces are engaged in hostilities or in situations where imminent involvement in hostilities is clearly indicated by the circumstances, during the preceding 180-day period.

(b) Matters to be included

The report required by subsection (a) shall include, with respect to the time period for which the report was submitted, the following:

(1) A list of each country or organization with respect to which force has been used pursuant to the Authorization for Use of Military Force, including the legal and factual basis for the determination that authority under such law applies with respect to each such country or organization.

(2) An intelligence assessment of the risk to the United States posed by each such country or organization.

(3) A list of each country in which operations were conducted pursuant to such law and a description of the circumstances necessitating the use of force pursuant to such law, including whether the country is designated as an area of active hostilities.

(4) A general description of the status of operations conducted pursuant to such law as well as a description of the expected scope and duration of such operations.

(5) A list of each partner force and country with respect to which United States Armed Forces have commanded, coordinated, participated in the movement of, or accompanied the regular or irregular forces of any foreign country or government that have engaged in hostilities or there existed an imminent threat that such forces would become engaged in hostilities, including-

(A) a delineation of any such instances in which such United States Armed Forces were or were not operating under the Authorization for Use of Military Force; and
(B) a determination of whether the foreign forces, irregular forces, groups, or individuals against which such hostilities occurred are covered by such law.

50 USC 1550(a) to (e):
https://uscode.house.gov/view.xhtml?req=granuleid:USC-prelim-title50-section1550&num=0&edition=prelim

Soooo... who was the President on December 20, 2019? 180 days added to December 20, 2019, is June 17, 2020. Do you know what happened in March 2020?

Donald John Trump via the same 50 USC Chapter 33 became a Wartime President via Section 1541 when he Federalized 1 million Reserve Components to Active-Duty as you can find in Executive Order 13912... which was a DIRECT ORDER from the Commander-in-Chief to the Military AND made it a Federal Order which has NOT been revoked.

Sooooo.... WHY is "Joe Biden" giving complete authority and functions vested in the President to the Secretary of Defense? Maybe because Donald John Trump did the same thing on April 30, 2019, in Executive Order 13919? The problem people have with these are TERMINOLOGY... but it's mainly due to the fact they have not seen the chronological timeline of ALL Laws and Orders... You cannot have one without the other, especially in this case.

Executive Order 13912 specifically says: "...authorized to order to active duty not to exceed 24 consecutive months, such units, and individual members of the Ready Reserve under the jurisdiction of the Secretary concerned, not to exceed 1,000,000 members on active duty at any one time, as the Secretary of Defense and, with respect to the Coast Guard when it is not operating as a service in the Navy, the Secretary of Homeland Security consider necessary."

Not to exceed 24 CONSECUTIVE months... meaning the order is a continuous order until revoked or rescinded or mission accomplished... Those soldiers called to duty will not exceed 24 consecutive months... has NOTHING to do with the overall order and operation.

This is WHY the *Military Justice Act of 2016*, passed in the 2017 National Defense Authorization Act, was so important. First time in United States Military History this was established:

1. Military Laws and Courts are separate from Civilian Laws and Courts.
2. President and Commander-in-Chief are two separate titles, roles, duties, obligations, and laws.
3. Commander-in-Chief separated from the Federal Government roles, duties, obligations, and authority.
4. Placed the sole decision of Courts-Martial in the hands of the Judge Advocate Generals (JAG).

So, when one reads that Joseph Robinette dog pony soldier boy, all the kids wanted to touch his golden hairy legs in the pool, 81 million votes with 12 car rallies, trips upstairs but walks on sandy beaches fine, Biden Jr. gives THE authority and functions to the Secretary of Defense in July 2021, when the Executive Document SPECIFICALLY says:

> "*I hereby delegate to the Secretary of Defense the authority and functions vested in the President by section…*"

See how that reads. See why terminology is important?

> "*Vested in the President*"…

In what President? THE President by section 1285(a) through (e) of Public LAW which is the SAME 50 USC 1550(a) to (e) which specifically says in 1550(a):

> "*Not later than 180 days after December 20, 2019…*"

Who was the President in December 2019? THE President. THE same President from the line: "vested in THE President."

Donald John Trump.

WHY in the tarnation would Joe Biden tell the Secretary of Defense to abide by the authority and functions vested in THE President of Section 1550 of the War Powers Resolution Act which is the LAST Amended Section where a President declares War in the United States which 1550 is declared by DONALD JOHN TRUMP?

That ONE clause / memo ALONE proves who the acting Commander-in-Chief is.

January 25, 2021

On January 25, 2021, the "Biden" Administration announced 4 Star General Flynn would be taking command of the United States Army Pacific.

That would be 4 Star General **Charles Flynn**… the brother of the very whistleblower on the Iraq and Afghanistan Wars while under the Obama/Biden Administration, 3 Star General Michael Flynn…

He assumed command on June 4, 2021. Now, why would "Biden" name the 4 Star brother to the Pacific Theatre? Only the hottest topic and region in the world: Russia, China, Japan, Australia, Guam, New Zealand, and Indonesia.

April 16, 2021

Press Secretary Psaki in live presser: "***Wow. There is a plane right over head.***" There's also a 33 mile no fly zone radius around the District of Columbia. Even Military Aircraft must request access to… unlessssssss, there's a Military Occupation taking place. Of course, there is… and I have multiple aircraft on file and in the documents proving so.

Federal Aviation Administration:
https://www.faa.gov/newsroom/restricted-airspace-0

Marker 2 minutes and 10 seconds:
https://www.youtube.com/watch?v=6ZRK_ZONePc

September 2021
It is CIC Donald John Trump who established the National Quantum Initiative Act that led to the National Quantum Initiative Advisory Committee with Executive Order 13885.

"With the launch of Quantum.gov, the White House has created an online home for the National Quantum Coordination Office and a new digital hub for the growing quantum community to connect with wide-ranging activities underway across the Federal Government. The newly published Quantum Frontiers Report lays out critical research questions for the entire U.S. innovation ecosystem to tackle in the years ahead, and will serve as an important roadmap for researchers around the country," said Michael Kratsios, U.S. Chief Technology Officer.

Quantum.gov will feature resources and news on QIS activities from across the Federal government, geared towards both the research community and the public. It will serve as a one-stop-shop for key strategic documents and reports, agency programs, and NQCO initiatives."

HPC Wire:
https://www.hpcwire.com/off-the-wire/the-white-house-announces-quantum-gov-and-quantum-frontiers-report/

November 2021: National Guard

Fox News · 18 hrs

Oklahoma National Guard won't enforce Biden's vaccine mandate

Clearly a massive Optic. If "Biden" was President and Commander-in-Chief, the Adjutant General would most definitely take an Order, or be Courts-Martialed for a move such as this. This comes down to simply knowing Military Chain of Command, Orders, and Procedures.

March 2022: Ukraine

"Russia, Russia, Russia, Russia, Russia, Russia, Russia"... Who's tired of hearing about Russia?

You could easily never think about Russia if you knew about the Operation via the Continuity of Government plus Laws and Orders the whole time… you could literally laugh, roll your eyes, and walk away knowing you know the REAL story behind Russia. But I mean hey… just think about all those poor lost souls on Facebook who changed their photo to look "cool" and "supportive" over a DIRTY, FILTHY and CORRUPT criminal organization between the Obama Administration with whom as Vice President?

The short version for everyone to begin with to understanding Ukraine is this: Why did Obama write 3 Executive Orders in a row with an additional 4th later in the year of 2014 alone?

Executive Order 13660:
https://www.federalregister.gov/documents/2014/03/10/2014-05323/blocking-property-of-certain-persons-contributing-to-the-situation-in-ukraine

Executive Order 13661:
https://www.federalregister.gov/documents/2014/03/19/2014-06141/blocking-property-of-additional-persons-contributing-to-the-situation-in-ukraine

Executive Order 13662:
https://www.federalregister.gov/documents/2014/03/24/2014-06612/blocking-property-of-additional-persons-contributing-to-the-situation-in-ukraine

Executive Order 13685:
https://www.federalregister.gov/documents/2014/12/24/2014-30323/blocking-property-of-certain-persons-and-prohibiting-certain-transactions-with-respect-to-the-crimea

Why did Vice President Joe Biden travel to Ukraine 7 times in 7 months in 2014 on your taxpayer dollar?

Why was there only 1 of 2 rounds in the election of the Ukrainian President in 2014? Why did Obama call to congratulate him a few days later?

What was the $1 Billion dollars in defense Victoria Nuland secured for Ukraine on behalf of the Obama Administration?

Did that $1 Billion have anything to do with why there's proof the United States were funding the Biochemical Laboratories in Ukraine? The same Victoria Nuland caught on recording saying, "F*ck the European Union."

Is there some weird irony why all the key names and players under the 8 years of the Obama Administration were all hired or appointed under "Biden"? Naw? Just a coincidence?

Why did the "Biden Administration" including Victoria Nuland deny throughout 2021 and early 2022, there were zero Biochemical Laboratories in Ukraine?

What are the odds that Victoria "F* the EU" Nuland was appointed as "Biden's" Under Secretary? And why did she finally admit on March 8, 2022, under Oath, that there are indeed Biochemical Laboratories in Ukraine, but "afraid the Russians would attain them?"

Why did Republican Mitt Romney deny there are NOT Biochemical Laboratories in Ukraine on the SAME day AFTER Democrat Victoria "F* the EU" Nuland admitted under Oath there ARE Biochemical Laboratories in Ukraine? Also, look what else took place the SAME day she's testifying that there ARE Biolabs in Ukraine:

"We took note of Russia's false claims about alleged U.S. biological weapons labs and chemical weapons development in Ukraine. We've also seen Chinese officials echo these conspiracy theories," Psaki tweeted.

Jen Psaki @PressSec
United States government official

We took note of Russia's false claims about alleged U.S. biological weapons labs and chemical weapons development in Ukraine. We've also seen Chinese officials echo these conspiracy theories.

4:48 PM · Mar 9, 2022

Read the full conversation on Twitter

♡ 44.1K   ⬚ Reply   ⬆ Share this Tweet

Read 5.3K replies

So, which one is it? LOL How about Ukraine breaking the CIS Treaty with Russia in 2018? What are the odds that 2018 is the same year President Vladmir Putin handed CIC Trump the Soccer Ball?

It's all about ORIGIN. That soccer ball looks cool now that you know the timeline.

March 8, 2022: Victoria Nuland Testimony under Oath

Ole Vicky testifies under Oath that "there are Biochemical Laboratories' in the Ukraine."

March 14, 2022: Mitt Romney

RINO Mitt Romney responds about the Ukraine Biochemical Labs:

Republican Sen. Mitt Romney strongly condemned former Democratic Rep. Tulsi Gabbard, seemingly responding to comments she has made in recent days about US biological laboratories in Ukraine.

"Tulsi Gabbard is parroting false Russian propaganda. Her treasonous lies may well cost lives," Romney said in a <u>tweet</u> on Sunday afternoon.

This is literally 6 days after Victoria Nuland testified under Oath there ARE biochemical labs in Ukraine.

Business Insider:
https://www.businessinsider.com/mitt-romney-says-tulsi-gabbard-spreading-russian-propaganda-biolab-ukraine-2022-3

May 2022: Infant Formula "Shortage"

This is another one of those Optics that requires a person knowing what Continuity of Government and Military Occupancies are… The distractions from this Operation have been epic to say the least… LOOK OVER HERE!!! Much of the population looked, bought into it, started chattering… and that's been the ONLY good thing about the short attention spans and drama filled lives Americans have led. That's a positive for the Military and other Law Enforcement teams during Devolution and Reconstitution… they're able to work effectively and efficiently without goons of all kinds getting in the way.

In May 2022, the MSM distractions made the world panic with the 'Infant Formula' shortage… And all you would have had to know to know who's really in control… is this one article via NBC.

"Due to the urgency of the situation, the Secretary of Defense approved U.S. military aircraft for this mission on Friday evening," Jean-Pierre said, explaining the decision was made after commercial aircraft were unavailable.

Meanwhile, President Joe Biden on Saturday signed into law a measure that would allow more formula to be purchased with funds from a federal program that helps low-income women and children."

Keywords: *Due to, Meanwhile*

This was the United States Military flying the formula from Europe… not a Commercial / Business flight… How come the "Commander-in-Chief" did not approve the mission?

If "Biden" authorized this mission a week before as this article says in the first paragraph, then these two paragraphs would have not been necessary and would have read differently. This is just ONE article of the VAST articles that had similar scenarios to show the Orders in place from CIC Trump in March 2020 are live, current, and active.

NBC:
https://www.nbcnews.com/politics/politics-news/military-aircraft-arrive-baby-formula-europe-shortage-rcna29990

May 30, 2022:

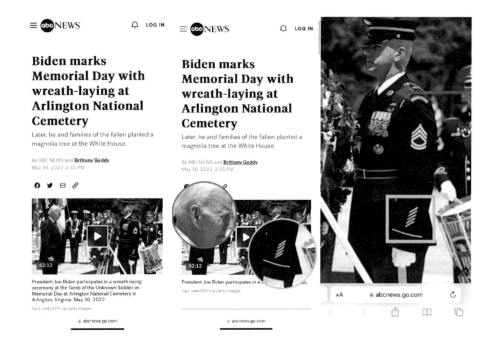

Look at that ear, all attached and all. Then remember, Military Regulations and Customs. *They matter.*
Now let's take a gander back at Vice President Joe Biden.

Now look at that ear and the sleeve on the Honor Guard.

September 2022:

"Battle for the Soul of the Nation Speech" – September 2022:

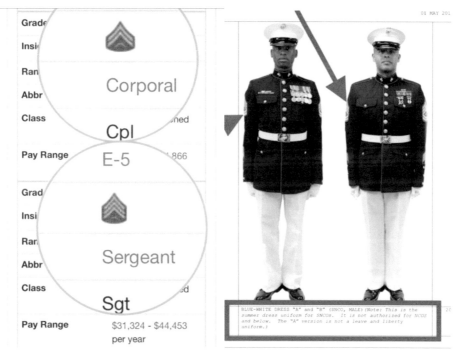

It is NOT authorized for NCO's and below. Summer Dress for SENIOR NCOs only. A Sergeant is an NCO; a Corporal is below an NCO, as shown with "Biden." Marine Corps Sentries do wear white for White House duties, but this speech was in Philadelphia. Many argue this, but the regulations say what they say. It's the uniform regs that matter.

February 2023 (and others): The "Chinese" Balloon

"Hey!!! Look over here!!!" And you all did. Here's the "Chinese" Balloon that day:

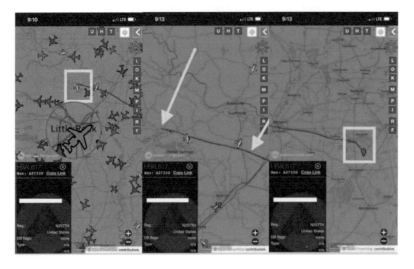

What's that Registration say? N257th United States HAHAHAHAHA

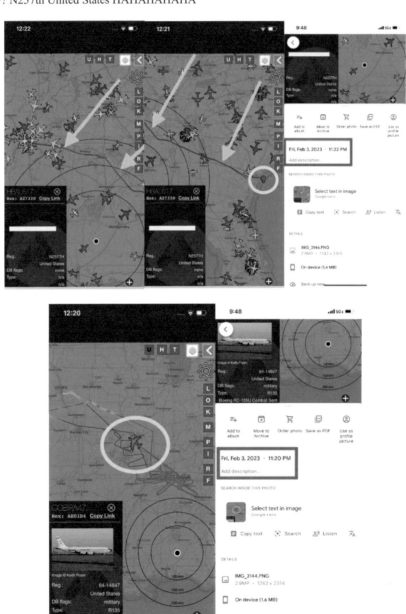

And there's the Aircraft the "News" told you was sent to track it, but never got anywhere near it HAHAHAHAH

This is kind of like those black headed greasy hair guys with their blue button downs on Infomercials… But wait! There's more! Since you Americans love 'news' so much and only care about things until you're told to, look at a few more you missed that the 'news' NEVER told you about, but I did, and VERY few Patriots shared those posts.

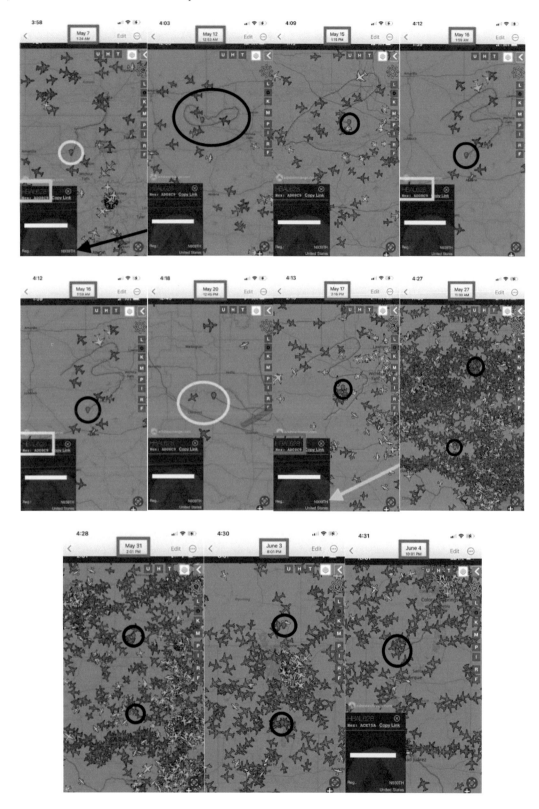

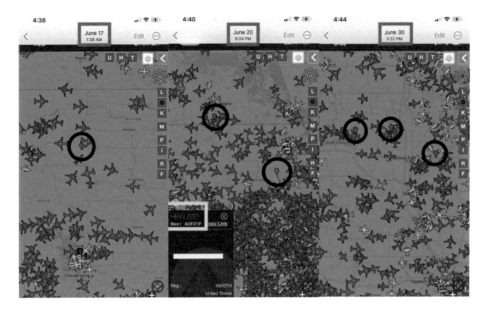

I have MANY more saved but must save room on this book.

April 2023: Reconstitution Manager's Guide

An issue under the Federal Continuity Directives. And if "Joe Biden" was President from January 20, 2021, to April 2023, how come the most recent Law inside of this is from Donald John Trump, December 7, 2020?

Reconstitution Manager's Guide:
https://www.fema.gov/sites/default/files/documents/fema_reconstitution-managers-guide.pdf

How many Americans have ever heard of Reconstitution before these issues or this book? And ask yourself… after all these years, why is Reconstitution a heavy topic? It's being issued by bipartisan legislation.

Now ask yourself, do you know what a Constitutional Convention is?

Convention and Ratification:
https://history.state.gov/milestones/1784-1800/convention-and-ratification

Although the Constitutional Convention met for the last time on September 17, 1787, public debate over the Constitution was just beginning. The Constitution specified that at least nine states ratify the new form of government, but everyone hoped for nearly unanimous approval. As the states called their own ratifying conventions, arguments for and against the document resurfaced. Writing under the pseudonym Publius, Alexander Hamilton, James Madison, and John Jay defended the proposed plan in a series of newspaper articles, later collected as the *Federalist Papers*.

The Constitution was officially adopted by the United States when it was ratified by New Hampshire on June 21, 1788, the ninth state to do so. The first Congress under the new Constitution convened in New York City on March 4, 1789, although a quorum was not achieved until early April. On April 30, 1789, President George Washington delivered the first inaugural address, and within his initial term the first ten amendments—known as the Bill of Rights—were adopted, establishing the fundamental rights of U.S. citizens and assuaging many fears associated with the relatively strong central government the Constitution provides.

U.S. Constitution:
https://www.loc.gov/item/today-in-history/september-17/#:~:text=Although%20the%20Constitutional%20Convention%20met,the%20Constitution%20was%20just%20beginning

July 10, 2023: The Nuclear Football

Ask yourself 'why' this is suddenly so important as a headline piece for 'news?'

The Nuclear Football is very key as it holds the 'One Voice' Emergency Alert System. Good thing this is all a Military Occupation and COOP and CIC Trump has the actual Nuclear Football, and this "soldier" is solid proof as the Uniform is (Drum Roll) all jacked up.

Uniform is ALL jacked up.

Might need a magnifying glass, but that's not the same.

Everything has a Regulation.

Not even close!

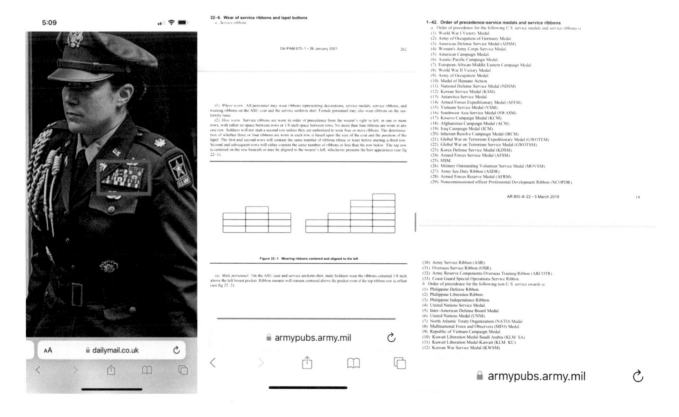

1. Wear the ribbons on the left side of the uniform, above the left breast pocket. 2. **Arrange the ribbons in order of precedence, from the highest to the lowest.** Feb 16, 2023

All of "her" **ribbons** are not in the correct precedence.
https://armypubs.army.mil/epubs/DR_pubs/DR_a/pdf/web/ARN18147_R600_8_22_admin2_FINAL.pdf

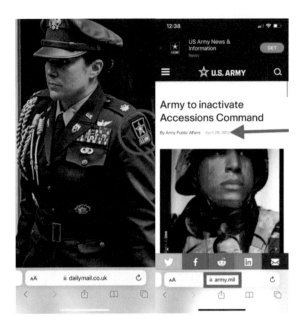

Appearing on scores of thousands of vehicles from half-tracks to tanks and jeeps, the symbol became inextricably linked to the U.S. Army. And in 2006, the imagery was updated (and trademarked) to create the current logo by rendering it black, white, and yellow to represent gunpowder, saltpeter, and sulfur.

Not considered a distinctive insignia in the same way as a shoulder sleeve insignia, the U.S. Army logo (without the trademark symbol) is worn by members of U.S. Army Accessions Command, its Support Brigade, Officers and Enlisted personnel assigned to Department of the Army Headquarters (but only HQDA staff), and Soldiers at Initial Entry Training or One Station Unit Training. It measures 2.5 inches by 3.25 inches.

12:37

News   Images   Shopping   Videos   Books   N

⭐ Army.mil
https://www.army.mil › article › ar...   ⋮

Army to inactivate Accessions Command | Article

Apr 20, 2011 — U.S. Army Accessions Command will be inactivated as part of Defense and Army efficiency reviews, officials announced today.

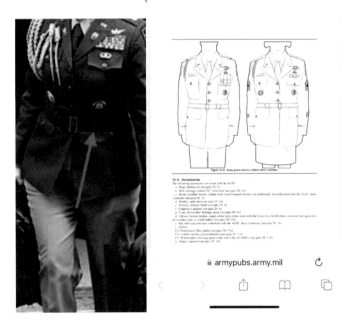

Paying attention to details matters.

August 8, 2023: "Biden" visits Grand Canyon

And as always, comes out the 'Ass End' of "Air Force One"… When it happened to Obama in China, it was an insult, but for 2.5 years, "Biden" has been coming out the official "ass end" of the aircraft, but it's 'normal.' SMH

Mainstream Media said he signed an Order for Grand Canyon. "He" signed a Proclamation not an Executive Order.

Here's the differences:

Executive Orders generally:

(1) are "directed to, and govern actions by, Government officials and agencies external";
(2) have the force of law if the topic of the Executive order is "founded on the authority of the President derived from the Constitution or statute"; and
(3) are required by law to be published in the Federal Register (1936 to present) and in Title 3 of the Code of Federal Regulations (1938 to present).

Proclamations generally:

(1) deal with the activities of private individuals;
(2) do not have the force and effect of law, unless the President is given the authority over private individuals by the Constitution or a federal statute; and
(3) are ceremonial in nature now, but historically did much more "heavy lifting".

Library of Congress:
https://guides.loc.gov/executive-orders/order-proclamation-memorandum

That's the cheapest sign *ever*… 2x4's and the graphic is cheap. LOL. But what a beautiful piece to the movie.

Source:
https://news.azpm.org/s/97122-biden-creates-new-national-monument-near-grand-canyon/

"He" didn't sign an Executive Order. "He" signed a Proclamation. The Politico article went onto say:

But the national monument designation has already been criticized by House Republicans who have called for a probe for information on how the monument boundaries were selected and how it will affect mining and energy development. They've argued it will block new uranium mining at a time when the U.S. should be looking to become more energy independent, especially given the prominence of Russia in the market to provide low-enriched uranium to nuclear reactors.

Politico on Grand Canyon:
https://www.politico.com/news/2023/08/08/biden-protect-grand-canyon-sacred-00110342

CIC Trump said the Uranium One was the actual Russia Scandal…

> "*Your real Russia story is uranium.*" — President Donald Trump

Several of Uranium One's owners were also donors to the Clinton Foundation, giving $145 million to the charitable foundation, and critics have alleged that Clinton greenlighted the sale to appease donors to her family's charity.

Hillary and Uranium One:
https://www.politico.com/story/2017/11/14/hillary-clinton-uranium-one-deal-russia-explainer-244895

In her attempt to discredit reports of the controversy surrounding the Uranium One deal, Clinton said Trump and "his allies," are diverting from the investigation.

"The closer the investigation about real Russian ties between Trump associates and real Russians … the more they want to just throw mud on the wall," she said. *"I'm their favorite target, me and President Obama."*

Well, maybe if it weren't true… HAHA!

Obama-era Russian Uranium One deal: What to know:
https://www.congress.gov/116/meeting/house/109694/documents/HHRG-116-II06-20190625-SD004.pdf

And "Biden" signed a proclamation banning Uranium Mining in the Grand Canyon? Oh, the irony the Federal Continuity Directives address Tribal Governments. Already planned.

July 27, 2023: Fact Sheet: Continuity and Reconstitution Planning Integration

A viable continuity program includes synchronizing the reconstitution team with continuity staff. Coordination between the two teams is critical to ensure both continuity and reconstitution activities occur seamlessly after a catastrophic incident.

Background:

Presidential Policy Directive 40 (PPD-40), "National Continuity Policy," requires all executive branch departments and agencies (D/A) to provide for "reconstitution capabilities that allow for recovery from a catastrophic emergency and resumption of normal operations." PPD-40 also requires D/As to "develop continuity plans, including devolution and reconstitution." This requirement stresses the importance of reconstitution plans being fully synchronized with the D/As' continuity plans. Ensuring fully synchronized planning requires coordination between the continuity manager, reconstitution manager, and both the continuity and reconstitution teams. An organizational-level reconstitution program has several components and certain activities must be performed in steady-state [or preevent] and during continuity operations, not just after a catastrophic incident occurs.

Reconstitution in the Continuity Process

Reconstitution is defined as the process by which surviving and/or replacement personnel resume normal operations. Figure 1 details how reconstitution is an ongoing process that occurs simultaneously with the other three stages of continuity. Reconstitution planning begins during readiness and preparedness and continues through the resumption of normal operations.

Reconstitution: Continuity for Everyone Else

A comprehensive reconstitution plan should parallel the Continuity of Operations (COOP) plan. The COOP plan addresses what personnel on the Emergency Relocation Group (ERG) will do to perform essential functions and where they will operate following a catastrophic incident. Likewise, the reconstitution plan should address what everyone else in the agency will do and where they will operate following a catastrophic incident, including how the reconstitution team prepares for the resumption of normal operations. This way, a reconstitution plan helps to ensure the resilience of the overall organization and ultimately the federal government. Pre-event planning and training for the rest of the organization can happen concurrently with the ERG training.

Fact Sheet: FEMA Continuity Reconstitution:
https://www.fema.gov/sites/default/files/documents/fema_continuity-reconstitution-synchronization-fact-sheet.pdf

Not sure how much plainer it can be… the Federal Continuity Directives 1 and 2 were issued on January 17 and June 13, 2017, with both their Bullet Point 3's saying they supersede anything issued prior to, and the operational dates of those were posted on the Federal Register as: 2018-2022 and 2020-2024…

The new title of the Continuity of Government is a Continuity of Operational Plan, as it's outlined in those. These are current and bipartisan. So, if we're not in a COOP… How come there's been those foundational issues with 6 issues under those to July 2023? And how come none of those have any legislation by "Biden" in those?

You wouldn't have mismatched branches. Plus, their Uniforms are ALL jacked up, non-regulation. The Coast Guard does NOT guard the President. LOL Remember those Coast Guard Regulations!

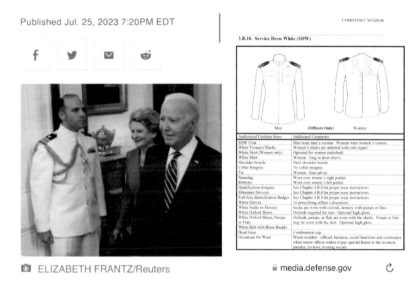

Is that Carl from the movie 'Slingblade'? Shout-out Coast Guard! You guys never *any* get love! Especially around the "President." LOL

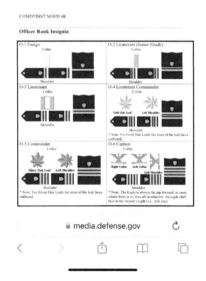

Now look at this "Marine" and his belt and off colored uniform.

Do you see a shiny belt and gold latch attached to it in Regs? #Nope.

And what about actress, Debbie Stabenow.

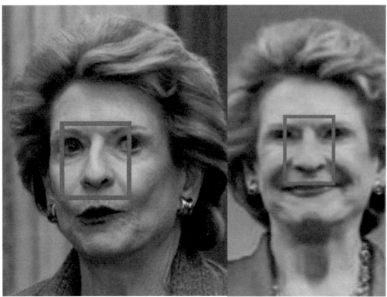

October 7, 2023: Israel – Hamas

The "Mainstream Media" told the United States public, Americans, that a Music Festival was attacked.

Hamas attack music festival:
https://www.cnn.com/2023/10/07/middleeast/israel-gaza-fighting-hamas-attack-music-festival-intl-hnk/index.html

So, let me get this straight… a music festival that took 1,400 lives leads to all these Nations launching a war on a group Israel could take out alone:

United States, Romania, Hungary, Brazil, Argentina, Colombia, United Kingdom, United Arab Emirates, Canada, Poland, Czechia, Japan, France, Italy, Spain, Mexico, Belgium, Netherlands, Germany, Thailand, Greece, Tunisia, Algeria, Slovenia, and Nigeria.

Once one grasps the current bipartisan Legislation that outlines the Laws and Orders of the Military Occupancy and the Continuity of Operations Plan formerly known as a Continuity of Government, all this is a cherry on top of the whipped cream and sundae.

Here's the proof: "Joe Biden" and his Israeli-Hamas press conference on October 10, 2023, gave the ULTIMATE Optic and Comm to the Military Occupancy when he said,

*"Democracies like Israel and the United States are stronger and more secure when we act according to the rule of Law. Terrorists pur-purposely target civilians, kill them. We uphold the **Laws of War, the Law of War**. It matters! There's a difference!"*

Yes, yes, it is folks. There's your Military Occupation comm right there to prove the whole Israel and Middle East theatre was planned by the good guys as they're destroying the Federal Corporation.

If this was about a small attack in Israel over 1,400 'victims'… all those countries listed above would not have been in and out of Israel in that week and weeks after. Those countries are the same countries in and out of the United States since the Section 1550 Order was given on December 20, 2019, by Donald John Trump in the War Powers Act of 1973.

October 2023:

'Special K' tells US will NOT be sending combat troops to Israel or Gaza. Troops are Troops. Combat is an action. These are the same people who think AR stands for Assault Rifle, when all rifles can be used for *assaulting* someone. And P.S. AR stands for ArmaLite Rifle.

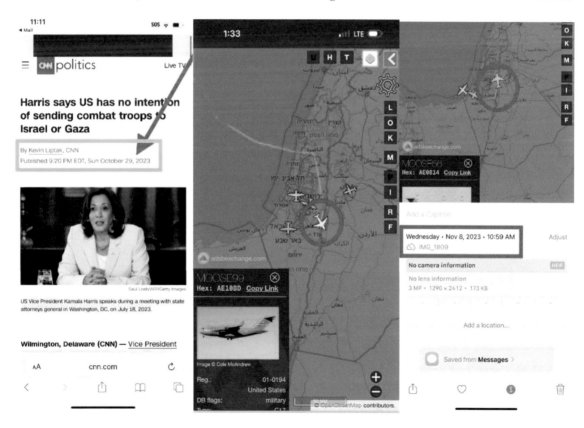

Clearly not LOL. US Troops were in Israel before and after "she" said this. All planned. All part of the Military Occupation. This is why it pays to listen to Veterans who know Military Laws, Orders, Regulations, Customs, paired with Federal.

Here's how you know. Remember the June 24, 2018, and August 2019, articles about the Army spending half a billion training soldiers for our next wars will be in mega-cities, not inside them but beneath them?

Subterranean Warfare = **Tunnels.**

Look at this Manual from 2019 called: ***Shaping the Deep Fight: Operational Implications for the 21ˢᵗ Century Subterranean Conflict.***

Acronyms

A2AD	Anti-Access Aerial Denial
AAR	After Action Review
ADRP	Army Doctrine Reference Publication
DMZ	Demilitarization Zone
FM	Field Manual
IDP	Internally Displaced Person
IED	Improvised Explosive Device
IDF	Israeli Defense Force
OPT	Operational Planning Team
ROE	Rules of Engagement
TC	Training Circular
ISIS	Islamic State in Iraq and Syria
US	United States
WWI	World War I
WWII	World War II

Look at Paragraph 2 under the Introduction.

To some, the solution to the subsurface problem lies at the tactical level of war. In 2017, the US Army allocated $572 million into training and equipping active duty brigades to fight in large scale subterranean facilities.

Shaping the Deep Fight: Operational Implications for the 21ˢᵗ Century Subterranean Conflict.
https://apps.dtic.mil/sti/trecms/pdf/AD1083592.pdf

Now let's look at **Israel** in the **November 2023** news:

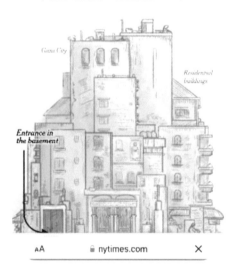

Amazing how that Manual from 2019 aligns with the Articles from 2018 and 2019 and fast forward to November 2023, with one of the chapters from this manual about Hamas paired with the tunnels in Israel.

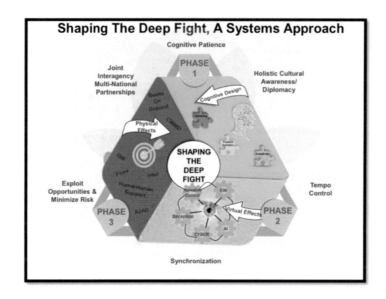

As depicted by the operational subterranean typology in Figure 2, surprise is nonnegotiable and necessary for gaining and maintaining contact with the enemy. Surprise is a primary principle of joint operations and creates the conditions for success at the tactical, operation, and strategic level of war. Surprise affords the attacker the ability to disrupt rival defensive plans by achieving rapid results and minimizing enemy reaction time.147 According to Carl von Clausewitz, "surprise lies at the root of all operations without exception, though in widely varying degrees depending on the nature and circumstance of the operation."148 Surprise is also essential to deception operations. Offensively, the United States must begin to effectively integrate their air defense systems into joint operations and leverage their electronic warfare capabilities, an uncommon but necessary practice. Deception operations must integrate electronic warfare capabilities and signature residue manipulation. Electronic signatures are everywhere on the modern battlefield making it difficult to hide from the enemy. From Fitbits, to Apple watches, to RFID tags, to global positioning systems, surprise is difficult to achieve unless operational planners can creatively alter virtual fingerprints to affect enemy actions.

While still an important facet, the answer to the subterranean threat is not in the next technological advancement or tactical solution, rather it is in the operational artist's creative and critical thinking and ability to reframe the problem, apply systematic thinking, and provide better options to the commander. Success against a subterranean threat lies at the operational level of war.

ALL Planned. No coincidences. But the MOST beautiful part of that graphic found in the 2019 Manual via a dot Mil site… are the two terms:

Cognitive Design
Cognitive Patience

November 2023: More jacked up uniforms

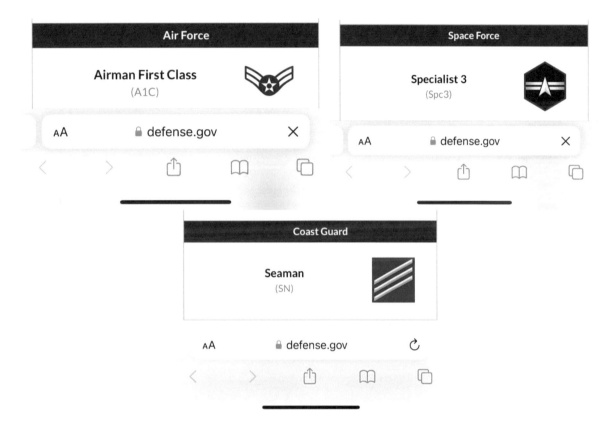

Even though this was planned and done on purpose, as they made the uniforms look in unison… but they're not.

Now, did you just ask yourself, '***what in the hades did I just read***?' That's quite all right! You made it through the reading (unless you skipped to the end like many used to do #guilty are ya?). _Remember_, read as many times as you need, it's like studying.

But just for bonus, I have some friends who would like to help you learn a little bit more in depth of Military Operations and paired with what brought me to you…

Allow me to introduce you to some of my friends in high places. Without further ado, I introduce to you Lieutenant Colonel Riccardo Bosi (Retired) from the Australian Forces.

'HOW DONALD TRUMP RODE TO VICTORY ON A PURPLE DRAGON'

A CONTRIBUTION BY LTC RICCARDO BOSI (RTD) TO
'THE MIDNIGHT RIDER RIDES AGAIN'
BY DEREK JOHNSON

INTRODUCTION

Conceal your dispositions, and your condition will remain secret, which leads to victory. Show your dispositions, and your condition will become patent, which leads to defeat.

Sun Tzu, The Art of War

Force and fraud are, in war, the two cardinal virtues.

Thomas Hobbes, Leviathan 1651

Disclaimer

The scope and scale of the War for the World, in which we have all been engaged, and which is the subject of this piece, beggars' belief and to be frank, would be beyond the comfortable comprehension of most people.

None of us, participant nor observer can claim complete knowledge. We are all doing our best, piecing together what we can from scattered fragments of information, to make sense of it all.

So, what follows here is incomplete and at best, only a small part of a much bigger story, some of which might never become public.

For ease of comprehension, I have used the terms Black and White Hats to denote the adversaries and friendlies.

PURPOSE

Having said that, I have been asked to explain how the Commander-in-Chief, President Donald J. Trump, the US military along with civilian components, and in conjunction with their international allies, successfully executed the most secretive and most difficult operation in human history, while keeping both friend and foe alike, completely in the dark.

To do this in full is a task for future historians and requires more time and space than we have here, and so the short answer in two phrases is 'operational security' and 'center of gravity'.

DEFINITIONS

Operational Security (OPSEC)

OPSEC is the capability that:

- identifies and controls critical information,
- identifies and controls indicators of friendly force actions attendant to military operations, and
- incorporates countermeasures to reduce the risk of an adversary exploiting vulnerabilities **(1).**

The purpose of OPSEC is to reduce the vulnerability to successful adversary exploitation of critical information. OPSEC applies to all activities that prepare, sustain, or employ forces.

1. **U.S. Joint Publication 3-13.3 Operations Security 06 January 2016 p. I-1**

Operations Security:
https://media.defense.gov/2020/Oct/28/2002524944/-1/-1/0/JP%203-13.3-OPSEC.PDF

Operation Security 2017:
https://media.defense.gov/2020/Oct/28/2002524943/-1/-1/0/NTTP-3-13.3M-MCTP-3-32B-OPSEC-2017.PDF

Center of Gravity (COG)

COG is the source of power that provides moral or physical strength, freedom of action, or will to act (**2**). Analysis of the threat (adversary) COG identifies what needs to be weakened or destroyed to defeat the enemy while conversely, friendly COG analysis identifies what needs to be strengthened or protected to ensure victory.

TWO TALES FROM TWO WARS

In order to assist non-military readers to fully comprehend the nature and importance of the concepts of OPSEC and COG, I will relate two stories from two wars. The first concerns the inexplicable ineffectiveness of B-52 bombing missions during the Vietnam War and the second concerns the successful neutralising of the most dangerous ship in the Nazi fleet during the Second World War.

OPSEC – Vietnam

Conceal your dispositions, and your condition will remain secret, which leads to victory. Show your dispositions, and your condition will become patent, which leads to defeat. - **Sun Tzu, The Art of War**

The need for secrecy in war is as old as war itself but it was only as a result of security failures, and therefore operational failures by the US during the Vietnam war, that the US '*began to make a concerted effort to review its security posture from the vantage point of an adversary in order to:*

- identify that information concerning U.S. intentions and capabilities that an adversary considers vital,
- to discover how he gains such knowledge about U.S. military plans and capabilities, and, finally,
- to develop strategies by which U.S. commanders could prevent him from gaining that knowledge (**3**).

The concerted effort referred to above was the birth of a more professionalised and systematic process to keep knowledge of US strengths and weaknesses from the adversary. That was when the process became known formally as operational security, and the operation was known as PURPLE DRAGON.

Operation PURPLE DRAGON. On 17 June 1965, under the cover name Operation ARC LIGHT, US B-52 bombers launched their first mission against a Viet Cong (VC), stronghold in South Vietnam.

These strikes against VC and North Vietnamese Army (NVA) targets in South Vietnam and the ROLLING THUNDER strikes against targets in North Vietnam were regular occurrences.

Despite the increased bombing, it very soon became clear to US commanders that the enemy was successfully avoiding the '*worst consequences of (these) US and Allied operations.*' (**4**)

After a year of bombing neither the morale nor operations of the VC or NVA, nor North Vietnamese military and industrial activity seemed to have been impacted.

The concern was on many people's minds - was U.S. intelligence concerning the enemy's whereabouts and strength faulty or, more ominously, were the ARC LIGHT and ROLLING THUNDER missions being given away in advance, providing the VC/NVA the opportunity to avoid them? (**5**)

The PURPLE DRAGON team began searching through all elements of operations: conception, planning and execution, which might be insecure and therefore, if intercepted or observed by the enemy, could provide them with actionable intelligence.

2. **Department of Defense Military and Associated Terms p. 30**
3. **US Cryptologic History Series VI The NSA Period Volume 2 PURPLE DRAGON: The Origin and Development of the United States OPSEC Program 1993 pp3-4**
4. **ibid p4**
5. **ibid p5**

DOD Military and Associated Terms:
https://www.tradoc.army.mil/wp-content/uploads/2020/10/AD1029823-DOD-Dictionary-of-Military-and-Associated-Terms-2017.pdf
NSA Period Volume 2 PURPLE DRAGON:
https://www.nsa.gov/portals/75/documents/news-features/declassified-documents/cryptologic-histories/purple_dragon.pdf

(**ibid** means *same source* for future reference)

Much of what PURPLE DRAGON discovered remains classified, however suffice to say that operations codes were upgraded as were the teletype and secure voice links between Bien Hoa and Da Nang. Consequently, the effectiveness of ARC LIGHT and ROLLING THUNDER improved.
Both US Navy/Marine Corps Amphibious Operations and US Army/Navy Riverine Operations also benefitted from PURPLE DRAGON OPSEC surveys.

Evidence of enemy prior awareness of the operations significantly decreased as the surveyed units implemented suggested changes in procedures. U.S. intercept of enemy alert messages dropped off and contact with the enemy usually increased.

These positive results, however, were almost invariably only temporary. In most cases, the enemy, being denied one valuable source of foreknowledge of U.S. intentions and capabilities by the improved operations security of the units involved, would cast about until they had found a new source of information to take its place. Then, evidence of the enemy's prior knowledge would again surface and the OPSEC procedure would begin again (**6**).

National Security Agency (NSA). PURPLE DRAGON would not have succeeded without support from NSA but during the period following the Vietnam War the US OPSEC Program suffered from a lack of focus. However, by 1982, its efforts to establish a formal OPSEC training curriculum were rewarded when the Joint Chiefs of Staff (JCS) directed that NSA "establish and maintain an OPSEC training program for NSA/Central Security Service (CSS) civilian and military personnel.

*During the 1980s, therefore, a consistent view of operations security - its theory, its method, and its goals - was being propounded throughout the U.S. government (**7**).*

*Finally, on 22 January 1988 President Ronald Reagan signed National Security Decision Directive (NSDD) 298, decreeing that "each Executive department and agency assigned or supporting national security missions with classified or sensitive activities shall establish a formal OPSEC program (**8**).*

Thus, with the promulgation of NSDD 298, operations security became the third major component, along with signals intelligence and information systems security, of the National Security Agency's mission.

*NSDD 298 also marked the culmination of over twenty years of development of the concept of operations security, from a single operation, meant to address the lack of success of aerial bombing operations· in Vietnam, to a national-level program widespread within the U.S. government, meant to protect all national security missions and operations from compromise by any hostile nation (**9**).*

It was at this point OPSEC, the PURPLE DRAGON, which was vital to White Hat operations came of age.
COG – World War 2

> *Victorious warriors win first and then go to war,*
> *while defeated warriors go to war first and then seek to win.*
>
> Sun Tzu, *The Art of War*

In every tactical land battle, there is almost always a piece of vital ground or decisive terrain which is of such importance that it must be retained or controlled for the success of the mission.
Imagine, for example, a narrow mountain pass dominated by high ground on both sides. Also imagine that the enemy must use that pass to reinforce and resupply a garrison located in a fort some distance away.
Possession of this pass would ensure a successful siege and the eventual surrender or withdrawal of the garrison from its position.

6. **ibid pg. 50**
7. **ibid pg. 91**
8. **ibid pg. 92**
9. **ibid pg. 92-93**

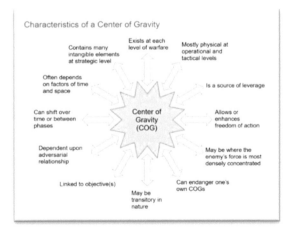

Figure 1 Characteristics of a Center of Gravity

Similarly, at the strategic level of operations there is the centre of gravity (COG) which is the source of power that provides moral or physical strength, freedom of action, or will to act. Success requires protecting the friendly COG while defeating the enemy COG and it comprises specific characteristics. See Figure 1 drawn from DOD Joint Publication 5-0 Joint Planning.

Correctly identifying the COG informs specific objectives to be achieved.

Let me provide the example from the Second World War.
Tirpitz. The Battle of the Atlantic was the longest continuous military campaign spanning the full length of the war 1939 to 1945. Nazi Germany's counter blockade of the United Kingdom by the use of its U Boats was for a time successful and the UK was denied both food and war materiel being sent from the US.

The convoy system used by the allies began to reduce the losses of their merchant ships to the U-Boat wolfpacks, but the introduction of Nazi Germany's battleship the Tirpitz, the fastest and most modern battleship in the war, could potentially turn the tide back in favour of the Germans. The Royal Navy could not match the Tirpitz for speed, defences or destructive power and if it attacked the convoys sailing beyond the range of the Royal Air Force's protection, it could compel the UK's capitulation. Britain would have starved.

The Tirpitz did however suffer a strategic disadvantage because of its massive size. If it were to be damaged in the Atlantic, it could not return to Germany and its large dry docks for repairs because it would be compelled to pass through the English Channel where the Royal Navy and the Royal Air force would be waiting together to destroy her.

The only alternative was for the Tirpitz to use a dry dock on the Atlantic coast of France, and there was only one large enough to accommodate it, the Normandy dock at St Nazaire. So, in order to protect the vital convoys crossing the Atlantic from the US to the UK, the Tirpitz had to be neutralised (**10**) by destroying the COG – which was of all things – a dock. There was one small problem, no-one in the conventional forces, Royal Navy, the Army nor the Royal Air Force, thought it could be done.

The Greatest Raid Of All. But a group of inventive and courageous men thought it could, and in what later became known, as 'The Greatest Raid of All', took the job on.

The dock was attacked by a joint force from the Royal Navy and the recently formed Commandos. It was an operation where more Victoria Crosses, the UK's highest aware for valour, were earned and more quickly than any other action during the Second World War.

And the result? Well, mission accomplished. The dock was destroyed, the great battleship Tirpitz - the pride of the Kriegsmarine - never entered the Atlantic, the convoys continued to transport food, men and materiel from the US and the UK was saved.

As you have seen, correct COG selection is critical to mission success.

Now that we've discussed OPSEC and COG, let's discern the Commander-in-Chief, Donald Trump's and the White Hats' approach to this War for the World.

10. **To render enemy personnel or material incapable of interfering with a particular operation. US DOD ADP1-02 Terms and Military Symbols August 2018 p 1-68**

ADP1-02:
https://irp.fas.org/doddir/army/adp1_02.pdf

WINNING THE WAR FOR THE WORLD

Black Hat Intention

The situation in which the White Hats found themselves was perilous to say the least. If I was to attempt to discern their intention it would be thus.

In examining this intention, I have deliberately omitted any discussion of structures and organisations above that which the average person can validate from their own experience.

Purpose. The Black Hats' purpose was to rule the planet.

Method. Over many decades, the Black Hats have infiltrated and taken control of every aspect of life on earth.

They recruited a small handful, relative to the global population, of skilled, talented and amoral people into secret societies.

The secret societies established networks across these <u>critical functions</u> required for global control.

- Polity,
- Bureaucracy,
- Judiciary,
- Constabulary,
- Military,
- Finance,

- Industry,
- Unions,
- Mainstream media,
- Social media,
- Academia,
- Education,

- Health,
- Science,
- Technology,
- Entertainment
- Religion.

They employed deception, manipulation, brainwashing, bribery, blackmail, as well as threats of, and actual violence and death, in order to fabricate, disseminate and entrench stories and lies about the nature of life on earth into the consciousness of the people.

To ensure the people were sufficiently docile and readily accept the stories and lies with minimal resistance, the Black Hats degraded the people:

- Physically,
- Emotionally,
- Socially,
- Mentally,
- Educationally,

- Psychologically,
- Professionally,
- Financially,
- Spiritually

The stories and lies were sold to the people of the world as real, and reinforced through news and entertainment, and the people believed and invested themselves in these lies. The Black Hats next intended to exterminate 6.5 billion people through the use of compulsory injections of poisons concealed as vaccines.

The final step was to enslave the remainder of the people as 'servant drones' through a program of transhumanism.

Endstate.(11)

The Black Hats' endstate was:

- an elite ruling class,
- assisted by artificial intelligence,
- served by an electronically controlled transhuman servant class, and
- a global population of 500 million.

Identifying COGs

Black Hat COG. So, what is the Black Hat Centre of Gravity? Control of the global leadership.

Black Hat Critical Capability. The primary abilities that are essential to the accomplishment of their mission are:

- Global finance because controlling the flow of money guarantees the obedience from global leadership, and
- News, entertainment, main-stream-media, social media because controlling the flow of information guarantees the obedience of the global population.

Black Hat Critical Requirements. Essential conditions required to employ the critical capability are bribery, blackmail and threats that control the leadership.
Black Hat Critical Vulnerabilities. The aspects of critical requirements vulnerable to attack are worse threats and/or public exposure.
Risk Management. *At this stage, consideration must be placed on whether total collapse of the enemy or system is commensurate with the objectives and end state.*

To attack and collapse overtly the global leadership with the concomitant impact on the financial system would cause total economic collapse and therefore public disorder and possibly starvation for the people.

While the objective mentioned above remains valid, it is clear that an indirect approach by the White Hats would be required. This indirect approach would employ the following methods:

- covert operations, (12)
- clandestine operations, (13)
- unconventional warfare, (14)
- guerilla techniques, (15)
- espionage, (16)
- counter espionage (17)
- infiltration, and
- cyber operations.

All these methods are inherently and extremely high risk, and compromise, or detection would result in White Hat mission failure.

Secondly, significant time would be required to penetrate all critical functions, exacerbating the already high risk.

White Hat COG. Therefore, it may be concluded that the White Hat COG is OPSEC – the PURPLE DRAGON – that is, nothing must be allowed to compromise the nature of the operation to the Black Hats.
White Hat Critical Capability. The primary ability that is essential to the accomplishment of their mission is the global military because the threat of deadly force guarantees the obedience from global leadership.
White Hat Critical Requirements. Essential conditions required to employ the critical capability are worse threats and/or public exposure of the global leadership.
White Hat Critical Vulnerabilities. The aspects of critical requirements vulnerable to attack are operational security compromise.
Risk Management.
OPSEC. Given the vital importance of OPSEC, standard procedures were likely employed, such as:

- Compartmentalisation of information, restricting information to only those involved in operations, and even then, not revealing the whole truth to the participants,
- Using planned joint and combined military training exercises as cover for both subterranean and surface international operations,
- Conducting false flag operations,
- Leaking false information through both trusted White Hat as well as Black Hat sources,
- Spreading rumours of dissent between trusted White Hats,
- Creating expectations which consistently failed to live up to expectations,

- The list goes on and on…

Providing Hope. Given the long lead time for the indirect approach to bear fruit, and the impossibility of providing moral boosting progress reports and updates which would telegraph to the Black Hats, the White Hat intentions, the people might believe that defeat is inevitable and become demoralised to the point of surrender.

To mitigate against this, the White Hats would be compelled to provide some information that would not be construed by the Black Hats as a real threat.

The information could be coded and disseminated through open sources which could provide hope to the people.

The coded messages would need to be so opaque as to appear a hoax and anyone putting credence into them would be considered a laughingstock.

Q: What could the source of the messages be called?

This sounds a lot like what they have done… and magnificently.

11. **ibid p IV-26**
12. **op sit ADP1-02 p 1-25 Covert Operation – An operation that is so planned and executed as to conceal the identity of or permit plausible denial by the sponsor.**
13. **ibid p 1-17 Clandestine Operation – An operation sponsored or conducted by governmental departments or agencies in such a way as to assure secrecy or concealment.**
14. **ibid p 1-101 Unconventional Warfare – Activities conducted to enable a resistance movement or insurgency to coerce, disrupt, or overthrow a government or occupying power by operating through or with an underground military, auxiliary, and guerilla force in a denied area.**
15. **Guerilla techniques in that guerilla forces utilize adversary resources for their operations, eg the White Hats allowed the development of social media by the Black Hats, only then to take control and use the capability to achieve their objectives viz Elon Musk and Twitter (now X).**
16. **CIA Glossary of Intelligence Terms and Definitions June 15, 1978 p-6 Intelligence activity directed toward the acquisition of information through clandestine means and proscribed by the laws of the country against which it is committed.**
17. **Op sit Dictionary of Military and Associated Terms p 51**

ADP1-02:
https://irp.fas.org/doddir/army/adp1_02.pdf

CIA Glossary of Intelligence Terms and Definitions:
https://www.cia.gov/readingroom/docs/CIA-RDP80M00596A000500020003-7.pdf

Summary

The White Hats planned exquisitely and executed their operation in secrecy. They synchronized countless complex missions such as:

- Taking control of the various corporate entities masquerading as sovereign nations,
- Taking control of the major corporations,
- Eliminating high risk/dangerous Black Hats and employing doubles to confuse all,
- Recovering national wealth stolen over centuries,
- Leaking information to the media through such means as the Hunter Biden laptop,
- Special operations 'soft knocks' to effect armed arrests of some Black Hats,
- Special operations 'hard knocks' to achieve a different 'outcome',
- Engineer police actions such as high-profile arrests and/or rescues, for public consumption,
- And once again, the list goes on and on…

And so, it was the prosaic twin pillars of OPSEC and COG selection that underpinned the victory the Commander-in-Chief Donald J. Trump and the White Hats in the War for the World.

CONCLUSION

We the people, have rightly experienced deep frustration and even fury at the apparent inaction by the White Hats over the past four years. We helplessly watched:

- Our businesses and livelihoods being dismantled, and our homes and possessions being stolen by unlawful government fiat;
- Our freedoms being trampled under the tyrannical boots of the Black Hats and their truly treasonous political, judicial, military, constabulary, and media minions; and
- Our health and even our lives and the lives of our loved ones being decimated by a psychopathic and mercenary medical profession.

But now, having examined just some of the facts of the matter, and as a result of the analysis, it has been revealed and we have seen that, for perhaps the first time, the manner in which this War for the World was fought was not only the best way it could be fought, but also in reality, the only way we could have won.

The cost to us in lives and treasure was far greater than any of us would have wanted to pay, but we must remember that the alternative was the unthinkable, the complete destruction of the human race.

We, the people should be grateful we survived, and we only did so due to the sacrifices of life and limb of the White Hats, and also of the uncounted and uncountable men and women who comprised the digital army, who worked tirelessly and bravely to defeat our collective enemy. This was indeed their greatest hour.

We, the world as well as the US, owe the Commander-in-Chief Donald J. Trump and the White Hats a debt we can never repay but one we will always remember.

And we should always keep in mind the words of Winston Churchill in 1943, when he was Prime Minister of the United Kingdom, with the fate of his nation at stake and the result not certain…
In wartime, truth is so precious that she should always be attended by a bodyguard of lies.

Now, **former Deputy Commander of Delta Force, Colonel Charles "Chuck" Sellers**:

Despite the changing developments in how future wars are to be fought, some things remain constant. The twin sisters, Strategy and Tactics, which have existed since the very beginning of warfare, remain relevant. Strategy, derived from the Greek word Strategos, meaning "General", lays out the overall approach as to how a war or a campaign will be conducted.

Tactics refers to actual methods to be used in specific actions on the battlefield. Both rest on the bedrock of established rules as to how war should be conducted, such as the most ancient treatise on the subject in existence today, Sun Tsu's Art of War.

His analysis of the rules of war, thought to have been written over 2,400 years ago in approximately the sixth century B.C., is arguably the most concise, systematic, and comprehensive ever written. It was studied by the ancient Greeks and Romans, by Napolean and numerous other notable Generals in history, and is still in widespread use today.

While we concede that the face of modern warfare is indeed changing, and will likely continue to do so, based on the evolving threat and Operational Environment, it would be wise for military leaders, at all levels, in all militaries, in all countries, to study and learn these well-established rules, and be prepared to apply those that are appropriate in facing the inevitable unknowns likely to confront them as the new operational paradigm takes shape.

Success in these widely dispersed global operations is likely, in addition to highly sophisticated weapons and technology, to be focused on the use of highly trained, agile, and well supported Special Operations Forces of the various White Hat militaries. Though usually operating within their respective Theaters and Operational Areas, they will do so with unity of command under a single responsible commander, well-coordinated through close and continuous collaboration between the vetted senior leaders of the military organizations of the nations involved. In addition to the principle of unity of command and unity of effort, these forces will also employ the principles of surprise and deception as to whether an attack is to be made and where it will occur, as well as the principle of massing overwhelming force at the point of attack. All of this will require meticulous planning between all the international militaries involved, as well as the resources necessary to quickly move the required forces to the Zones of Action in which they are needed.

The emphasis will be on "Mission Orders" where leaders at all levels, in all White Hat military organizations worldwide, understand the goals and objectives of the Campaign or Operation and make their decisions accordingly to accomplish their specific missions in support of those goals. The recent operations in San Luis Obispo, California, to retake a US military base that had been captured by Deep State elements within the US military with the support of a US three-letter agency, as well as the assault near Lutsk, Ukraine, carried out by combined US and Russian Special Operations Forces resulting in the destruction of 250,000 liters of adrenochrome and the elimination of the leadership of a major Ukrainian human and adrenochrome trafficking Cartel, were undertaken on the same night, under the military authority of the same senior US Commander.

These two operations, conducted nearly simultaneously half-way around the world from each other, were not directly related but contributed directly to the overall mission of disrupting and/or destroying the Cabal's ability to operate. For all intents and purposes, they were part of a Joint Operation.

Tools exist to assist in Joint Operation Planning. For example, within the US Military, the joint planning and execution community (JPEC) conducts joint planning to understand the strategic and operational environment (OE) and determine the best use of existing capabilities to achieve national (and international) objectives. Joint planning identifies military options that can integrate with other instruments of power (diplomatic, economic, informational) to achieve those objectives. In the process, likely benefits, costs, and risks associated with proposed military options are identified and analyzed.

Again, success in the planning effort will require intense collaboration between vetted key leadership in all the militaries of the countries involved in the joint planning effort. – *former Delta Forces Deputy Commander, Charles Sellers*.

Part One Summary to date:

First things first, for those who think 'Q' is a "conspiracy theory?" Try looking at the Department of Energy where it's explained 'Q' is a Clearance equal to Top Secret.

Q: What if my last investigation was completed 5 years ago?

A: DOE can still accept your current security clearance under the principles of reciprocity. But, Executive Order 12968 and its implementing documents, which govern the administration of security clearances and access authorizations within the Executive Branch, require that individuals who hold Top Secret clearances or Q access authorizations be investigated every 5 years. So, if your current employer hasn't already started an update investigation for you, you'll be asked to submit paperwork right away so that DOE can request the update.

Q: Back up a minute! You just mentioned a "Q" access authorization. What is that and how does it relate to the Top Secret, Secret, and Confidential clearance terminology I'm familiar with?

A: Top-Secret, Secret, and Confidential security clearances refer back to the level of National Security Information to which an individual may have access. Because DOE is granting access to Restricted Data and special nuclear material, it uses different terminology. Generally speaking, there are two types of access authorizations, the L and the Q. The L access authorization corresponds to the background investigation and administrative determination similar to what is completed by other agencies for Confidential and Secret National Security Information access clearances and the Q access authorization corresponds to the background investigation and administrative determination similar to what is completed by other agencies for a Top-Secret National Security Information access clearance. In addition, because RD information is more sensitive than NSI information, access to Secret Restricted Data requires a Q access authorization.

Q: I'm employed by a DOE contractor, and I currently have a Q access authorization. I saw a job advertised in the paper that required a Top-Secret clearance. Based on what you just said, would the agency that advertised that job accept my Q?

A: Under the reciprocity guidelines, a Q is the equivalent of a Top Secret. The investigation required for a Q is the same as the one required for a Top Secret, and with a Q an individual can be given access to Top Secret National Security Information if his or her duties require it. Unless the position in question has special requirements, your DOE Q should be accepted by the agency filling that job in the same way that DOE would accept a Top-Secret clearance for a position requiring a Q.

DOE:
https://www.energy.gov/ehss/departmental-personnel-security-faqs

Short answer from 2016 to present day:

It's quite *this* simple. It's a Military Occupancy and Continuity of Operations Plan. That's the base and foundation. *Everything* falls under those two. And those are well outlined in current, bipartisan Legislation.

There's TWO scenarios playing out at same time:

1. Special, Controlled Operation where all civilians must see the Laws and Orders visually played out where everyone will learn and know their individual responsibilities and how to get involved and appreciate their Foundation, History, and simplicities of Government again.

2. You know how to read, follow, and comprehend Legislation, Laws, and Orders, more specifically Military Laws and Orders supporting Constitution.

The end goal's the same. On January 21, 2018, Q said, "we have it all," and on the 2020 campaign trail, CIC Trump said, "we have it all, we've caught them all." January 21, 2018, is 9-days before CIC Trump signed Executive Order 13823, to revoke Obama's EO, to keep Guantanamo Bay open. All of this has ALREADY taken place via LEGISLATION.

The Law of War Manual, which is the Department of Defense's Manual was reissued on June 12, 2015, and Donald John Trump made his famous escalator ride to announce his candidacy for the 2016 Election, 4 days later, June 16, 2015. *No coincidence.*

The Military Justice Act of 2016, written in May 2016, bipartisan legislated on December 23, 2016, had these 3 things clarified by the United States Supreme Court, that (1) Military Courts are separate from Civil Courts (2) President and Commander-in-Chief are separate (3) Commander-in-Chief is separate from Federal Government, which settles the debate about President vs. Commander-in-Chief and the declaration of war.

Also in December 2016, the Global Magnitsky Human Rights Accountability Act was legislated which would come the following December 21, 2017, in CIC Trump's first declaration of a National Emergency in Executive Order 13818, which was "with respect to serious human-rights abuse and corruption around the world." (This also paired with the sanctions from Executive Order 13936 with Hong Kong issued July 14, 2020).

Also, following up from his first big speech in February 2016, also that same December is when CIC Trump made his speech about keeping Guantanamo Bay aka Gitmo and "The Spa" open.

Remember ALL the 'Russia Collusion' that dominated the media airwaves? That's why it pays to know legislation and how your government operates and functions. Those key entities were VERY important to know plus they prove the Military Occupancy and Continuity of Operations Plan because of how epic those were and CIC Trump was just President-Elect at the time Congress passed those two.

Then came the Federal Continuity Directive 1 issued on January 17, 2017, three days before the big day. In which clearly outlines the National Essential Functions for the 3 Branches of Government and their duties, along with chapters: **Devolution** – what the left-wing media and other clowns called "conspiracy theories" and **Reconstitution**. The Operational Dates are in the Federal Register as: 2018-2022.

The Secretary of the Department of Interior's letter on a dot Gov site proves the 2018-2022 under President Donald John Trump. Issues like this wouldn't have inaccurate dates that would still be available after January 20, 2021, if this were not the intention.

"The Department of the Interior's Strategic Plan for Fiscal Year 2018- 2022 is our bold vision for the future under President Donald J. Trump."

2018-2022 Strategic Plan:
https://www.doi.gov/sites/doi.gov/files/uploads/fy2018-2022-strategic-plan.pdf

Then came the famous speech at the beautiful Inauguration on January 20, 2017, by THE Commander-in-Chief, Donald John Trump, when he said,

> *"We are taking the power from the District of Columbia and giving it back to you the people."*

And standing behind him were those BEAUTIFUL optics via the UNITED STATE MILITARY and those headbands displaying *what was to come.*

Left – Military Intelligence
Right – Judge Advocate General

In May 2017, CIC Donald John Trump, was seen in the sword ceremony in Saudi Arabia, proving the take down of the Saudi Government in the timeline above.

On June 13, 2017, the Implementation Phase was issued of the Federal Continuity Directives, called the Federal Continuity Directive 2 with Operational Dates: 2020-2024.

August 2017, it was reported that Guantanamo Bay would have a $500 million dollar expansion.

On December 6, 2017, CIC Trump DECLARED Jerusalem capital of Israel in the year of jubilee, which is beyond monumental and historic, this put the epic, visual stamp on this being a Biblical operation.

Fifteen days later, on December 21, 2017, he declared his first National Emergency via Executive Order 13818, pairing with the Global Magnitsky Human Rights Accountability Act, which would be the leading kick-off to directly go after these dirty money in which they've used fiat currency, deep state, swamp rats and their trafficking rings.

From December 21, 2017, to November 12, 2020, CIC Trump issued 11 National Emergencies via Executive Orders.

On January 31, 2018, he revoked Obama's Executive Order that was signed to close Guantanamo Bay, aka GITMO, and signed Executive Order 13823 to keep it open.

September 12, 2018, he signs the most lethal Executive Order, 13848, declaring a National Emergency via Election Interference which proves this was never for President Trump or 2020 alone. That EO was signed 2 months before ANY election under his Presidency which makes 2 years and 2 months before 2020, and 2.5 years before January 6, 2021.

That ONE EO nullifies mine and your votes and January 6, 2021, "insurrection" with ONE key line.

"Although no foreign power has altered the outcome or vote tabulation in ANY United States Election."

> **Altered the outcome** = mine and your vote.
> **Vote Tabulation** = Objections.

On January 6, 2021, 2 objections happened in the Arizona count and conveniently the "insurrection" took place immediately.

That one line in an Executive Order declaring a National Emergency 2 years before both 2020 and 2.5 years before J6, proves *"we have it all, we've caught them all"* – it was a plan from the start.

That ONE EO trapped all Governors, Attorney Generals, Secretary of States, Judges and Lawyers who did not apply and enforce the new Legislation.

President Trump was the first sitting President to walk into North Korea on June 30, 2019. His global appearances with Pope, G7, stepping in front of the Queen etc. were also part of the plan and happened... RIGHT IN FRONT OF YA.

He never started a foreign war. He was chosen to bankrupt the Federal Corporation as defined under 28 United States Code 3002, the Organic Act of 1871 and 1878, and dismantle the Crown, the Vatican, and the District of Columbia, and their fiat currency where the cabal has controlled these swamp rats for years aka the Federal Reserve, what John Fitzerald Kennedy set out to do.

He never started a single foreign war and had a BOOMING economy along with a $770 Billion dollar defense budget. But what really matters, that brings this whole operation to where the rubber meets the road, and the reason you're reading this book, is to take all the above, understand it's a massive, complex, multi-layered Special Global Operation, and here's how you prove it:

Donald John Trump became a Wartime President with the key dates of December 20, 2019, and March 27, 2020.

The War Powers Act of 1973, 50 United States Code Chapter 33 Section 1550. That is the Foundational Order given by the Commander-in-Chief. This is the actual Order that says Donald John Trump is the Commander-in-Chief.

On December 20, 2019, all these things took place:

1. Space Force, 6th Branch of Military established.
2. Uniform Code of Military Justice, overhauled, reissued, first time since its establishment in 1950.
3. Courts-Martial Handbook reissued.
4. The War Powers Resolution Act amended and established who the Commander-in-Chief is by LAWS and ORDERS.
5. Global Fragility Act established.

The War Powers Resolution Act being one of the MOST key Laws. The Constitution does say Congress declares war, but the Constitution also says in, Article I, Section 8, Clause 14:

[The Congress shall have Power . . .] To make Rules for the Government and Regulation of the land and naval Forces;

In which they have done so… starting with First and Second War Powers Act which was amended in 1973 with the War Powers Resolution Act. And with the amending of the War Powers Resolution Act, it specifically says the President and Congress can declare war via National Emergencies in Section 1621; that the President must give a notice no later than 48 hours to the Speaker of the House of Representatives and the President pro tempore of the Senate a report.

So, when President Trump says, "if they're going to investigate me, they must investigate *__every__* President before me, _immediately_" – November 18, 2022, that's EXACTLY what he was referring to.
War Powers Act of 1973 aka Title 50 / 50 United States Code.

Presidential Emergency Action Documents signed by the President would have expanded his powers as President. Hence the Operational dates 2018-2022 and 2020-2024 of the Federal Continuity Directives 1 and 2, issued on January 17 and June 13, 2017.

Plus, the 11 Executive Orders with 11 National Emergencies and the Proclamations made by President Trump.

Then **50 USC Section 1550** titled: **Reports and Briefings on use of military forces and support of partner forces**:

"Not later than 180 days after December 20, 2019, and every 180 days thereafter, the President shall submit to the congressional defense committees, the Committee on Foreign Relations of the Senate, and the Committee on Foreign Affairs of the House of Representatives a report on actions taken pursuant to the Authorization for Use of Military Force (Public Law 107–40) against those countries or organizations described in such law, as well as any actions taken to command, coordinate, participate in the movement of, or accompany the regular or irregular military forces of any foreign country or government when such forces are engaged in hostilities or in situations where imminent involvement in hostilities is clearly indicated by the circumstances, during the preceding 180-day period."

In the first 180 days, DJT became CIC.

On March 2, 2020, the Defense Production Act amended. That's 50 United States Code Chapter 55. It was extended to September 30, 2025. That means all funds were appropriated on that day and everything from March 2, 2020, to September 30, 2025, was approved.

The MSM has reported "Joe Biden" has invoked the DPA 8 times. Odd, in the Act, his name is in there twice. Those two entries were an Act signed and passed by Donald John Trump and the other was the baby formula shortage in which the MSM reported the Secretary of Defense approved the mission due to urgency.

On March 13, 2020, Proclamation 9994 was declared, and on March 27, 2020, Donald John Trump became a Wartime President by definition, when he Federalized 1 million Reserves to Active-Duty with Executive Order 13912 declaring a National Emergency.

The ONLY person who can Federalize the Reserves and National Guard to Active-Duty is the President, which is found under Title 10 Sections 12302, 12304, and 12406. He is the ONLY who has Federalized the Reserves and National Guard to Active-Duty, visualizations prove this, but more importantly Laws and Orders do, as they have not been revised, revoked, or rescinded.

On April 30, 2020, still in that first 180 days, CIC Trump DIRECTED the Secretary of Defense equal authority to Federalize Reserves to Active-Duty with Executive Order 13919.

Those were Direct Military Orders from the Commander-in-Chief and placed in Federal Laws and Orders. The Military Justice Act of 2016 is reinforcement that the Commander-in-Chief is separate from President and Federal Government. And you best believe some PEADs were signed because the 'media' made that a hot topic in March 2020 when 60 plus percent of Americans cannot even simply name the 3 Branches Government.

On January 20, 2021, "Joe Biden" "swore in" at 11:47 AM EST which is a violation of the 20th Amendment, the Nuclear Football was not exchanged, he was not given the traditional flight as Presidential-Elect via Air Force One and was given 3 Cannons which is NOT a 21-Gun Salute, it's a Military FUNERAL Honors.

On July 19, 2021, a Memorandum for the Secretary of Defense was placed under Section 1550 in the Fiscal Year of 2020... which makes zero sense outside of a Military Occupation and Continuity of Government.

By the authority vested in me as President by the Constitution and the laws of the United States of America, including section 301 of title 3, United States Code, I hereby delegate to the Secretary of Defense the authority and functions vested in the President by section 1285(a) through (e) of Public Law 116–92 [50 U.S.C. 1550(a) to (e)] on the use of military force and support of partner forces to the Congress.

This is "Joe Biden" delegating the Secretary of Defense the Authority and Functions of Section 1550 = Donald John Trump to the Secretary of Defense. Well, DJT had already done so with Executive Order 13919.

This Memo was needed for future purposes via the 2-year clause of how a President can declare war via National Emergencies in 50 United States Code Section 1621.

Every part of this Special Operation must be done with integrity of Military and Federal Laws and Orders that support the Constitution and our Foundation. If none of these procedures were followed and nothing was recorded to look like a President was doing anything... you'd have your clear answer.

The Secretary of Defense is a nominated and appointed by the President. It's a Military position. That Memo is telling the SECDEF to adhere to the Order of Donald John Trump from December 20, 2019, in the War Powers Act where a President declares war, yet CIC DJT had already given direct orders to the SECDEF.

To prove "Joe's" not President, it's really this simple:

When you go to 10 United States Codes 12302 and 12304, the sections where the President calls into duty the Ready Reserves and Selected Reserves to Active-Duty, the last amended sections of those is Executive Order 13912 under 12302 and Executive Order 13919 under 12304...

If "Joe Biden" was President, those Executive Orders 14097 and 14102 should be listed under Executive Order 13912 in 12302, and 13919 in 12304, but they're not.

Executive Order 14097:
https://www.federalregister.gov/documents/2023/05/01/2023-09318/authority-to-order-the-ready-reserve-of-the-armed-forces-to-active-duty-to-address-international

Executive Order 14102:
https://www.federalregister.gov/documents/2023/07/18/2023-15347/ordering-the-selected-reserve-and-certain-members-of-the-individual-ready-reserve-of-the-armed

Everything "Joe Biden" has signed Military related has been an extension of the Orders under the Military Occupation and everything signed Federally related has been an extension of the Continuity of Operations Plan as outlined in the Federal Continuity Directives. There's been some optics of him "revoking" certain things signed by CIC Trump that paint the picture of someone who doesn't care about all-Americans and looks anti-American.

If they didn't mean anything and if Joe Biden were acting President, he wouldn't be extending 11 Executive Orders with 11 National Emergencies declared, two and three years in a row.

ESPECIALLY Executive Orders 13818 – Global Human Rights Abuse, 13848 – Election Interference, 13959 – Securities Investments that Finance Communist Chinese Military Companies and amend it with a new Order as well, especially if you know ANYTHING about real Joe Biden's history with China, and the extension of EO 13848, Election Interference, absolutely makes ZERO sense whatsoever.

If you can read all that and believe it was just 'another' four years OR all coincidence that those happened... as my dear sweet, late Grandmother used to say, "*God love 'em.*"

Still having trouble comprehending? If "Joe Biden" was President, he would have the same power as every other President, so ask yourself:

1. Why didn't he receive the traditional escort into D.C. by the United States Air Force on Air Force One as every other President?
2. By Military Customs (zero party or religious affiliations) on January 20, 2021, why did he receive 3 Cannons at Arlington National Cemetery, which is a 3 Volley Salute, which is a Military Funeral Honors for a Foreign Dignitary, NOT an Inauguration?
3. Why did the National Guard and Reserves NOT salute "his motorcade" as "he" passed by which is Military Regulation and Custom?
4. Why did his signature change after 46 years as Senator and Vice President from Joe Biden to J.R. Biden Jr.?
5. If Ancestry DNA and 23 and Me have write-ups about how there's only 2 types of earlobes, attached and detached, how come the Joe Biden of 46 years in Senate and VP had a detached earlobe, and the "President" Joe has an attached earlobe?
6. All Executive Orders with National Emergencies declared by Donald John Trump had expiration dates, why didn't he let them expire?
7. Why did he extend not just one, two, or three, but all 11 Executive Orders with National Emergencies, two years in a row?
8. Why did he campaign half of 2020 to 'shut down Guantanamo Bay?'
9. How come he cannot sign an Executive Order to revoke Executive Order 13823 by DJT to shut down Guantanamo Bay?
10. Why would he name the 4 Star General and full blood brother of the 3 Star General, as VP, he and Obama smeared, destroyed his image, good name, and whole career in the Military, only to be pardoned by President Trump, to the Commanding General of the United States Army Pacific, which covers the regions of the hottest topics in news: Hawaii, Russia, Japan, China, Taiwan, Australia, New Zealand, Guam?
11. Why would he hire Victoria Nuland as Under Secretary, who worked for Obama Administration, known for securing $1 Billion in defense for Ukraine, while he was Vice President, also known for being recorded saying, "F*ck the EU?"
12. Why throughout 2021 and 2022 did his Press Secretaries and his Administration tell the public, "There are no biochemical labs in Ukraine," but the same Victoria Nuland testified under Oath to Congress, March 8, 2022, there ARE biochemical labs in Ukraine?
13. How come the media shows him coming off the 'ass end' of Air Force One in which the media showed the Chinese did not provide a staircase for Obama in September 2016 as reported 'coming out the ass end,' but it's normal for every "Air Force One" excursion for "Biden?"
14. How come "Air Force One" has not flown with Presidential SAM Call Sign since May 2021?
15. Why are all Department of Defense Aircraft flying with SAM Call Signs?
16. Why would "Biden" tell the Nation he is to sign an Executive Order (yet to do so) to prevent Uranium Mining companies taking over Grand Canyon, when Uranium One was the largest scandal in history involving $145 million sale from Clinton Foundation to Russia?
17. Why has the media shown "Biden" and "Kamala" on the same Aircraft?
18. Why has the media shown "Biden" and "Kamala" in the same automobile going to lunch together?
19. Why are there always mismatched uniforms and not the Marine Corps sentries around "Biden?"
20. Why are the uniforms always non-regulation and all jacked up around "Biden" and "Kamala?"
21. Why isn't there a Director of the White House Military Office?
22. Why do I have proof of a friend of a friend who worked for CIC Trump's Military Office with email ending with @whmo.mil and under "President Biden" with email @state.gov?
23. Why has there been 5 issues under the Federal Continuity Directives 1 and 2, with Operational dates of 2018-2022 and 2020-2024, the most recent being April 2023, which would mean "Biden" has been "President" for 2.4 years, but the most recent Law inside the April 2023 Reconstitution Manager's Guide under the FCDs, is from December 2020, which was CIC DJT's Law… how come "Biden" does not have one single Law in the Continuity of Government?
24. Why does "Wikipedia" show "Biden" invoked the Defense Production Act 8 times, but the actual Defense Production Act (50 USC Chapter 55) show his name twice, and one of those is an Act signed and passed by Donald John Trump, and the other is the Baby Formula shortage, which the Secretary of Defense approved the mission? The Act was amended March 2, 2020, and extended to September 30, 2025, meaning the appropriations of anything from March 2, 2020, to September 30, 2025, have already been funded and approved.
25. Why does every Military Order the MSM says he signed, not appear in any Act or Code on .Gov sites?
26. Why did MSM tell the world Israel was a Music Festival Attack and within a week to 3 weeks: United States, Thailand, United Arab Emirates, Germany, Italy, Netherlands, Mexico, Canada, Argentina, Colombia, Czechia, Tunisia, Romania, Poland, Spain, Belgium, Japan, France, Hungary, Brazil, Nigeria, Algeria, Russia, and Greece, were all in Israel?
27. Why did "Kamala Harris" say on October 30, 2023, that no U.S. Troops would fight in Israel-Hamas War, but our Troops have been in Israel weekly?
28. How come "Biden" and "Kamala" aren't on TV daily? Why does their 'pressers' take days and weeks?

Yes, it's really that simple.

E-v-e-r-y SINGLE thing falls under the Military Occupancy and Continuity of Operations Plan… ***EVERYTHING***.

This operation at this kind of magnitude did not spring out of nowhere… It wouldn't have been a 'let's see if we can get Trump elected, *then* start issuing Laws and Orders'… *No*.

This was an operation that's been in plans for years. May never know the exact number as there's always been Patriots in and out of Military in high levels ready to roll when the 'Perfect Storm' presented itself.

The 2016 Campaign trail quote by Donald John Trump also proves such…

> *"I have over 200 Generals backing me right now and more to come."*

To put that comment into perspective, there were 14 Generals in charge of World War II.

Army – 6
Air Force – 3
Navy – 5

That '200 Generals' comment was a "conspiracy theory" for many years. And we all know who created the term 'Conspiracy Theory.' It was to keep you the people in the blind.

Tables turned in November 2016. Election night. And when it's revealed, you shouldn't have ANY problems with the Military taking over the systems of the Deep State and their rigging of systems for many years to 'get their people' in positions of power. The Military did exactly what they were supposed to do. Protect our Constitution. And the only way to get this party started was to utilize where we are in technology to get their guy (CIC DJT) in place to lead this Revolution.

Everyone must keep in mind... the Military did NOT have to do this as a multi-level complex-controlled operation. Based on the history of our Military, our Military foundation, and the Declaration of Independence, the Military could have from the get-go swooped right in and tried to force people to educate themselves on history, legislation, laws, and orders. But that's just it... those are individual responsibilities that Americans should take pride in knowing their history, foundation, and legislation. That's not something that should be forced. And it's not any time of "boots on the ground" type situation. This was never a "boots on the ground" type battle except for the Trafficking decimation as that's how these evil rats in the deep state kept their dirty side money.

It's not new. It's only unique, different, foreign, and all the other definitions to you. It's not to those who comprehend strategic operations and plans. It's the *Art of War*.

"Joe Biden" is a World War II History repeat the same as "President Laurel" was for the Philippines. President Quezon was brought back and forth to the United States, creating a Government in Exile, while maintaining full control of his Military, under United States Law, while a puppet, "President Laurel" met the press etc.

WWII Puppet States:
https://en.wikipedia.org/wiki/List_of_World_War_II_puppet_states
Government in Exile of the Commonwealth of the Philippines:
https://en.wikipedia.org/wiki/Government_in_exile_of_the_Commonwealth_of_the_Philippines

How do you catch these lying, deceitful thieves who are wasting your hardworking taxpaying dollars and turning it into millions for them with their "do as I say not as I do" mentalities that keep us all divided and pinned against each other?

You catch them from within and make them show *their* cards to the world without ever showing yours. No different than the infamous quote, "*if we ever lose America, we will lose it from within.*" It works both ways. Because once again, at the end of the day, corporations, organizations, facilities, and systems do not corrupt themselves, it's people with free-will. We have a choice every single day to 'do unto others' with transparency, honesty, integrity, accountability with responsibility.

That's HOW you catch thieves. You set traps. But for you to comprehend what's taking place in that regard, you had to know how the thieves fooled you and have tricked you for years. Even though it was non-traditional, it was a psychological operation that duped you the people for many years, those who have no clue what's been taking place in this reverse operation.

You best them. If you know a Conspiracy Realist like me and my buddies, you'd know that CIC Trump is a 5D Chess Player. The '**best**' is yet to come.

Best is a chess term. See, when the King gets trapped, that's called Stalemate. And instead of beating someone... there's more humiliation with a crook to have to surrender than to be taken down by direct force. That's called... best move. *"You just got bested."*

Chess engine — A chess computer, or program designed to analyze games to calculate the **best** moves. Modern chess engines are generally considered to be significantly stronger than even the best human players.

New York Times: Chess Glossary
https://www.nytimes.com/2022/06/13/crosswords/chess/chess-glossary.html

What you're witnessing is actually a Counter-Psychological Operation... with a majority of the PsyOp having to educate and re-educate the mass population (remember the Cognitive Design and Patience diagram pages back in the 2019 Manual) with history and foundation of our Nation that many have taken for granted or have been lied to over and over with misconstruing and misquotes from our Founders by these career Politicians and Deep State Swamp Rats, especially now that many of the "historians" are not direct descendants from those who have deep roots in this Nation where the stories were passed down. We have so many in this Nation who've tried to re-write and re-tell History and have butchered it horrendously.

It wouldn't take many people to form a good alliance to devise plans, that are critically and strategically laced with layers of plans and missions and keep growing along the way once others saw this is achievable when the right people come together in these positions that "we the people" have placed SO MUCH TRUST into for many years.

The Revolutionary War is a great example. The population of the United States from 1775 to 1783 was 2.7 million. Only 1.7% to 1.9% fought each year in the 9-year war. Do your math… that's 98.1% and 98.3% who sat in their homes, whined, complained, griped, fussed, 'debated,' yet weren't willing to fight for what those Founders created, founded, and established.

The 4th of July is not celebrated for the Constitution. It's celebrated for the Declaration of Independence which SPECIFICALLY gives 'we the people' the right and duty to overthrow any such government that goes against its foundation which has been LONG overdue. This Nation was founded WITH weapons in the middle of a WAR brought to you by those same WEAPONS. Anyone who says otherwise clearly knows nothing or simply wants to change history. When one learns that simple setup… Then the strategy to take down these deep state swamp rats that nobody can identify but their own counterparts who can see all the machine from the inside view, will make more sense that the same way you would destroy something good is to interrogate and infiltrate from the inside out.

That same strategy also works with the good guys and gals doing the same thing from the inside out, yet in the sense of setting a broad perimeter that the Military's taking over all systems and infrastructure, they're going to be watching from the broad perimeter and will close in when needed, if needed, then give the certain individuals the opportunity to do what's right, while exposing those who have never done what's right from the start, and those who are in a position to do so, but won't or refuse to, to expose their actions to the public.

Many people will justify those or simply not use logic. Others will try to answer a question with a question such as:

"Why are we sending billions to Ukraine?"

"If Trump was in charge, why would it look like this?"

"If Trump was in charge, why would he let this country be destroyed?"

And the wheels on the bus go round n' round. That's someone who read through this book looking for a quick answer versus reading to absorb and expand their thinking… because the Military Occupancy and Continuity of Government via bipartisan legislation proves an operation along with the Legislation, Laws, and Orders, in a chronological order under those as they fall according to their level and need, are always front and center.

The integrity of our system lays in the hands of people. The only way those people prove themselves are by actions that they're upholding the core values and principles of honesty, transparency, integrity, accountability, and the responsibility, of the foundation and legislations that supports that foundation and the Constitution.

The only people in the field of knowing everything are the Commander-in-Chief of the Military, the Generals, the Department of Defense, the Military Intelligence Agencies, the National Security Agency, the United States Cyber Command, etc.

Don't be that American saying: "FJB" and "Let's Go Brandon." How about "Let's Go Americans, learn your history and how your Nation operates and functions" Then you wouldn't look lost with public, bipartisan Legislation that benefits all of us. America was NEVER supposed to look like the hatred and dog eat dog it does.

It's a mindset. It's positive versus negative energy. If just 75% of Americans knew all the above… just think where this Nation would be and how truly educated and intelligent people would be and the quality of life. You MUST fight for it but fight for the right things. One cannot fight for it if the history is twisted, butchered, misconstrued, and used for agendas.

I can GUARANTEE that a Veteran who knows the Military Laws, Orders, Regulations, and Customs, plus how they tie in with Federal, is the number one person to protect all lives in not just the United States, but the world. But America is an idea on a piece of paper in the Smithsonian that is always a living form that must be fought for every single day. That paper specifically gives us the right and the duty to overthrow any government that goes against her Foundation. That Foundation includes all those who want to be an American and buy into HER Foundation.

We're draining the swamp and resetting America back on her Foundation. That's why the CHRONOLOGICAL ORDER via Military and Federal Laws from 2015 to present day are important. It's the Blueprint of the Plan.

It may not be everything… but this is enough to prove who's in charge! Now go back… page one of the Blueprint… open your laptop and pull up each entity one by one. Read, Research, Study, Repeat.

Official Websites and Social Media:

Websites:
Thedocuments.info
www.rattletrap1776.com
www.derekjohnsoncountry.com

Facebooks:
www.facebook.com/the1776nation
www.facebook.com/rattletrap1776
www.facebook.com/derekjohnsoncountry

Telegram:
www.t.me/rattletrap1776

Rumble:
@rattletrap1776

Twitter (X):
@rattletrap1776

TruthSocial:
@derekjohnson

Snapchat:
iamderekjohnson

Instagram:
@derekjohnsoncountry

Merchandise:
www.rattletrap1776.com

Booking and Management:

1776 Nation
My1776nationmedia@gmail.com

I'd like to give a very Special Thanks to my Family and Friends for your sacrifice of time usually spent together that I deviated to keep my Oath to the Constitution and this Nation and allowing me to serve beyond my service. It's been quite the journey, and I couldn't have done it without you, especially my Mom and Dad.

Thank you all, 1776 Nation and RattleTrap1776 Nation, for your unwavering love and support as we've also enjoyed this journey together from August 24, 2022, in my pickup truck to growing the platforms to what we've grown to.

As I've always said, the only way to support me is via music and merchandise. So, I definitely appreciate y'all. And P.S.: If you trust the Man, trust the Plan! We got this!

See y'all soon… picking up right here, *soon*… Rattle! #BornForThis

Made in United States
Troutdale, OR
11/19/2024

24990244R00109